Faith Deconstruction

Faith
Deconstruction

by Rev. Mashaun D. Simon

Faith Deconstruction For Dummies®

Contents at a Glance

Table of Contents

Introduction

As far back as I can remember, I've felt some amount of fear or shame about my faith. I was either afraid to inadvertently do something that would be perceived as wrong or sinful, or I was stressed out about certain choices I'd made and the impact they would have on my future and soul salvation. I didn't grow up in the most religious house, but there were religious influences all around me or in my view, especially on television. I always saw myself as someone with a genuine heart and good morals, but none of that negated the fears. My struggles became more prevalent once I started to realize my same-sex attraction and identity.

I placed a lot of pressure on myself to do right, be right, and live right. I made the conscious decision to chase after opportunities and accolades to prove to the naysayers that I was indeed good and not a statistic. I believed (and wanted to prove) that I could do good things and be a good person in the world, and even though society said there was this one thing about me, God would or could still be pleased.

I was crushed the day someone dear to me said, "God doesn't hear your prayers!" because of my identity as same gender loving.

Mine isn't an isolated story. Countless people, many of them I know personally, have been harmed by toxic and harmful theology disguised as faith. Because you're holding this book — whether you purchased it yourself or someone gave it to you as a gift — you're probably one of the many as well.

Welcome to the club. I receive you with open arms.

For more than a decade, I've been actively deconstructing my faith. I say *actively* because as I look back, I realize that some of what I consider to be faith deconstruction, or at least some aspect of it, I've been doing as far back as high school. This book is highly informed by my experiences, my questions, my revelations, and my discoveries.

About This Book

When I was approached about writing *Faith Deconstruction For Dummies*, I was initially resistant. The invitation practically came from out of nowhere. It wasn't anything I was anticipating, even though I'd dreamed of writing a book one day. Once I realized the invitation was a serious request and not a hoax, I immediately knew what I didn't want this book to be. One of the first things I declared in the early stages of this project was my disinterest in writing a book with the sole purpose of stripping someone's faith or their relationship to their religious affiliation from them.

I think I've successfully accomplished that.

This book is written from the perspective of a Christian-raised, married, same-gender-loving preacher and former pastor, theologically trained, who critically questioned and challenged much of what he was once taught. The marketplace has a lot of books on faith deconstruction. Some of them informed this project. What makes this one unique is that it's informed by my experiences. In certain respects, I'm still working out some of what I believe, and it shows up on the pages in real time.

No other book I've come across has an entire chapter dedicated to the stories and testimonies of others who have deconstructed their faith.

This book seeks to introduce faith deconstruction, providing background on the topic and where it originates, insight into some factors that may lead you to deconstruct your faith or at least rethink your relationship to religion, and questions to ask yourself as you deconstruct and make the necessary choices for the health and vitality of your faith.

I've organized the book into the following six parts:

>> **Part 1: Venturing into the World of Deconstruction**

>> **Part 2: Understanding the Difference Between Faith and Religion**

>> **Part 3: The Nuts and Bolts of the Faith Deconstruction Journey**

>> **Part 4: Discernment and Deconstruction**

>> **Part 5: Things to Consider When Deconstructing**

>> **Part 6: The Part of Tens**

I also used a few conventions to help you better navigate the text:

>> Any new terms are *italicized* and defined upon their first mention in a chapter.

>> Keywords and numbered steps appear in **bold.**

>> Sidebars in the chapters provide further details or information that's good to know but that you can skip if you want.

Foolish Assumptions

I try my best not to make assumptions, but I did make one assumption about you, the reader. I've assumed that you've picked up this book because you are curious about deconstruction, are just realizing you're deconstructing, or have questions and don't really know what's going on.

If you're not one of those people, you're potentially a critic seeking to find ways to discredit anything and everything written in this book.

If you're the latter, welcome. I hope you find something enlightening and worthwhile you didn't anticipate. If you're one of the former, I hope what's within these pages is helpful to you as you attempt to gain greater awareness and knowledge. But you may know more than I'm giving you credit for.

All in all, this book is for the people who haven't felt brave enough to take their faith into their own hands. I'm doing this project for the people who have hidden from themselves and loved ones thoughts, struggles, and changes in their theology and relationship with religion. I invite you to think critically about what you believe and why you believe it.

Icons Used in This Book

For Dummies books provide icons intended to highlight important points in each chapter. For this book, I use just a few.

REMEMBER

This icon points out information worth digesting. It's also used throughout to recall information or points made in other chapters.

TIP

This icon is also used to point out important pieces of information, but more than that it indicates information that may be helpful and further insightful as you read.

WARNING

Not used often, this icon is intended to provide insight and advice to you, but more along the lines of wise counsel.

Beyond the Book

In addition to what's printed here, I took the time to develop a Cheat Sheet for you to utilize in whatever way you see fit along with this book. Visit www.dummies.com and search for **Faith Deconstruction For Dummies Cheat Sheet**.

There's also a bonus chapter online about the benefits of faith. (As I said, my goal isn't to discourage faith.) If you're interested, head to www.dummies.com/go/faithdeconstructionfd.

Where to Go from Here

How you choose to approach this book and its contents is up to you. You may read it from beginning to end (even though I'm told that rarely happens), or you may skip around to the sections that interest you most in any given moment. I've tried to set up the book in such a way that any option and approach works. My only hope is that what you engage in the pages of this book meets what you're seeking and need for your process and journey. My hope is that through this book, you're better equipped for your faith deconstruction and better enlightened along the way.

Bon voyage!

1

Venturing into the World of Deconstruction

Delve into deconstruction for better understanding.

Identify causes for faith deconstruction.

Determine if you're in crisis or not.

Recognize what may be motivating your faith deconstruction.

Chapter **1**

Deconstruction 101

I might as well acknowledge the elephant in the room. Faith deconstruction isn't exactly the sexiest topic to talk about, which is a problem. Or at least it should be. Thinking critically about faith and religious beliefs should be something that everyone is open to and willing to do. But most people are sensitive about their faith, their beliefs, and the religious institutions they attend.

How a person identifies in relation to their faith is important even if they're a nonbeliever. Being a nonbeliever is a big part of a person's identity, whether they want to admit it or not. Beliefs — and disbeliefs — influence everything.

As a reader of this book, you likely have some questions. I'm pretty sure one question has something to do with what you once believed about God. Maybe you aren't sure you believe what you were once taught. Or maybe you have a few questions and are looking for something or someone to offer you support, guidance, and answers. You're in the right place. But first, let me assure you of something: You're not losing your mind. You're not crazy. And God isn't going to punish you for having questions.

This chapter lays the groundwork for what you'll encounter in the rest of this book. Here you'll get a minor overview of faith deconstruction and some thoughts on what makes deconstructing your faith necessary and beneficial in the grand scheme.

Defining Faith Deconstruction

As I was writing this book, I selectively had a few conversations with people I trust about the project. During one of them, a friend asked me, "How are you defining faith deconstruction?" The question caught me off guard. At that point, no one had inquired as such, and I hadn't expected anyone to do so. I hesitated briefly. I wasn't prepared to give them an answer. I didn't *have* an answer. I didn't know how I was defining deconstruction.

In the back of my mind, I assumed everyone familiar with faith deconstruction understood what it was. I also assumed each of them was working off the same definition. And because of those assumptions, I hadn't formulated a definition or description for myself. I knew what I knew about deconstruction. I knew what I believed about deconstruction. But this question was different. He wasn't asking me what I knew. He was asking me how I planned to define it. In the same way I'd assumed, he'd assumed. He assumed I'd already formulated a working definition and that the definition I'd formulated was informing this project.

But I didn't know. Not at that point at least. Now, isn't that something? The person writing an entire book on faith deconstruction and presenting it as a help guide for others experiencing it didn't have an answer.

I also realized in that conversation that the definition of faith deconstruction has variations. At the core is a universal understanding. Universal tenets inform the definition for some. Proponents of faith deconstruction also use a version of the definition. And a version is informed by the opinions and perspectives of those who oppose faith deconstruction. This section addresses some of those binaries, as well as insight on how I understand and define deconstruction today.

What is faith deconstruction?

So, then, what is faith deconstruction? Well, it really depends on who you ask and what their position is on the topic. Those who are critical of faith deconstruction and would, potentially, consider themselves opponents, define faith deconstruction as the process of someone walking away from God or from their faith. Other opponents often describe faith deconstruction as trendy and a threat to Christianity or faith overall. They perceive deconstruction to be damaging to traditional, doctrinal Christianity.

One essay I read on faith deconstruction declared that faith deconstruction lacks any trace of true Christianity. It was written by a woman who grew up a devout Christian, experienced a deconstructive journey of her own, and eventually returned to what she described as a "historically Christian understanding of the gospel." She shared that she was introduced to deconstruction by a former pastor, accusing him of being on a mission to "propel" the congregation into deconstruction so he could "convert them to progressive Christianity."

I found her claim that faith deconstruction lacked any trace of true Christianity, and her challenge that faith deconstruction has completely abandoned any connection to scripture, to be dangerously inauthentic and misleading. Much of her influence and approach to those who have deconstructed is informed by her relationship to and reverence for scripture. That reverence and her interpretations of said texts inform her faith.

Proponents of faith deconstruction have an entirely different perspective and definition of faith deconstruction. For some, faith deconstruction is a critical examination of their faith and theology. It's about more than doubt. As they define it, faith deconstruction is an investment. Some deconstructionists describe faith deconstructing as weeding. When they deconstruct their faith, they take a deep look at not just their faith, but the influences of their faith understanding and what they've been taught about God. Reexamining doctrines, traditions, and tenets of religious systems is part of that process of evaluating.

REMEMBER

While opponents suggest faith deconstruction is solely motivated to tear down doctrine, proponents see the work differently. Some have used the phrase "breaking apart." But I think there may be another way to describe it that's possibly more accessible: diagnostic. Take, for example, the work that mechanics must do when working on an automobile. Before they can do any actual work, most mechanics first perform a diagnostic inspection. They check everything, externally and internally, to assess what needs repair and what doesn't. In some instances, they'll get an inkling to a problem and do more investigating. They'll check every part of the car from under the hood to beneath the body of the car, including breaks and electrical systems.

TIP

Faith deconstruction is a lot like the work of a mechanic. There may be alerts and sensors that will communicate the need for repair or at least some attention. But you really can't get to the root of the problem without investigating, running tests, and getting under the hood.

That's how I see faith deconstruction. Especially now. Nuance is important. I didn't always have access to nuance, or the information/knowledge needed to acknowledge what makes nuance so important. Before I knew anything about faith deconstruction, I paralleled those who were questioning their faith as atheists. If at any time it seemed like someone had any kind of doubt about what they believed or what anything meant biblically, I immediately lumped them into the category of atheist. I didn't really know what *atheist* meant either. It just seemed like the most appropriate way to understand and label critical thinkers. Part of this is because I was taught implicitly and explicitly to never question God or anyone of religious authority. Things were what they were because God said, and that was all there was to it.

I also held that anyone who no longer believed was destined for hell. It's what I was taught and conditioned for years. I also felt this way about anyone who didn't believe in and profess Jesus Christ as their Lord and Savior. That meant anyone who lived in a faith outside of Christianity, whether they were Jewish, Muslim, or anything else, was outside of the will of God. Jesus was "the way, the truth and the life" (John 14:6). Jesus was the only way. I had these concerns for others, and they manifested within me.

Now, I was never one of those Bible-thumping believers. But quietly and internally, my heart ached for anyone who was outside of Christianity. And my heart ached for myself, struggling with my own humanity, identity, and spirituality. I allowed the messaging I was exposed to in church and in the media to inform much of that heartache. I even fell in love once with someone who considered themselves an atheist. Initially, I ignored what my mind told me was wrong as we spent time together. But eventually I feared what would happen if I allowed myself to love them more than I did because we were "unequally yoked" (2 Corinthians 6:14). I've come a long way since then.

What does it mean to "deconstruct" your faith?

When I began accepting that I was deconstructing, which I share more about in Chapters 2 and 15, I looked at the process more like taking a puzzle apart and putting it back together. Or, in the examples I use in later chapters, taking ingredients from a beloved meal and putting them together, but in a different way — like deconstructing an apple pie. Faith deconstruction for me in 2022 and 2023 was more about making something I considered beloved, using the same ingredients, and being surprised that the outcome didn't look the way I expected it to. Looking back, I don't think that was the most accurate example simply because some of what I was doing included not using or reusing some of the old or classic ingredients any longer.

REMEMBER

Thinking critically about what you believe will mean abandoning some of the ingredients you once cherished. The "dessert" will taste different, but it will still be just as satisfying, if not more.

Thinking critically about your faith means evaluating and reevaluating. For me, the faith deconstruction process is a form of auditing. It's taking an inventory of what you believe and how your faith works for you. Faith isn't something to engage passively. Despite what you've been taught, faith is something that's happening *for* you versus something that's happening *to* you. It's beneficial to your development.

When I began deconstructing my faith, I did an inventory of what I'd been taught versus what felt right in my heart. I was always challenged by the way leaders in the church treated the neighborhood drunk whenever he sneaked into the church through the back door on some Sundays. Yes, his presence interrupted the flow of service sometimes, but didn't Jesus encourage those with burdens to come to him so he could give them rest (Matthew 11:28)? I began to feel as though there was a commitment to being orderly over being servants and stewards within the community.

When something didn't make sense to me or, put another way, whenever I experienced something that felt contradictory to what I was taught, it brought up questions. Sometimes I asked my questions aloud, but not very often. Usually, I kept them within and sought answers within my heart. But I had questions about a lot of things as I experienced them. I couldn't understand why some churches had musical instruments while others didn't. I wanted to know why some services had devotion and others didn't. I had so many questions because there were so many contradictions — even before I began engaging the Bible more narrowly.

Having questions is part of the deconstruction process, at least for me. As I observed, I questioned. The same is true for many others who deconstruct. For some, says my friend Verdell Wright, who you will hear more from in Chapter 11, it can be jarring. "Something jarred you in a way that you could not unsee. Whether it was subtle or built up over time, you noticed something you hadn't before." Eventually, the weight of your inquiry becomes too much to carry and what you once believed begins to crumble.

Borrowing an example from Wright, think about a house in danger of falling apart. You begin to survey the damage and ask yourself what's worth saving. What does the insurance policy cover, and if the damage is irreparable, what can you get for the house if you get rid of it? Deconstructing your faith means surveying the damage done to you and others. It means taking your faith into your own hands and investigating. For me it began with asking questions. For Wright it meant surveying what others had given him to believe.

TIP

In Chapter 11 you hear from others who have deconstructed. Their stories provide insight on what it meant for them to deconstruct and the outcomes of their inquiries. Some studied other religions, comparing and contrasting what they were given to believe with what they found through exploration. Others read and studied more about the faith system they were born into, using history, context, and divine knowledge to better evaluate their relationship to their faith. Some even took all they'd learned and turned it into purpose — committing themselves to helping others who may be struggling with some of the same questions they wrestled with. They were active, as everyone should be, in their deconstruction process.

Common Deconstruction Questions and Misconceptions

I'm often challenged by the "us versus them" rhetoric found in society at large, but especially in religious communities. And it's not just a mentality for anyone outside of the group, but within the community as well. It can be very cultish, which is discussed more in Chapter 9. How is it that one of the tenets of religion is community building, but many spend more time sowing division?

The beauty of humanity is the beauty of diversity. If God is all powerful, all knowing, ever present, and the architect and creator of the world, doesn't that also make God intentional in *your* existence? God is the orchestrator of all things diverse. And if people are created in the image of God, doesn't that also mean everything living and breathing reflects God's identity?

These are a few of the many questions I continue to have in my journey of seeking and understanding God and humanity. But I digress.

Several misconceptions about faith deconstruction are worth highlighting. This section provides insight and an overview into a few as a means of expanding your understanding and comfort in deconstruction.

Isn't deconstruction just the latest religious debate?

Contrary to what anyone tells you, faith deconstruction isn't a new phenomenon. Chapter 2 discusses some of the origin of faith deconstruction as a contemporary concept, but the fact of the matter is, faith deconstruction isn't new. It's just the hottest topic for now. If faith deconstruction is thinking critically about your faith and, as a result, altering your understanding and relationship to your faith, then faith deconstruction has been present in and throughout world history for generations.

In my seminary training, I was exposed to philosophers, thinkers, and theologians who impacted the way society thinks about theology. Some of the names that come to mind include Karl Barth, John Calvin, and Martin Luther (the latter two discussed in Chapter 7), whose thinking and critical analysis led to movements that formed some of the world's mainstream Christian denominations still today.

There are also the likes of major thinkers and leaders of yesterday and recent contemporary history who used faith and religion to fight against the many ills of society:

THE BIBLE AND WORLD AFFAIRS ACCORDING TO KARL BARTH

Considered to be one of the most influential theologians in a generation, Karl Barth is attributed with once saying, "We must hold the Bible in one hand and the newspaper in the other." While he believed that God's message and desire for humanity is made clear in the scriptures, he also believed that the Bible isn't enough. To have true and authentic impact, Barth believed faith leaders and believers must understand the world and what's happening in it. It was paramount, according to him. Most fundamentalists, however, disagreed, believing scripture to be the only authority and scripture alone. The Swiss-born scholar is credited with having written more than 20 books that provided insight and intrigue into faith, scriptural authority, and the church.

- >> Frederick Douglass

- >> Rev. Dr. Martin Luther King, Jr.

- >> James Baldwin

- >> Bayard Rustin

- >> Teresa of Ávila

- >> Sojourner Truth

- >> Jurena Lee

- >> Harriet Beecher Stowe

- >> Susan B. Anthony

These are just a few of the names that come to mind of people who thought critically about faith and used what they thought to bring forth change in the world and society. This may be a stretch, and I'm sure I may get some pushback for making this suggestion, but I can see some of what they were doing in their work — thinking critically and, to some extent, birthing movements that reformed and challenged — in the vein of deconstruction. What they did may not have been faith deconstruction explicitly, but it has some parallels and similarities. And that, for me, suggests that deconstruction was alive and well before anyone put a label on it.

FREDERICK DOUGLASS, ABOLITION AND DECONSTRUCTION

Anyone familiar with Frederick Douglass and his work understands him almost exclusively as an ex-slave whose post-slavery life and work was largely focused on abolition. While that's mostly true, what many are unaware of is that his abolition ethic was informed largely by his faith. According to historians, he critiqued the manner to which the Christian faith was used to support and promote slaveholding. He often called it slaveholding religion and argued that, as he understood Christianity, slaveholding religion

(continued)

(continued)

was counter to the "pure, peaceable, and impartial Christianity of Christ," which he loved. He loathed the "hypocritical Christianity of this land." Eventually, he joined and became licensed in the African Methodist Episcopal Zion (AMEZ) Church but left after a few years. He began to feel as though the messages within AMEZ were too close to the messaging received in white churches. He's quoted as saying he "consented to the same spirit which held my brethren in chains" some years after leaving the AMEZ.

Do only former Evangelicals deconstruct?

You may have heard of Evangelical Christianity, Christian Conservatism, or Christian Fundamentalism. Maybe you even assumed they were all the same thing as I did. In the same way that I once lumped anyone and everyone who wasn't Christian or who questioned God and Jesus as atheists (and maybe even heretics a times or two), I lumped all evangelicals, conservative Christians, and Christian fundamentalists in the same group and category. Yes, the three have some overlap, but considering them the same is a gross generalization.

I point this out because another misconception of faith deconstruction is the belief that everyone deconstructing is coming out of one of these groups. There may be *some* truth to that, but it's not universal overall. But why do people think this, and what's the difference between the three? I'll start with the differences:

>> **Evangelicalism** is defined as a movement within Protestant Christianity. Evangelists are informed by Matthew 18:19–20: "Therefore go and make disciples of all nations, baptizing them in the name of the Father, and of the Son, and of the Holy Spirit, and teach them to obey everything I have commanded of you." This scripture is widely known and understood as the Great Commission. Evangelicals believe one of their sole purposes is to "go out and make disciples," and they do so by sharing the gospel of Jesus Christ. They believe the Bible is the ultimate authority, the inerrant word.

>> **Christian fundamentalists,** on the other hand, are believed to be a stricter subset of Christianity than evangelicals. While evangelicals are more culturally engaged, fundamentalists are not. Fundamentalists are intentional about being set apart from society and culture. They believe the Christian Bible to be literal and, like evangelicals, subscribe to personal conversing — that is, being born again and in right relationship with Jesus. They're traditional in nature and usually found within Christian denominations like Pentecostalism.

>> **Conservative Christians** may also consider themselves members of evangelicalism or even identify with fundamentalism, but they're usually less theologically engaged. They're more driven politically and concerned about social issues. Some groups you may have heard of that are commonly associated with conservative Christianity include Focus on the Family and Liberty University. They're also described as the religious right. They're often associated with Pentecostalism, but their churches are much more independent in nature.

REMEMBER

Understanding these groups — what makes them similar and what makes them different — provides context. This is mostly true for anyone who consciously understands their deconstruction as a product of these communities. But some have no awareness of that possibility. You may not be a member of a community explicitly labeled as conservative or evangelical or fundamentalist. What does that mean for your deconstruction? Even without being a member of a church or one of these groups, you could have been exposed to their messaging.

How or why? Because of colonialism. Chapter 13 discusses a little about decolonizing your faith, which can be an important part of faith deconstruction. *Colonialism,* the practice of imposing your worldview, practices, systems, and beliefs onto another group, is deeply rooted in Western Christianity, and to some extent global Christianity.

REMEMBER

For a religious system that's reported to be the youngest of all religious systems in the world, colonialism was highly effective at spreading Christianity and its beliefs, systems, and structure around the world. As a result, Christianity became dominant and baked into society — especially within oppressed communities.

Therefore, while you may not have been a member of an evangelical church or a fundamentalist movement, or consider your faith community to be evangelical or fundamentalist in nature, your faith community may have been informed by many of the traditional teachings born out of the impact and presence of historical colonialism. No one is exempt. Even the most "liberal" or "progressive" spaces have been informed and influenced by a colonized version of Christianity.

Does faith deconstruction only apply to Christianity?

Even though opponents of faith deconstruction like to suggest an almost symbiotic relationship between faith deconstruction and evangelical, conservative, or Christian fundamentalism, it's not exclusive to Christianity. If deconstruction is defined as thinking critically about what you believe, what you've been taught religiously, and how it aligns with your faith, it's worth assuming that the same occurs in any and every religious system. Why? Because no one system is perfect, for one. Second, thinking critically about what you believe just makes sense. Third, as Chapter 6 covers, all religion is the product by which faith is formed, and it's made up of systems, rules, and practices that work to maintain the homogeneity of that religious community. It's inevitable to have some dissonance that prompts people to deconstruct.

What does faith deconstruction look like in other faith systems?

If you're Jewish, you might challenge the traditional and societal norms of the community. This may also result in your rethinking your connection to the community and its importance in your life. It could be a difference in how you understand your place in society or an identity that's not widely accepted in the larger faith community.

In Islam, deconstruction also involves challenging beliefs, interpretations of religious texts, and reevaluating authority. If you deconstruct within Islam, you'll look beyond the faith to other forms of thinking, religiously and culturally, to assist in your process of evaluating what you believe and your relationship to the faith. In some Muslim societies, faith deconstruction is seen as a form of apostasy, the abandonment of religion. Apostasy is illegal in many of those communities.

Like Judaism and Islam, deconstruction within Hinduism involves self-interrogation of the systems that govern the faith. In this case, it's the caste hierarchies. Deconstructing Hindu means exploring other forms of understanding beyond the faith. It also means reassessing the faith's deities and their value in your life.

For Buddhism, which in some circles isn't considered a religious group or system, deconstruction or a reevaluation of the practice of Buddhism is the first step. This could mean considering the effectiveness of the practices that are at the core of Buddhism, including meditation, chanting, and rituals.

What makes deconstruction beneficial?

I began my faith journey believing God could only be encountered through Jesus. As I engaged other spaces and did some work and research of my own, much of that changed for me. Some years ago, people used to joke that I had the ability to see God in everything — even a flower on the side of the expressway. That's true. As I've engaged other spaces, I've encountered something I can never truly understand or describe — something that feels like what I would like to believe is a divine presence.

As far as I'm concerned, God isn't something that can be simply relegated to a religion or a church or a specific community. God, or the Divine, is in all things and in all spaces. If there *is* a God. I'm working through some of what I believe. Deconstruction, like faith, is an ongoing journey of seeking, learning, relearning, unlearning, and discovery. While at one time I was a devoted Christian who believed Jesus was the only way, today I'm somewhere between a humanist and an agnostic. It may be more accurate to suggest I'm along the lines of a religious humanist or a spiritual agnostic. Maybe even a theistic or polytheistic humanist.

Honestly, I'm still figuring a lot of it out. I'm still informed by the teachings of Jesus as recorded in the New Testament gospels, but I'm also informed by some of the tenets of other faith systems as well. I also wrestle with whether it's necessary to label myself anything, understanding that labels are more for the purpose of helping others understand us. Categories can sometimes be limiting and ineffective.

REMEMBER

One of the benefits of faith deconstruction is the ability and courage to explore. I have a greater understanding of who I am, what I believe (or better yet what I don't believe), and what role I want to play in the world because of my deconstruction. My Christian upbringing is still a big part of me and how I am in the world. Those lessons didn't just go away. And I still have a lot of love for some Christian spaces. Choirs and gospel music will always have a place in my heart, especially in those moments when I need a reminder, a pick-me-up, or inspiration to get me by.

TIP

Deconstructing your faith makes you better and authentic, besides making you more solid in your beliefs and foundation. It provides freedom, clarity, and purpose. The mysteries of God are intended to be just that: mysteries. How else will you know what that means for you and your relationship with God if you don't explore it and critique it some? It's how you learn and how you grow. If your faith isn't tested at some point in your life, you're not doing it right.

Let the Journey Begin. . .

If you're here, it's likely you have some big questions. Or maybe you're just a little curious. Maybe you've heard the phrase *faith deconstruction* before but really don't know what it is or what it means. Maybe no one has ever really explained it to you in a way that felt tangible. Or maybe they have, and you wanted or felt you needed to know more.

You're in the right place. You're right where you're supposed to be!

This book is by no means the sacred text of faith deconstruction. That would be entirely too presumptuous on my part. But when I was beginning my own faith deconstruction journey, I wish I'd had the knowledge and awareness I now possess. Who knows what my journey may have been like if I'd had a book like this?

As you begin your deconstruction journey, I hope this book provides you the guidance, clarity, and direction needed to make that journey a little more bearable — regardless of where it takes you. You may find answers. You may not. But hopefully, what you find in these pages will make a positive difference for you.

Now go see where it leads you!

Chapter **2**

Examining the Origins of Faith Deconstruction

There's something about an origin story. In some of my favorite movies or TV shows, the origin story is the background. Origin stories are especially important in many of my favorite superhero productions, providing just enough foundation to understand who the characters are, what situations birthed their identities and motivations, and who the important people are in their lives.

When done right, origin stories are one of the most important aspects of any narrative. And they don't just show up in superhero stories. I think of the first five minutes of one of my favorite movies, *The First Wives Club*. Watching just a few short scenes reveals the necessary background of why the loss of a New York socialite affects the characters of Goldie Hawn, Bette Midler, and Diane Keaton.

I want to know not only the why, but the how of the why. I want to know how a situation has surfaced and what led to it. I'm a nerd like that. This has been especially true for my faith deconstruction journey. When it became apparent that I was deconstructing my faith, one of the first things I learned was the name Jacques Derrida. In those early days of my process, I didn't dig as deep as I normally would have, but I knew enough to pique my interest. When it came time to work on this book, I accepted that I needed to know more background.

How do you get to where you are in faith deconstruction, and who is responsible? This chapter offers a little information about the origins of deconstruction and faith deconstruction as a practice. It isn't an exhaustive history by any means, but enough to help you get a better understanding and context as you discern where you are in your journey.

A (Fairly) Brief History Lesson on Faith Deconstruction

In the spring of 2023, I went public about deconstructing my faith. It was a scary experience, which I share a little about in Chapter 15. I was participating in a writing fellowship, and the assignment was to write and publish three essays on whatever topic we felt passionate about. One of my essays was a first-person narrative on my faith deconstruction journey. What's missing from that essay is what I learned about faith deconstruction in the process of writing the essay.

To understand faith deconstruction, it's necessary to understand the philosophical concept of deconstruction. It's like the question, "What comes first: the chicken or the egg?" You can't get to faith deconstruction without being introduced to and understanding deconstruction. (I mean, you can, but I think you're better equipped when you know a little of how we got here.)

In my initial research, I kept coming across the name of French Algerian philosopher Jacques Derrida. According to Catherine

Turner, Derrida first outlines the concept of deconstruction in his book *Of Grammatology*. But his critique has nothing to do with faith or religion. Derrida's deconstruction philosophy is rooted, initially, in language and understanding. I was surprised that I'd never heard of Derrida before I began working on my essay. Never in high school, graduate school, or seminary had his name come up, at least that I could remember. Derrida was a stranger to me.

Who is Jacques Derrida, and how is his writing about deconstruction in the 1960s relevant to faith deconstruction today? The following sections provide an overview of his work, his definition of deconstruction, and how it evolved to what's now known as faith deconstruction.

Introducing Jacques Derrida and his philosophy of deconstruction

Every faith deconstructionist I've come across has credited Derrida with being the inventor of deconstruction. Several of them have referred to him simply as the "father of deconstruction." One of the many critiques that cultural critics, including me, have when it comes to how history is told is how credit is often assigned. At the core of just about every narrative of how something was formed, discovered, or named is usually a male of European descent. Some critics may even label these acts as whitewashing. Derrida's designation is, seemingly, no different. But I digress.

Whether credit is given where credit is due, Derrida is believed to be the first to pen anything pertaining to deconstruction. As a result, he made most of his career writing and lecturing on the topic. But when he died, not every obituary written of him was celebratory. One that appeared in the *New York Times* described Derrida as abstruse (meaning difficult), hard to understand, and obscure. His work had made major contributions, but Derrida wasn't blindly lauded for his scholarship. Not broadly anyway.

Who was he, and how did he become the father of deconstruction? As stated previously, Derrida first outlines the concept of deconstruction in *Of Grammatology,* published in 1967. I've never read the book, but I've read a few summaries and reviews. And

I must admit, I struggled to get my mind around what he was trying to say. Initially, as I read and researched, I landed on the idea that meaning isn't static. His overall argument is that readers aren't always capable of deciphering what an author's meaning or intent is because of what *they* bring to the exercise. It's an analysis on interpretation and, to some extent, projection. Derrida believes that as readers engage the written word, they place their own understandings and perspectives and meanings upon the piece that may not align exactly with what the author intended.

Derrida wrote that understanding the intent of an author's words requires pulling it apart. This is the act of *deconstructing.* By pulling it apart, the reader is intentionally determining and deciphering meaning, while also critiquing how well the author makes the argument they're attempting to make.

In other words, to understand the intent of a written piece, it's necessary to take it apart and read it through the lens of the author.

TIP

As Kristen Lavalley points out in her essay, "the cultural history of deconstruction," Derrida wasn't looking to destroy what was already known or understood about language but to provide context to the complexity of language and its relationship to meaning making. Derrida's work regarding deconstruction seeks to provide nuance on the power of language and contextual true meaning.

Taking a closer look at Derrida

By many accounts, Derrida was critiqued as being conflicted and complicated. One biography I read described him as a voracious reader. The bio also pointed out he wasn't the best student — so much so that he failed almost every entrance exam or oral exit examination he ever took; at least once. And he faced a fair share of scandal, not only for his writings and lectures on deconstruction — sharing positions that weren't very popular in some parts of the western world and were considered at times nonsensical — but because he found himself on the wrong side of history, some would say. According to reports, Derrida publicly supported a fellow professor who was accused of sexually harassing a student. I also learned that Derrida shied away from being photographed for many years and never talked to the media. His first-ever on camera interview may have taken place almost 30 years after he published *Of Grammatology*. In life, Derrida was described as an elusive scholar. Many of those who have written about him suggest that Derrida wanted his work — his words — to speak for him.

Born in 1930, Derrida published nearly 40 books over the course of his career. And even though he taught and lectured at the École Normal Supérieure and the University of Paris, it would be 30 years before he successfully defended his dissertation. In 2004, he died in Paris, France, from pancreatic cancer. Not long after Derrida's death, Mark C. Taylor, professor emeritus in the Department of Religion at Columbia University in New York, wrote an op-ed for the *New York Times* titled "What Derrida Really Meant."

In his op-ed, Taylor makes the case for how and why Derrida's work in deconstruction is significant. He suggests that many of the critics of deconstruction not only misunderstand Derrida and his research but also miss how far-reaching Derrida's work has been.

Near the end of his life, Derrida — who was Jewish — started focusing on religion. He saw a relationship between religion and uncertainty as almost necessary.

As Taylor puts it, Derrida believed that it's impossible to have religion or religious thought without some uncertainty. I can relate to that with my own deconstruction journey. Religion is fickle, or at least it should be. Faith is precarious, which is what makes it faith. And God and the things of God are a mystery, also as they should be. It seems that even though Derrida spent much of his career engaging deconstruction through the lens of that which he cherished — literature and language — he saw ways to best apply his challenge to theology.

For the first time in my reading and researching of Derrida, I found myself with an inkling of understanding what he was trying to say and do through his work around deconstruction.

Adopting Derrida's deconstruction concept to faith

Derrida's work had such a great impact on Taylor that he used the tenets of Derrida's scholarship in the formulation of his own research. In 1982, some 20 years after Derrida's *Of Grammatology,* Taylor published what's believed to be the first book ever on faith deconstruction, titled *Deconstructing Theology.* In the book, Taylor refers to the "death of God." Friedrich Nietzsche, a philosopher from Germany, made that phrase popular. He believed that heaven was unreal, questioned the validity of good versus evil, and was commonly categorized as an atheist.

Nietzsche, along with Søren Kierkegaard and Georg Wilhelm Friedrich Hegel, was an early influencer of Taylor's work. Kierkegaard was a theologian and philosopher who originated from Denmark. Hegel is described as a German idealist.

I was puzzled by Nietzsche's "death of God" language. What I found in research was fascinating, however. The "death of God" suggested a weakening in the impact and influence of tradition as well as authority. In other words, tradition and authority's influence was waning, which meant that meaning and faith were also in jeopardy. Religious spaces were collapsing, and awakening and awareness were taking their place. A postmodern deconstruction movement was already at play. Taylor weaved together the previous work and commentary of Nietzsche, Kierkegaard, and Hegel with Derrida to increase awareness and provide what he referred to in the book as philosophical insight for other theologians of their time to benefit.

REMEMBER

Taylor began laying the foundation for what has become somewhat of a modern movement of faith deconstruction. A ripple began in the 1980s that has continued today.

"There can be no ethical action without critical reflection" is one of the lines from Taylor's op-ed on Derrida. It's probably one of the strongest lines in the entire piece. What makes deconstruction *deconstruction* is critical analysis, which many opponents of faith deconstruction find troubling. Faith, discussed in Chapter 5, is believed or understood to be unabashed trust and assurance. In some respects, faith is taught to be unshakable and immovable. The reality: That's not always true.

REMEMBER

Faith is intended to be blind but never doubtless. An important part of faith is both assuredness and doubt. And yet, because of religion, many have lost the capability to assess critically what they believe and why. Derrida's deconstruction becomes a tool by which Taylor critiques theology, faith, and religion because it calls for thinking critically. Derrida's deconstruction provides, at least for Taylor and others who followed Derrida, a means by which to communicate what it means to think critically about God. And that's precisely the definition of theology.

Anything that's worth cherishing or living by should be open to interpretation and reflection. Most people who are deconstructing their faith are evaluating and reevaluating their beliefs and their relationship to their beliefs. When someone has taken the time to critically evaluate and reflect on who they are, what they believe, and why they believe it, their relationship to their beliefs is enhanced.

MORE ON NIETZSCHE, KIERKEGAARD, AND HEGEL

In many ways, Nietzsche, Kierkegaard, and Hegel were contemporaries of one another. Each is described as a 19th-century philosopher and critic. Their research overlapped in a lot of ways, but they were also worlds apart in their perceptions, areas of expertise, and approaches. Hegel, who was born in 1770 and died in 1831, wasn't a theologian. However, much of his work and writing is referenced by historical and theological scholars throughout history. For Hegel, Christianity was the absolute faith. He felt that through this absolute faith, society achieves self-realization. He believed religion to be not just a set of beliefs, systems, and practices, but a crucial and integral part of one's development, especially spiritually.

Kierkegaard is said to have been a major critic of Hegel, especially as it pertained to what's described as Hegel's systematic approach, which suggested that all things are connected and that people get to the understanding of all things through historical inquiry. Kierkegaard believed faith was more individual and personal. He believed in personal freedom in faith, felt that faith is subjective and can't be proven,

(continued)

(continued)

and described the life path of most in three stages: aesthetic (pursuit of pleasure), ethical (embracing moral duties), and religious (the highest stage reached through faith and connection to God).

Nietzsche was critical of Hegel and was also not a theologian. But his work greatly influenced theologians, like Taylor and others, as well as other philosophers and psychologists. In addition to the "death of God" concept and his rejection of heaven as real or good versus evil, Nietzsche believed that every being is ruled by pure will and that pure will is fundamental in every being's motivation and drive.

Delving into the Critique of Faith Deconstruction

A classmate of mine said something to me early in my deconstruction journey that I've never forgotten. I can't remember how we got on the topic of deconstruction exactly, but I remember immediately being quietly excited that we were having the conversation. This was the first time I'd been able to have this kind of conversation with someone I not only trusted but also saw as one of the smartest people I'd ever met. The conversation happened during a one-week intensive course as part of the Doctor of Ministry degree program we were enrolled in.

I like having smart conversations with smart people. It makes me feel like I'm walking away enlightened and informed in a way I wasn't when the conversation began. By the end of this conversation, however, I was unnerved. "I don't even think deconstruction is the right or most appropriate word for it," he said.

I remember asking myself, "What if what I thought I was experiencing wasn't in fact what I was experiencing? What if I'm wrong?" I also remember asking myself, "If we don't call it *faith deconstruction*, what do we call it then?" This section touches on the debate of whether faith deconstruction is the most appropriate identifier for this process. This isn't about the validity of deconstruction itself (I cover that in Chapter 1 if you're interested), but rather about whether deconstruction is the best descriptor or moniker and my qualms about the chatter.

The debate . . .

Prior to the conversation with my classmate, I hadn't heard anyone else express his sentiment. I'd seen or heard commentary about the validity of deconstruction in a great number of spaces, especially via Facebook and other social media platforms. But I'd yet to hear anyone say, "We shouldn't be calling this *deconstruction*, but something else."

As discussed in Chapter 1 and throughout this book, faith deconstruction has many opponents overall. Most of the people are against the process because of their perceptions of it as a concept. They don't see the validity in thinking critically about faith and religion and the benefits that can come with it. Or they see the validity, understand the repercussions of allowing people to think about what they believe critically, but are afraid of what it may mean for them and the spaces they're invested in.

There are also those who are champions of the practice of faith deconstruction and support it as a concept but are challenged by the name or what to call it. They understand Derrida and Taylor's intent and support it, but they're challenged by the choice of the descriptor. Some of these individuals have made a name and reputation out of the very practice of questioning and challenging toxic theology. They're self-proclaimed champions of those harmed by the practices, teachings, and interpretations of harmful theology. And some have been victims themselves, which is what made them champions of deconstruction as a concept.

I've come across another group in my own journey and research that's equally interesting to me. Some of them are theologically trained and heavily invested in the faith communities for which they hold membership. They perceive faith deconstruction to be dangerous because of their fear that faith deconstructionists may be irresponsibly supporting religious abandonment and doing so recklessly. They're against the use of the name *deconstruction* because of what they perceive to be destructive and rebellious acts rather than critical and pastoral engagement and guidance. As far as they're concerned, deconstruction is too focused on eliminating and isn't focused enough on the rebuilding, often understood as reconstruction. Reconstruction is discussed in-depth in Chapter 18.

TIP

It seems that, overall, what's at the core of the argument is a belief that the word *deconstruction* is limiting *and* misleading. For many opponents of the word but proponents of the work, there's a feeling or a belief that the work of thinking critically about what they believe and why isn't deconstruction. Deconstruction is, in their view, too final. What's happening is a critical evaluation and reevaluation that doesn't have to result in complete destruction of beliefs but does make room for an expansion of those beliefs and an understanding of faith and religious affiliation.

Those who are evangelical and deconstructing have adopted Derrida's definition because it speaks to their experiences with deconstruction or, at least, based on how they've chosen to understand and define it for themselves. It can be a means of not simply questioning but also dismantling understanding and the perception of authority of those who proclaim to speak for God.

While I understand the critiques of many, I take issue with some of their assertions. I also can't help but wonder if something more sinister is at play.

Often, discussions such as what to call deconstruction and if the name fits are intended to do something else. It's possible that this debate over what to call it is an attempt at discrediting deconstruction and its validity. Sometimes when people aren't comfortable enough to say exactly what they mean, they find another way of saying it — a workaround to the real issue at hand. And again, society has been thinking critically about literature, faith, understanding, and belief since the beginning of time. Those things will always be debated. It's what makes areas like philosophy and theology and the work that people do within them important. How else will people learn and expand and adjust if not for the critical analysis of all things — faith and religion included?

What should deconstruction be called then?

Words mean things. They have meaning and intent. And sometimes, to borrow a bit from Derrida, people project meaning onto something that distorts the author's intent and meaning.

In my research, I came across several suggestions for other words that could be better used. *Undoing* is one. I also came across *reforming* or *reformation*. I understand why some suggest the word *reforming* or even *reformation*. When you reform, you improve by removing faults or abuses. *Reform* can also be defined as putting to an end by enforcing or introducing better methods. When you reform, you change, and you're made better. When you reform, according to most definitions, you're refined.

REMEMBER

There are parallels between faith deconstruction and reformation; sure! In the process of reconstruction, you're reforming. There's another part of the definition, however, that doesn't exactly align with deconstruction, or maybe it does. And that part is: to induce or cause to abandon evil ways.

Be honest. Reformation? Isn't that somewhere society has been and something it has done already? Religious history, especially Christian history, has had its fair share of reformations. And each time, for the most part, the result has been something new but just as flawed. There's also another piece of the deconstructing part that's important. Faith deconstruction introduces new information or a fresh perspective. It's not just that you're experiencing a reformation. Before you can even get there, you shed all forms of toxic theology, as well as rules and doctrines that limit your freedoms and your imagination. Shedding is an important part of the journey, which is why I think Derrida and Taylor felt deconstruction was the best fit.

I like *undoing*. When I think about it, I also think about *unraveling* as well as *unwrapping*. *Undoing* provides the right amount of description and understanding of what faith deconstruction is like for many people. You aren't just rethinking, reevaluating, or reworking what you believe. You're also undoing. You're unwrapping layers of thinking and teaching and influence that have become so affixed that they were burrowed into your psyche, your very being. Part of the deconstruction process is then unwrapping yourself from all that influence.

But does it matter what the process is called? Is the naming rooted in a desire to define all things to feel better prepared and more comfortable? Whether Derrida had any idea when he chose the word *deconstruction* to make the point he was trying to make for his work, or whether Taylor had any idea how his applying it to theology would result in me now writing this book doesn't matter. Whether the process is called *deconstruction* or *reformation* doesn't matter. What it's called doesn't remove its necessity, its importance, and the influence that the practice has had on countless individuals and their faith journey.

Chapter **3**

Modern Motivators for Deconstruction

D econstruction doesn't just happen, regardless of what anyone tries to make you believe. Every deconstruction story has a moment that served as a spark. It may not always be definitive, but it's impactful. Something is shaken, causing the foundation to become compromised.

It's like the lead-up to a divorce. Initially, the trigger moment is dismissed, but a seed is planted. Over time, the seed starts to grow. Instances that were once written off as coincidences can't continue to be overlooked. The couple stops making excuses for all the things they used to let slide and, eventually, they reach the point where they can't tolerate anymore. They no longer have the patience they once had. They don't want to even try any longer, so they file for divorce.

Patchwork efforts are made, but the inevitable is, well, inevitable. Most often the couple decides that the relationship is worth fighting for. They seek counseling. They attempt to find a fix by negotiating. But eventually, they come to terms with reality.

They realize it's just not working anymore regardless of how hard they try.

Like divorce, faith deconstruction is the crack in the foundation, the lifting of the veil. Maybe you've had enough, and your only option is to let your faith go.

TIP

To be clear, in faith deconstruction, you may not divorce yourself from your beliefs completely. Some of what you once believed or some of what you once cherished is retained. But something is ended. Something(s) is/are lost.

But how did you get to the point of no return? While Chapters 1 and 2 provide a baseline understanding of faith deconstruction, this chapter highlights some of the factors that can lead to faith deconstruction. It's not an exhaustive list. (*Note:* Chapter 11 digs deeper into what has led some people specifically to deconstruct their faith, while this chapter discusses the role these factors play in faith deconstruction.)

Examining Some Factors That May Lead to Deconstruction

Have you ever heard of the phrase *cognitive dissonance*? I learned this concept during my first year of seminary. Cognitive dissonance happens when your beliefs and values no longer align. You experience a form of emotional, mental, and psychological discomfort that causes you to either find a way to adjust or to change.

If you're deconstructing your faith, more than likely you decided to make a cognitive–dissonance–provoked change. What might that look like? There are so many examples. Maybe you're someone who once believed that homosexuality is a sin but then learned that the Greek word that many have translated as homosexual was introduced to the Bible in 1946. Or maybe you learned that the story of Sodom and Gomorrah wasn't about homosexuality but was instead a lesson on hospitality. Being exposed to this "new" information may impact your understandings and entire identity.

The reasons for faith deconstruction are personal and individual. It's possible your deconstruction is informed by experience. Maybe an authority figure in your religious community mistreated or mishandled you. Or maybe your spark was ignited not by something you experienced personally, but something you witnessed happening to others. Perhaps it was a sermon you heard that made you uncomfortable, or you witnessed or overheard something that didn't feel right.

Your deconstruction may be informed by a shift in your beliefs or new considerations after reading a scripture or sacred text for the umpteenth time. Maybe it was a subtle and random revelation you were incapable of considering previously. Or you had a conversation with someone that led you to see the text differently. For me, there were a series of moments from my years in high school to the time I entered seminary, but I consider one particular moment in 2009 to be the impetus of my faith deconstruction journey. I talk about it in depth in Chapter 8.

Whatever it was, things are now different.

This section covers some of the influences that can lead you to reevaluate your faith. Chapters 8, 9, and 10 elaborate on some of these in greater detail.

Religious abuse

As Chapter 2 discusses, faith deconstruction isn't a widely embraced enterprise. In fact, quite a few are vocal critics. Some of them view deconstruction as emotionalism; they don't believe that those deconstructing are approaching their situation pragmatically. As far as they're concerned, faith deconstruction is simply a childish reaction to a little discomfort. They're of the mindset that some have experienced worse in the church, and their discomfort is par for the course.

But this is gaslighting. And, to some extent, it's one of the tools of religious abuse.

Religious abuse can take on many forms. But at its core, religious abuse is mistreatment in the name of God. This can include any of the following:

>> Spiritual and emotional manipulation

>> Fearmongering

>> Shame or condemnation

>> Control and/or isolation

>> Exploitation (oftentimes financial)

Usually, religious abuse occurs at the hands of those in charge. If in a church, it's usually the pastor or someone with authority, which can mean a trustee of the church, a deacon, or an auxiliary leader. Even a church secretary or a minister is capable of religious abuse. Beyond the church or religious institution, religious abuse can be enacted by a community or political leader (which is discussed more in depth in Chapter 6).

What does religious abuse look like, and how can you tell when it's happening? Religious abuse occurs when religion is used as a tool of inappropriate influence. Whether through spiritual or emotional manipulation, shame and condemnation, or fear mongering, religious abuse occurs when your actions, thoughts, beliefs, and even perspectives are controlled by someone twisting religious concepts to obtain power and influence over you.

The preaching moment in a lot of churches is one example. This is especially true through the act of *proof-texting*, the practice of using scripture or a sacred text to prove a point. It becomes manipulation when the preacher takes a text and uses it completely out of context. They *eisegete* the text (interpreting a text by placing personal beliefs onto it) to sway the opinions and perspectives of the congregation. In some instances, pastors will use the sermon to shame or condemn, emotionally and spiritually manipulate the congregation, or create panic so that members will make personal, political, or financial decisions that align with their agenda.

Some suggest religious abuse isn't the most accurate label for this behavior. They believe that religious violence is a more fitting and appropriate description. But whether you call it religious abuse or religious violence, some have experienced harm at the hands of religious figures that has left them traumatized and vulnerable. Many who have experienced this harm have turned to deconstruction as a remedy. Maybe you're one of them.

TIP

Some faith leaders will suggest that what you may consider abuse or violence isn't anywhere close to being abuse or violence. They might suggest that their messages, protocols, and culture are rooted in tradition and divine inspiration. Perhaps they'll even reference the concept of long suffering as an excuse for their actions. *Long suffering* is the belief that some people are ordained by God to endure longer-term hardship. They'll suggest that suffering means being righteous and in line with what God intends.

WARNING

This sort of mindset is also abusive and manipulative. Religious communities are meant to be safe havens. They should be committed to empowering and uplifting their members, not belittling them for the sake of perceived power and control. If a community doesn't feel safe, it isn't a godly led or ordained space.

Sexism: The patriarchy

From Hagar, to Ruth, to the "Virgin" Mary, and Mary Magdalene, Christianity alone has countless examples of influential women who have played important roles in many of the Abrahamic faiths. These women named God, birthed a prophet, discovered a troubled tomb, and became the embodiment of loyalty and love. In many respects, they laid the foundation for strength, power, and purpose. And they aren't the only ones.

Throughout the history of religion, and history overall, women or women figures have led the way. They've organized movements that brought about revolutions. They've birthed and created not only leaders, but periods of enlightenment. They've been the embodiment of what it means to be a stalwart, a trailblazer, a visionary, and a leader. You can find a few examples of some of these impressive women in Chapter 19.

I think about women like Fannie Lou Hamer, who's known for saying, "Nobody's free until everybody's free" and "I'm sick and tired of being sick and tired." She was a staunch advocate for voting rights, going so far as to challenge a sitting president, President Lyndon B. Johnson. I also think about Prathia Hall, also an activist as well as a preacher. Little known fact: Hall was the originator of the famous "I Have a Dream" speech. In the 1960s, she repeated the phrase, "I have a dream" during a mass prayer meeting where Rev. Dr. Martin Luther King, Jr. was also in attendance.

Women have been the blueprint. Unfortunately, within some religious communities and sects, women have been perceived as less than what they deserved. Patriarchy has been an epidemic within some of the most popular and impactful religious movements. And women, unfortunately, have been relegated to roles that have done more to assuage the ego of patriarchy than truly celebrate them for their gifts and divine purpose.

But here's the thing: Globally, more women consider themselves religious than men do. According to the Pew Research Center, a little over 80% of women identify with some kind of religion, versus a little over 70% of men. And when you break it down by religions, the numbers are even more telling. A little more than 54% of those who identify as Buddhist are women. Roughly 53% of Christians are women. And the number is almost the same for Jews, at 52%.

However, several religious groups don't allow women to be leaders in the church. The Roman Catholic Church, the Mormons, the Eastern Orthodox Church, the Presbyterian Church of America, the Southern Baptist Convention, and the Evangelical & Reformed Synod don't ordain women to be priests, deacons, bishops, or leaders in their denominations. The same is true for Islam, Orthodox Judaism, and Hinduism.

TIP

These limits are due to sexism within the faith. For generations, scriptural text-proofing is another example of how women have been perceived and limited religiously. However, suggesting that scripture is the sole culprit is a misuse. Many of the religious texts existing today were influenced greatly by perspectives already present in society. One of those perspectives was patriarchy, or man-centered society. Many of our religions today didn't simply start where they are now. They were formed over time. As a result, many of the perspectives that made their way into our sacred texts were influenced greatly by the society that surrounded them. Meaning was placed onto and into these stories, and these meanings continue to plague us today.

Sexism within religion has motivated faith deconstruction for many women and some men. They've looked at the texts, traditions, and practices more closely and determined that the practices don't align with what they believe to be right and just. As society has changed over time, so has its views. Christian scriptural texts like Ephesians 5: 22–24—"Wives obey your husbands the husband is the head of the household in the same way that Christ is the head of the church"—have taken on new meaning in the wake of gender equality and women empowerment.

What has this looked like in real time? One example is the development of inclusive language in some practices, like Christianity. Some have replaced their gendered language for God with non-gender-informed language. Instead of calling God *He*, they've adopted language like *the Divine*, *the Creator*, and *Father-Mother God*. This has also been helpful for those who may have had a history of abuse at the hands of their fathers or father figures. The trauma of that abuse that was once projected onto God because of how God is seen as a father figure hasn't been relegated solely to the men/father figures who enacted the abuse upon them.

Sexuality and faith

Ever heard the phrase, "God made Adam and Eve, not Adam and Steve"? This statement was at one time a common retort for many within Christian spaces that were anti-LGBTQ+. The statement is a suggestion that God has always been on the side of what's considered tradition. It suggests that to be anything outside of what's considered "normal," meaning not heterosexual, is against God and, to some extent, is sacrilegious.

Regularly, whenever someone raises the topic of sexuality, most people automatically lean toward thinking of sexual identity or expression, such as queer, LGBTQ+, or same sex/same gender loving/attracted. However, sexuality is broader than that.

Merriam-Webster defines it as the quality or state of being sexual, such as sexual reproduction, sexual activity, and the expression of sexual interest. Webster also includes sexual identity, such as bisexual, straight, gay, and pansexual in its definition. This subsection focuses more on the identity concept. The following subsection, sexual purity, elaborates more on the first half of Webster's definition.

For those who identify as queer, LGBTQ+, or same-sex attracted, their deconstruction often begins around the time their faith or religious teachings begin to conflict with their revelations around their identity. Many find themselves questioning whether what they've been taught religiously as it pertains to homosexuality aligns with what they believe about themselves. At the root of their questioning is a central question: Does God love me or hate me? This question is often informed by the sermons they've heard during church, or the conversations had in and around them within their local community. Maybe a preacher, teacher, priest, or imam has talked about the sin of homosexuality, or a beloved community member has suggested that people who are gay or transgender are perverted or mentally ill. Many of these beliefs are inspired by what's taught in religious spaces.

For those who aren't members of the alphabet mafia (an affectionate moniker to describe the LGBTQ+ community) but consider themselves loved ones or allies, their deconstruction begins somewhat similarly. As they've heard some of the same commentary, many of them have struggled with what they've been told versus what they've experienced in proximity with members of the community. They question the validity of the opinions, beliefs, and narratives because their personal experience has provided a more genuine, authentic, and personal understanding of the people being ridiculed.

For the more conservative sects of most religions, homosexuality is perceived to be sinful because of the belief that same-sex attracted and same-sex loving individuals are sexual deviants. Chapter 10 discusses the concept of sin more in depth. Because these groups have standardized heterosexuality as the norm, any identity that is perceived as more progressive is considered counter to what they believe God intended.

However, in recent years, a lot of conversation has taken place within more progressive settings regarding sexuality and how diverse sexual expression and orientation was in bygone times. One example is the concept of two-spiritedness in Indigenous cultures. The concept of two-spiritedness is said to be exclusive to Native American culture. Definitions vary, but at the core of the concept is the acknowledgment of individuals who either possess both masculine and feminine qualities, or have diverse gender identities and sexual orientations. Some two-spirit individuals are revered in their community and hold special roles, which includes spiritual and religious leadership.

Purity culture

What does it mean to be free? As a concept, many would suggest that freedom is rooted in privilege. Being unfettered by the subjugation of others, their opinions and perspectives, and their rules and controls is a privilege. Being free means having agency over yourself and your choices. But freedom isn't simply physical in nature. It's also mental, emotional, and maybe even spiritual.

Sexual liberation, for many, is freedom. Purity culture has often fought against the agency to be sexually liberated and, to some extent, free.

In many ways, purity culture is an unwelcome companion to many of the motivators discussed thus far. Within Christianity, many proponents to purity culture have used 1 Corinthians 6:19–20 as their case for purity culture. They've argued that because one's body is indebted to God, they're to act and live righteously. And, for them, living righteously means "saving oneself" or abstaining from sex until marriage — heterosexual marriage, that is.

Other religious groups have their own versions of purity culture. In some religious communities, purity culture can be equated with modesty. In others, sexual desires are equated to suffering, and believers are instructed to refrain from sexual misconduct.

Sex, in general, is often perceived as taboo. It's a topic of discussion that can be a struggle to engage in, even within interpersonal relationships. The Christian relationship to sex or concept of sex is limited to one true purpose: reproduction. As a result, many of the strategies and language regarding purity are directed at women almost exclusively. Women are often instructed to see themselves and their bodies as vessels for men's fulfillment, gratification, and satisfaction. Sex is seen and perceived as being useful only for the purpose of making families and should only be exercised between two individuals of the opposite sex within the confines of a marital arrangement. Anyone who engages beyond these culturally prescribed parameters is considered sexual deviants and shamed for what those in authority see as failures.

REMEMBER

Desire and physical intimacy are a natural part of human life.

Many of those who have deconstructed because of purity culture have been informed by a few factors. For some, the policing of their bodies became trauma-induced experiences that caused them to have to dig from under the weight of self-esteem issues and self-doubt. Others, especially Black women who submitted to the whims of purity culture, have realized how the culture placed them at an unfair advantage and how their bodies were being policed and regulated by spaces that centered acceptance of the majority community (read: white, cisgendered, right wing, evangelical men).

Considering Other Causes of One's Faith Deconstruction

The previous sections discuss some of the factors that have led people to deconstruct their faith. Many of the factors have some tie to identity. Often, a person's identity, such as being LGBTQ+, influences their deconstruction. But other factors can lead to faith deconstruction.

Faith deconstruction is usually a result of something that happens to a person. It's often caused by a spark. And, more likely than not, that spark is the result of something someone did or said. But faith deconstruction can also come about through the observation of others, a desire to differentiate oneself from those you disagree with, or the disgust/frustration you're feeling that brings about a revelation or a desire for change, a cognitive dissonance.

The following section highlights a few additional motivations, from grief to experiences with religious extremists to the need and desire to decolonize your faith.

Loss/grief

Are you surprised to see loss/grief categorized as a motivation for faith deconstruction? Most would probably never think to consider grief as a conduit for deconstruction, but it is. The loss of something or someone is one of the most life-altering instances you can experience. It shifts you. In some instances, it knocks you off your axis.

In the grief process, depending on the severity and impact of the loss, you experience a period of seeking, wondering, wandering, and questioning. That season might include shifting your perspectives and understandings of life in general. Faith becomes a not-so-innocent bystander in all of it.

Take, for instance, the concept of healing. Chapter 5 discusses this more in depth, but when you feel hopeful about a certain outcome, the disappointment you experience when the outcome isn't what you expected can cause you to question and challenge what you've been conditioned to believe about God, Jesus, or whoever/whatever you worship. The disappointment is the seed planted in your deconstruction process.

Whether with death or any loss in general, grief becomes another means by which you might deconstruct your faith. The things you were taught to believe or expect become challenging to accept amid the pain of the loss. Not only that, you might become irritated by some of the tools that faith leaders use, from language to spiritual bypassing — "God loved them so much God wanted them to be in heaven with Him" — (discussed more in Chapter 10) to the lack of answers and perceived support. All of these are avenues by which you might re-evaluate your relationship to your faith and the religion of your upbringing. And rightfully so.

Religious extremism

Most groups that are extremists don't perceive themselves that way. They believe they're within their duty and that it's their responsibility to maintain tradition or to save society from the dangers of outside forces. Perhaps they fear that your actions could limit their freedom. As a result, they've committed themselves to the work of preservation by any means necessary.

Each of the main religious systems has some presence of extremism.

>> Al-Qaeda, ISIS, and the Taliban have adopted radical interpretations of Islam.

>> Some Christian nationalists have adopted fundamental interpretations of Christian scripture.

>> Some Jewish extremists believe they have religious claims to the land of Israel. Some consider Zionists to be religious extremists.

>> Some Hindus promote Hindu nationalism, engaging in violent acts against other religious groups in India and the surrounding areas.

Extremists believe that their way of life is the only right way. Although they present a narrative of unity and community, their cause is rooted in exclusion of others who don't fit what they consider to be acceptable, normal, and righteous.

Nationalism

If you're deconstructing, you may have heard of the concept of nationalism before. In the simplest of terms, nationalism is a form of homogeneity. It believes in oneness — that all should be unified under a single national identity. This shared identity is usually centered around one ethnic, cultural, or maybe even religious identity. Whichever and whatever it is, there's a belief and commitment to everyone within the group sharing the same understandings, beliefs, and perspectives.

The five elements of nationalism follow:

>> Common language

>> Territory

>> Culture

>> Economic interest

>> Shared history

Nationalists take pride in their culture, beliefs, practices, and standards. However, nationalism is different from patriotism. This is because nationalist pride extends beyond being prideful of their nation. Theirs is a supreme loyalty that extends beyond just love and devotion. It's an obsession.

Nationalism can take several forms:

>> Liberal nationalism

>> Conservative nationalism

>> Religious nationalism

>> Post-colonial nationalism

Two forms of nationalism familiar to most are Zionism and Christian nationalism:

>> **Zionism:** Those who identify with Zionism consider it to be an important and necessary movement. Central to its work is the establishment of an independent Jewish state. But Zionism isn't completely beloved or respected around the globe. Some critics suggest that it's void of any claim to religious morality, due mostly to the controversial issues that have plagued the movement, including charges of racism and discrimination against those outside of Zionism. Even members of Judaism — most specifically Orthodox Jews — oppose Zionism on religious grounds.

>> **Christian nationalism:** Christian nationalism is another movement plagued by great controversy. Christian nationalists believe that the United States is a nation

founded by Christians solely for Christians. It negates the cultures, tribes, and communities that inhabited the country before it was colonized. Critics of Christian nationalism consider the movement to be anti-democratic and anti-American. In most instances, Christian nationalism is a tool of white supremacy in America.

Decolonizing faith

Contrary to what you may be thinking, faith decolonization isn't the same thing as faith deconstruction. Whereas faith deconstruction, which is discussed more in depth in Chapter 2, is the process by which one evaluates their religious beliefs and their relationship to their faith and religion, faith decolonization examines the utilization of religion historically to oppress and capitalize off the oppression.

When one decolonizes faith, they're honoring the concept of Sankofa. Derived from the Akan people of West Africa, *Sankofa* is loosely translated to mean "go back and get it." Faith decolonization involves reclamation. Chapter 13 provides some examples of how members of the Black diaspora have benefited from faith decolonization to obtain a greater connection to themselves and their faith.

But what does this have to do with deconstruction? And where does it fit into the whole conversation regarding what motivates someone to deconstruct? As previously stated, many find themselves at a crossroads. As some faith communities become more extreme, others draw a line in the sand. Maybe you're one who has drawn the line. As you've evaluated your relationship to your faith and the religious communities of your upbringing, you've found it necessary to divorce yourself from the systems.

Deconstruction is a necessity. The reevaluation is an eye-opening experience that leaves you with no choice but to shift your relationship.

Chapter 4

Getting to the Whys of Deconstruction

I f you've ever raised a kid or you grew up in a house where there were little kids, you're familiar with the phase in their development where they question *everything*. I call it the *whys* phase. In their efforts to understand the world around them and how it works, *why* becomes their favorite word.

Mommy, why?

Daddy, why?

Really, why?

No, why?

Why, why, why, WHYYYYYYYY?!

To some extent, it seems *why* is the only word the kids know. And for most parents, it can be an annoying and draining time. But the beauty of the phase is that they're curious. Kids' natural curiosity is heightened, and because of it, they can't help but ask, "why." It's an important time of exploration, wonder and wander, processing, and discovery.

So many in society have lost the natural curiosity they had when they were young. To some extent, they lost it *because* it drove their parents crazy — the curiosity wasn't celebrated or nurtured; it was instead treated as a burden. The questions brought shame.

Asking questions is at the root of deconstruction. *Why* is one of the most important questions you'll find yourself asking either aloud or inwardly. Seeking clarity for the things you don't understand or find contradiction with could very well be the most integral practice of deconstruction. But many faith-based institutions aren't open to any questioning.

As you're investigating what you believe, evaluate the "why" of your deconstruction. What's motivating you? What's changed for you and why? Are you questioning God or your faith or something else altogether? In this chapter, I discuss the process of questioning and clarifying your "why."

The Crisis of Faith

Before you can get to the why, it's important to address the phase of faith deconstruction that's often the most uncomfortable: the crisis of faith. In his book *Praying the Psalms,* Walter Brueggemann writes about the three phases that everyone, at some point, experiences during their faith walk. They are:

>> Being securely oriented

>> Being painfully disoriented

>> Being surprisingly reoriented

The phases, better described as orientation, disorientation, and reorientation, provide a glimpse into what can be perceived as the natural state and order of the faith journey.

If you look at Brueggemann's three phases — orientation, disorientation, and reorientation — through the lens of faith deconstruction, then the crisis of faith is the disorientation phase of deconstruction. In orientation, everything makes sense. In reorientation, things are put back together or put back together and better. But disorientation involves pain.

REMEMBER

Disorientation is difficult because of the amount of unlearning, investigating, and negotiating you have to do with yourself to find both a set of beliefs and an identity that align more closely with who you are and who you want to be. It's painful because, if done right, shedding must take place. As it will be repeated throughout this book, disorientation involves questioning and reevaluating. Your very being and identity are being altered — for the better.

Disorientation *should* be painful because of the stance or belief that the faith journey isn't transitional in any capacity. Faith is often believed to be concrete, unchangeable, and immovable. This stance is part of the reason you may have heard during your developmental years not to question God or not to question what you were taught about God. The belief is that questioning is bad; it's wrong and has the capacity to lead you down the wrong path or away from God. But, in fact, deconstruction leads you down the path of greater clarity, understanding, and relationship with not only God but also yourself.

REMEMBER

You've been conditioned to believe that your faith involves remaining in the state of orientation for eternity. This perspective and perception are partly to blame for why the crisis of faith exists. But the beauty of faith is that it's meant to be fluid. Fluidity creates space for change.

The following sections further discuss the crisis of faith, its identity and name, and its causes.

MORE ABOUT WALTER BRUEGGEMANN

Walter Brueggemann was considered one of the premiere and most influential Old Testament biblical scholars and American theologians. From 1986 to 2003, Brueggemann taught at Columbia Theological Seminary in Decatur, Georgia. Upon his retirement, he was named the William Marcellus McPheeters professor emeritus of Old Testament at Columbia. Prior to Columbia, Brueggemann taught at his alma mater, Eden Theological Seminary. Ordained in the United Church of Christ, Brueggemann penned more than 100 books, including *The Prophetic Imagination*, *The Message of the Psalms*, and *Praying the Psalms*. He was a featured columnist with Church Anew.

Identifying the crisis

If you look at deconstruction through the lens of Brueggemann's disorientation phases, your crisis of faith is one where everything you thought you knew and believed is painfully altered. You aren't just questioning what you once believed; you're questioning everything you thought you knew about yourself and those around you. Such an experience can be painful and scary. For some, this process entails starting over.

So then, how do you determine whether you're experiencing a faith crisis or simply adjusting your relationship to your faith, which is also part of the deconstruction journey? Ask yourself.

Easier said than done, right? I get it. For much of your life, no one has ever really given you permission to decide or choose for yourself what you're feeling. Many religious systems tell you not only what to believe, but also how to feel. In that process, you're often taught to ignore your inner voice and spirit. Call it a sixth sense. Call it intuition. Call it a gut feeling. Whatever you call it, you've probably had a moment in your life where something didn't feel right, appropriate, or comfortable, yet you ignored it for whatever reason — most likely because you were taught not to trust yourself.

As a result, that has also meant ignoring the things that were the best decision for you out of fear — fear influenced by messaging that taught you that there are consequences divinely ordained because of your choice to change. Some people call that spiritual abuse.

Identifying your crisis of faith involves being self-aware — so aware that you have no doubts about the need for change. It entails being so tapped into yourself that your only option is to act. What does that mean? Simply put, leaning into the fear of the unknown for the purpose of climbing out of the pit of your crisis for the sake of your own personal, emotional, and mental survival.

TIP

Identifying your faith crisis is the first step of choosing yourself.

REMEMBER

What's causing the crisis?

Contrary to what anyone says, your crisis of faith is justified and justifiable. Think about it. For much of your life, you've been led to believe or you chose to believe certain things in life. One of those "things," more than likely, may have been that life would turn out a certain way for you simply because you espoused a certain set of beliefs. Or you believed that if you lived your life in a specific way or presented to have a certain kind of character trait, that struggle or disappointment would pass you by. Or because you were born with a certain gender, race, ethnicity, or class, you automatically deserved for the world to treat you special above all others. You were conditioned to believe these things, and many others, about yourself and others. When reality struck or you began to realize what you were told wasn't the case, your world came crumbling down. All hell broke loose.

Being faced with the possibility that what you were once told or taught to believe could possibly be untrue or fake is a daunting experience and can be shattering. Maybe religion taught you to have a specific kind of relationship to your faith and your faith identity.

In Chapter 3, I reference cognitive dissonance. As a psychological term, *cognitive dissonance* refers to the discomfort felt when a person's values and beliefs contradict. The contradiction creates such a tug-of-war within that anyone experiencing cognitive dissonance is forced to make a choice. There are believed to be three stages of cognitive dissonance and seven signs. The three stages are awareness or trigger, tension, and resolution. A few of the signs of cognitive dissonance include these:

>> Guilt

>> Shame or embarrassment

>> Avoiding new information

>> Decision-making discomfort

Cognitive dissonance is a big part of faith deconstruction and, in many instances, the starting line of faith crisis. What's causing your crisis is related to the experience of feeling disoriented. The world around you — the world within you even — doesn't feel like yours anymore. You don't feel like yourself anymore. The crisis of faith occurs when you're caught off guard, causing you to struggle to make sense of all the emotions flooding your senses.

One example of this is the ongoing debate regarding men and fingernail art. In 2021, the rapper and actor Kid Cudi caused a stir when he posted a picture on his Instagram account that showed his nails painted. For many, Cudi, who is believed to be a straight, cisgendered man, went against gender roles. They were shocked and confused. However, for Cudi, and many other men who enjoy nail art (me included), such a form of expression is not gender coded and just another form of personal expression, freedom, and creativity. This shift in perspective caused a dissonance for some.

REMEMBER

Anyone who experiences a crisis of faith has their own unique and individual process, but what's universal is that the experience is foundationally disturbing. It's painful, yes, but it's also an opportunity to learn, relearn, and create a more effective relationship with yourself and your faith.

Is Your Faith Still Working for You?

You may have been led to believe that faith and its function is the same for everyone, but that's a common misconception. Faith and its function is, whether on a surface level or deeper, different for everyone. That doesn't take away from the universality of faith. It just means that people have differing concerns that require them to access faith, for the most part, differently.

The following sections include insight on the process of deciphering and discerning whether your faith is working for you as you evaluate the why of your deconstruction and the value of your faith in your everyday life.

Evaluating what you were taught to believe

What do you believe? It's a simple question. What do you believe about God, about others, and about yourself? What is it that you believe? What do you believe about creation? Have you ever thought about it? Do you know? What do you believe about the history of humanity? How did the world at-large get here? Where did people come from? What were you taught to believe, and who taught it to you?

Have you ever wondered or questioned where those who taught you learned what they believe? Who taught them? And when did they learn it? Did they get it from a history book, school, or just by reading the Bible, Quran, Talmud, or another sacred text or collection of sacred texts? Have you ever asked them why they believe what they do? Have they ever told you why they believe what they believe? Were you even afforded the ability to ask such questions?

These may be simple questions, but they're worth considering. You might rarely think to ask questions, like "Why?" Doing so, in many instances, just isn't an option.

But it's important to evaluate why you believe what you do and to evaluate the origin of your beliefs so that you can have a better understanding of who you are and what your true and authentic relationship is to your beliefs. How can you know who you are and what your relationship to your faith is if you don't have awareness of why you believe it?

Where did you get the idea that Jesus was/is the son of God? Where did you obtain the belief of Moses and the prophets that followed? Where did the idea that there's one God who rules over a group of minor gods and that they all, once, inhabited the world? Where did you acquire the belief that there is only one God? Where did you get the idea of miracles? Where did you get the concept of sacred texts? Where did the idea of heaven and hell come from *for you*? Who taught it to you?

REMEMBER

This is where you start to understand where you are in faith deconstruction. Walking about blindly in belief isn't a sustainable enterprise for most. At some point, the foundation begins to crack. It always does. If you've never taken the time to evaluate the core of your beliefs and the overall source and motivation of your relationship to your beliefs, when a catastrophic moment presents itself, you'll have two options: crumble under the pressure of trying to reconcile your beliefs against the reality you're facing, which is the crisis of faith, or dig deeper into your avoidance of the questions, which will make your faith journey shallow, hollow, and flawed.

Asking how what you were taught has helped you

Let me be clear: It's not all doom and gloom. My intent is not to suggest that all you've been taught about faith via the religious community of your upbringing has been terrible. No, not all of it has been trash. Throughout life, religion can provide the necessary tools to navigate through life. Chapter 5 has some examples of when faith is beneficial.

But in the faith deconstruction journey, as you're questioning what you believe, why you believe it, and who provided your foundation for what you believe, it's important to also evaluate the many ways in which what you're taught has helped you. Why is this important? In any evaluation, there's a need to highlight the successes along with the areas of growth.

Each year, most companies do a performance review. You're probably familiar with those, but just in case you're not, the performance review, which usually takes place near or at the end of the company's physical year, is an opportunity to evaluate the work performance of each employee in the company. Every person within the company who's considered a long-term employee — this usually includes those who are full time, hourly employed, or salaried employees — is supposed to have a performance review. How they're completed can be different from company to company, but their main purpose is to provide an inventory of the employees' successes over the past year, as well as highlight areas of growth. Within the performance review, in some instances, there's room for goal setting for the next year of employment. And the complete performance review is *supposed to be* filed in the employees personnel file within human resources.

Performance reviews also have another purpose: They give the employer an idea of whether the employee is a viable member of the company culture. If they're not, the employee may be placed on some form of probation for their performance issues. Sometimes, if the issues outlined in the performance review aren't corrected, the employee's employment can be, and usually is, terminated. Companies also use the performance review to determine room for salary adjustments, like cost-of-living increases, or bonuses if the company offers them at the end of the fiscal year.

What would happen if you took time to evaluate what you've been taught about faith, via your religion, in the same way that companies evaluate the performances of their employees? What would happen if you took some of the questions asked in performance reviews, like, "Works well with others," and put them against what religion has taught you about faith? What about goal setting? In what ways can you juxtapose what you've been taught about faith against your wants and desires out of life? What would be some of your takeaways about what you've learned that could assist you in better understanding and utilizing your faith?

In this performance review of what you've been taught, it's necessary to evaluate how what you were taught is or isn't serving you. Are you better off? Do you have more clarity about yourself, others, and where you are in life? Do you feel equipped to face the numerous challenges life may throw your way because of what you've been taught? Are you happier, grounded, and fulfilled in your life because of what you believe and were taught?

Or are you seemingly more miserable each day and, if so, what role has what you believe had in your unhappiness, despair, and desperation? Is it serving you anymore? Where did you go wrong? What's the point of faith if it's not effectively serving you? Do you care that it's no longer serving you, or are you more focused on the performative aspects of faith and the approval you get from others for playing the game?

REMEMBER

Evaluating what you've been taught and how what you've learned has helped you in your life makes you not only a better believer, but a better practitioners of your faith.

Questioning whether what you were taught has limited or harmed you

While faith can't necessarily be done accurately or inaccurately, faith *can* be effective or ineffective. What you seek to get out of faith, or put another way, what service faith provides for you, determines its effectiveness. To determine how your faith is harming or limiting you, you must understand its effectiveness.

TIP

In simplest terms, you can understand faith as a tool used to help you face life. When the unexpected meets you, say a life-altering diagnosis or a challenge in your professional life, your faith helps you meet the challenge. As your faith is challenged, you can either grow from the experience or allow the challenge to stifle your growth.

As you evaluate your faith, investigate what purpose it has in your life. How are you using your faith, or how do you envision faith working for you? How else can you understand whether your faith has limited you if you aren't clear about its purpose in your life? During my childhood, there was an old sitcom joke where a young woman's father would meet her boyfriend for the first time. Countless times the father would ask the young man, "What are your intentions with my daughter?" The question had dual intentions. First, it was a tactic of intimidation. In other words, the father wanted to make it known that he didn't want the young man to try any "funny business," as many of the characters would say. It was his way of letting the young man know that he considered his daughter to be precious, special, and worth treating with respect and care. But the question also sought an understanding of the young man. Not only did the father want to protect his daughter, he wanted to gauge the character of the young man.

TIP

The same can and should be said about faith. You should want good intentions from your faith. You should want your faith to serve you in the best possible capacity.

Does your faith provide strength in difficult times? Is the purpose of your faith to help you find confidence in the things you're unsure of? Is your faith or the intent of your faith rooted in giving you hope when all hope is lost? How do you know if your faith is limiting or harming you if you don't know what you want out of your faith?

Yes, this is a different, more intentional way of looking at your faith. Usually there isn't a lot of thought put into it this way. Rarely do people take the time to consider faith and their relationship to it in this way. People just aren't provided these sorts of tools. Religion, for all its good, has its fair share of bad. One way religion has failed society is by not teaching people how to have effective faith. Teaching a person to have effective faith doesn't mean convincing them that because they have faith, everything they want, wish for, and desire will find them. It doesn't mean believing that life will be without challenges and disappointments. Instead, effective faith teaches that even when things don't work out, those setbacks won't be debilitating.

TIP

Effective faith should at least make your faith more mature and stronger. How? By making your faith accessible in a way that does more to help you grow and mature, versus limiting you, your choices, your perspectives, and silencing the inquisitive and curious spirit within you. Effective faith also opens the door to expanding your faith in ways that inspire and spark greater self-awareness and creativity in your faith practices.

Take, for example, ancestral veneration or the use of astrology. If you're more conservative in your religious practices, you might believe there's no room for ancestral veneration — the practice of communing with those loved ones no longer living. You might feel that communing with the dead is anti-Christian or idolatry. However, some religious communities celebrate ancestral veneration as a means of staying connected to their loved ones once they've passed away. Proponents of ancestral veneration who also practice Christianity consider ancestral veneration an extension of their faith, suggesting that the worship of Jesus is a form of ancestral veneration.

Some within Christian communities believe astrology, or divination — the practice of seeking guidance form the supernatural — is another form of idolatry. They argue that God is the only source of understanding, especially when predicting what's to come or seeking guidance for one's life and future choices. However, proponents of divination argue that many of the stories in the Christian bible point to people who sought guidance from the stars. They've often pointed out the story of the wise men who came to visit Jesus when he was born. They were led by the stars, in the same way that astrology and divination look to the stars for guidance.

These are simply two examples of how religion can limit how some seek to understand and practice their faith. But if these practices provide comfort, clarity, and awareness in the service of that faith, shouldn't they be valued, welcomed, and honored as viable options of access for the faith journey? There's beauty in expanding your faith, your relationship to your faith, and the practices of your faith.

Limiting how you practice or access your faith is a form of control and should be evaluated and questioned to better understand whether your faith is viable and working for you.

Reevaluating if any of it is working for you anymore

Having faith is a lifelong journey with no guarantees. But once you choose to carry your faith, it informs everything else in life. That's the key. Life happens. You can control how you allow those things happening to impact you, your moods, and your perspectives. But it's constant work.

Questioning your faith should be seen as a natural order of things in your journey. At some point, you should ask yourself if what you've been taught and told — by way of our religious systems — is providing for you the freedom, comfort, joy, and understanding you seek to have from your faith. It's necessary to, every now and again, question whether your faith is working for you. The following chapter attempts to define faith and what it means for the majority of those who identify as faith believers.

Faith is fluid. It's also fragile. Why is this? Because faith is riddled with uncertainties and, in relation to religion, riddled with false certainty. But there's also a beauty within faith. It allows you to explore, question and discern, seek and determine for yourself. You learn about yourself and others along the way. You may have setbacks, but you'll also have opportunities. You can't learn if you don't try. Faith affords you the ability to try.

Why deconstruct? The better question is why not. Life is hard. Every day there you face a new set of challenges. How you overcome them is a choice. Sometimes you can face them head on; other times, you're not so successful. How you respond is rooted heavily in the strength and health of your faith. You can't get stronger if you aren't challenged, given a chance to evaluate, test, and recalibrate.

Welcome to the Club — You're Not Alone

Faith deconstruction can be quite lonely. Actually, that's not completely true. Deconstruction isn't *quite* lonely; it's without a doubt, and matter-of-factly, *incredibly* lonely. The entire experience can and will make you feel like you're on an island all by yourself. Why? There are a few explanations for this. First, society is highly influenced by religion. The intermingling of religion in everyday life is discussed more deeply in Chapter 6. But the more vocal proponents of religion, most specifically Christians in the Western world, make anyone looking to deconstruct feel as though they're the enemy. This isn't just true in the Christian western world. As highlighted in Chapter 6, many majority governments in other parts of the world have made faith deconstruction, or some extension of it, illegal in their society.

But a vast number of people have embarked upon the faith deconstruction journey. Some of them have created entire communities, whether locally or digitally, for likeminded people to gather, share, and learn from one another. Chapter 16 discusses faith deconstruction and loneliness. Chapter 11 shares some first-person testimonies of the faith deconstruction journey. The following section offers some balance to the faith crisis experience and how it can be overcome as you journey through your deconstruction.

How others have shed the old in faith deconstruction

It's easy to assume that everyone who's experiencing faith deconstruction or who has had a faith deconstruction experience has had a crisis of faith. If you're looking at the crisis of faith as the painful process of reevaluating your faith and creating a new relationship to it, not everyone experiences a crisis.

However, anyone and everyone who embarks upon the faith deconstruction journey does have a process of unlearning and relearning. Within that process, they shed the teachings and understandings of old to embrace a different way of thinking and a different way of relating to their faith life and identity. In addition, they not only embrace a different way of thinking; they also embrace a different way of relating to others and how they express their beliefs.

What does that look like?

Making sense of their faith and newfound beliefs

Some embrace other religious practices. They embark on a quest of finding understanding within other religious/faith practices to determine which is a better fit for them. Perhaps they leave Christianity and become Muslim. Others study Buddhism or New Thought. Some lean into African Spirituality. Some would suggest this is nothing more than replacing one system with another. In some respects, that may be the case. In other respects, they may see their choices as starting completely over in their faith journey. They're exploring. In the process, they're ridding themselves of the exclusive teachings and perspectives of the religious systems of their upbringing and evaluating whether their new system is viable for how they understand themselves and their purpose in the world.

Others return to the religious system of their origin, but with a newfound understanding of themselves and their relationship to their faith. They might take with them some of the practices, tenets, and perspectives of the systems they explored during their break and find the commonalities and overlaps between the practices. They create for themselves a faith that's authentic to who they believe themselves to be. Chapter 11 discusses some of this in greater detail.

Understanding the Difference Between Faith and Religion

2

IN THIS PART . . .

Consider how faith is helpful and religion harmful.

Understand where religion comes from.

Obtain another view of the relationship between Christianity, Judaism, and Islam.

Chapter **5**

What Is Faith?

F aith can be a big part of who you are, how you see yourself, and how you live your life. It can be the lighthouse that guides you as you move through life trying to avoid obstacles. Perhaps you view a life without faith as an incomplete one. Maybe you start your day practicing your faith. Or maybe the opposite is true: You tap into your faith only in moments of struggle and disappointment.

But what exactly is faith? This chapter explores what faith is, where it came from, and what its benefits and problems are. It discusses how others understand and define faith, what faith looks like in practice, and how faith can redeem power in survival. It also discusses the failings of faith and its role in struggle.

Trying to Define Faith

People have faith and practice it without truly understanding it. It's hard to describe faith definitively. Type "What is faith?" in any search engine, and you'll find myriad examples and descriptions:

» Trust, assurance, and confidence in God

» Relying completely on who Jesus is and what he has done

>> Believing God exists and that He is wholly trustworthy

>> Believing something is true, and then committing your life to it

>> Confidence or trust in a person, thing, or concept

>> Complete surrendering and full humbleness of the heart for the Lord

Merriam-Webster Dictionary defines faith in a few ways:

>> Allegiance to a duty or a person

>> Belief, trust in, and loyalty to God

>> Something that's believed, especially with strong conviction

Even ChatGPT has its own definition. When asked, "What is faith?" the artificial intelligence tool provides this definition: "Faith generally involves a strong belief in something that transcends direct proof or logical explanation."

Paul Tillich, the renowned twentieth-century German American theologian, defined faith as the state of being ultimately concerned. His work and writings bridged the divide between traditional Christianity and the modern culture of his time. For Tillich, faith takes risks. He believed that faith requires action without certain knowledge.

MORE ON PAUL TILLICH

Paul Tillich (1886–1965), who spent the first forty years of his life studying, teaching, and pastoring in Germany, is often described as one of the most influential Protestant thinkers. As a theological leader and academic, he made significant contributions to society's understanding of faith and its relationship to reason. In 1933, Reinhold Niebuhr, a Reformed theologian and ethicist, invited Tillich to teach at Union Theological Seminary in New York City. In 1937, Tillich acquired tenure at Union Theological Seminary and was promoted to professor of philosophical theology in 1940. That same year he became an American citizen. His 1957 book, *Dynamics of*

Faith, is considered one of the quintessential pieces of writing on the topic of faith in the academy and theological circles. Throughout his academic life, Tillich sought to make theology relevant. He believed that human experience was just as valuable and valid to theology as the existential questions about God and God's being.

Understanding what faith is helps in understanding faith's role, importance, and power. Maybe you've walked through life with a surface-level understanding of faith. By having a clearer understanding of its definition, you can better appreciate the role of faith in your life.

Thinking About Where Faith Begins

Now that you have a baseline understanding of faith, it's important to uncover the origin of faith in your life. The following sections delve deeper into where the relationship to faith begins and how it shows up in everyday life.

The origins of faith

Your faith life, or your relationship to faith, most likely began locally. The world around you *introduced* you to faith. Following are a few places where you learned about faith:

>> At home life or from family

>> At church

>> In synagogues or other religious/faith-based institutions

>> From school, friends, or the community around you

>> From your favorite media, whether it's television, the internet, or social media

In the same way you were taught the alphabet, reading, color identification, and addition and subtraction, you were presented with a specific perspective on faith and how to live in or with faith. Put another way, you were taught your faith, what to believe, how to believe it, and why. You were conditioned. You were given an understanding and perspective rooted solely in what those around you deemed important and acceptable about faith. You weren't given a choice about your faith. Maybe you weren't allowed to have input about your faith in the beginning. What did that look like? In some instances, you may have been told not to ask questions and not to question God.

TIP

Is it possible to have faith without a revelatory experience of faith development? In other words, can faith truly be faith without you consciously and intentionally choosing your faith? Sure. But until you know for yourself and can develop your own belief system, you aren't operating in your own faith. Faith is experiential. No one starts to understand or know what they believe until they experience it for themselves.

As you grow, mature, and become more aware, you begin to develop your own relationship to faith, which is why some deconstruction happens. In those moments, the lessons you were taught about faith become practical. Before you were operating from an understanding of faith that was more idealistic or romanticized.

But once you can test the theories on your own, you develop a perspective and relationship with faith that's most fitting for you. Think of it as having something done or made just for you or with you in mind. When it's specifically for you, it not only fits better, but looks better and makes you glow when you see yourself in the mirror for the first time.

Faith in everyday life

Faith is personal and can show up in different ways. Maybe acts of faith for you are preprogrammed. You go through your day almost blindly without consideration. When you wake up in the morning, you open your eyes, wiggle your toes, breathe deeply, stretch, and move about freely. You don't think about whether you can do them or even tell yourself to do them. You just do. You don't even think about it. You simply have faith and move about your morning routine with certainty. You are living out your faith.

Every time you start the ignition to your car or walk to the bus stop or train station, you're walking (no pun intended) in faith. You have no doubt about the car starting or the bus or train being on time. These are just a few examples of latent faith.

TIP

Maybe your faith is so integral to who you are you don't consider how or when faith shows up for you every day. But when you take a moment to stop and think about it, just about every moment of everyday life has some connection to your faith.

Perhaps your faith is more intentional than that. You may pray or meditate first thing in the morning. If you're Buddhist, your day probably begins with the Nam-myoho-renge-kyo chant. If you're Muslim, you perform your faith by praying five times a day:

>> Fajr: Before dawn

>> Dhuhr: Noon

>> Asr: Late afternoon

>> Maghrib: Sunset

>> Isha: Nighttime

Hindus also have faith practices that they perform every day. These practices can range from meditating and practicing yoga to visiting a temple, doing charitable work, and exercising. They also perform a short ritual called puja every morning in their home. Puja may include any of these:

>> Lighting a lamp

>> Burning incense

>> Making offerings of fruit and flowers

>> Chanting mantras

>> Ringing a bell

Chapter 10 covers rituals in more depth, and Chapter 13 covers the origins, foundations, practices, and rituals of Hinduism and many other world religions in more detail.

The Faith Journey

Contrary to popular belief, faith isn't static; the journey is a life-long, ongoing, ever-changing enterprise. It must be. What worked for you when you were a teenager doesn't work the same way for you when you're in your thirties or forties — or at least it shouldn't. If your faith journey hasn't changed much, it probably hasn't grown much over the years.

If done correctly, your faith shifts, morphs, and adjusts over time. Your perspectives change, and you become curious about all sorts of new things. As you interact with new and different people, you become influenced by them and their ways of life. These experiences stretch you and your worldview. In that process, your faith is also expanded.

TIP

Although the genesis of your faith is influenced largely by how you were conditioned when you were introduced to faith, you can build your own understanding and relationship to faith.

Don't be afraid of this possibility. Your faith journey can and should be a beautiful exploration. The only way you can truly begin to understand your faith and what you believe is by evaluating and reevaluating what you believe. In Chapter 11 we get the first-person testimonies of nine people who have evaluated and explored their faith. The following sections address the role that belief and doubt play in aspects of the faith journey.

Faith and belief

Your beliefs are essential to your faith. Your entire faith system is influenced almost exclusively by the beliefs you hold near and dear. Merriam-Webster defines belief as follows:

>> A state or habit of mind in which trust or confidence is placed in some person or thing

>> Something that's accepted, considered to be true, or held as an opinion

>> Conviction of the truth of some statement or the reality of some being or phenomenon, especially when based on examination of evidence

The relationship between faith and belief isn't an exact science. Often, your faith is informed by what you believe. But you can believe in something and not have faith. Faith, as defined earlier in this chapter, is abstract, whereas belief is much more concrete.

Consider the previous example of latent faith. You have faith that when you go to start your car, it will. Your faith is rooted in experience because your car has started every time previously. Your belief is proven, and your trust is solidified. You're assured that your car will start.

REMEMBER

When it comes to deconstructing your faith, what you believe and how those beliefs change is a big part of what influences the deconstruction. However, it's not as simple as changing one or two beliefs. No, faith deconstruction happens when what you once believed no longer serves you. It's not as simple as questioning what you believe; it also involves completely dismantling the beliefs you once held sacred and reimagining your relationship to those beliefs.

Faith and doubt

Some say that doubt is the enemy of faith, that doubt has no place in faith, and that anyone who possesses even a small amount of doubt has no true faith. None of this is true. Doubt is a necessary companion to faith. It can strengthen faith and make faith understandable.

Doubt is an important aspect not only of faith, but of your walk in life. Doubt does each of the following:

>> Provides room for reflection

>> Encourages questioning and authenticity

>> Forces you to be humble in your beliefs

>> Strengthens your faith

>> Builds your trust

>> Avoids blind faith

>> Leads to greater clarity and understanding

Doubting or having doubts is natural and healthy. In moments of doubt, your faith becomes more tangible. How else do you truly know whether you have faith if you don't doubt? Often, however, doubt — or better yet fear — is treated as the big, bad boogeyman, and faith is called into question.

REMEMBER

Faith is like a muscle. For it to remain healthy, you must exercise it. Through your doubt, your faith is refined. Without doubt, your faith cannot be tested, and the opportunity for your beliefs to become proven is lost.

The Benefits of Faith

Faith is beneficial for several reasons. Beyond the obvious religion-based reasons, studies show that faith implants not only spiritual or religious identity, but also emotional, mental, and physical health. In addition, faith provides purpose and meaning to life. The following sections offer greater insight into the benefits of faith and how it shows up when it matters most.

Faith and survival

Faith becomes an essential tool for facing and overcoming challenges and struggles. Whether in the face of hardships, like grief, loss, and trauma, or struggles such as during the Civil Rights Movement, faith becomes a tool of sustenance, recovery, and hope. Faith is trusting or having confidence in what is seemingly impossible. Faith brings about survival.

In your most dire moments, you have a choice: Either you can succumb to the challenges you face, or you can find a way to overcome the situation in front of you. Faith is part of the motivation by which you decide to act instead of stagnate. Faith provides the motivation you need for survival. You're not moving about blindly. No, faith makes you believe that your survival is possible. And once your situation changes for the better, you can declare that you overcame through your faith.

"HOW I GOT OVER"

Written by Clara Ward in 1951, "How I Got Over" became part of the unofficial soundtrack of the Civil Rights Movement. The song was inspired by a situation that Ward and members of her family experienced in the segregated south during one of their travels. Utilizing the power of their faith, Ward and her family were able to escape what could have been detrimental in nature for the travelers. Ward used the experience to pen the words to the song, highlighting the power of faith in the face of challenge. Workers in the Civil Rights Movement adopted the song to ignite and inspire the work of fighting against oppression.

Faith and healing

Have you ever been in a situation where it seemed as though, inevitably, you couldn't overcome the situation you were in? All the signs before you pointed to something detrimental or devastating. But then everything changed. In an instant, the very thing you thought was bound to happen was no longer a care or concern. You overcame whatever it was by a Christmas miracle.

As stated previously, faith can be the tool used to overcome something. This is especially true if you've faced health challenges and believe that your faith healed you. Because you believed you could be healed or that your health was possible, you willed yourself into a successful outcome.

In the same way that faith can be the boost that the healing process needs, faith can be what you need to make sense of past health challenges and how you overcame them. Making sense of a health challenge requires placing meaning on what happened, why you faced it, and what led to your healing. You might determine that you faced the challenge because a divine being wanted to change your life or your habits or to get your attention. You might feel that God put you in the compromising situation to make you better.

A good example of this is the Academy Award- and Grammy Award-winning actor, singer, and comedian Jamie Foxx. In the spring of 2023, Foxx suffered a stroke that left him in a coma and hospitalized for several weeks. The following year, Foxx did a Netflix special. The special was Foxx's effort to make meaning of his stroke, suggesting that God used the stroke to get his attention and get his focus back on God.

TIP

Of course, if you're deconstructing your faith, this line of meaning-making is difficult. You'll find yourself questioning the validity of the belief, critiquing whether it's healthy or necessary to make sense of struggle and the healing that's the outcome of the challenge. This line of questioning is valid and fair, but it's also important to remember that making meaning of challenges is a coping mechanism. You might find it hard to imagine that the challenges you face are random and without meaning or purpose.

The next section investigates the problems with faith and how the effort to make meaning from challenges and struggles is seen as problematic for some but effective and almost necessary for others.

The Problem with Faith

Because faith is intangible, and in some respects mysterious, it's not exact. It isn't scientific, and it has no rhyme or reason. Faith is just a set of beliefs, ideals, and combined efforts. Sometimes the outcomes within faith are positive. When they aren't, the limits of faith can provide problems. The next section probes the moments of disappointment in a faith journey and the resulting struggles if you're attempting to put your faith into practice.

Disappointment and faith

The problem with faith is that sometimes things don't work out as planned despite your hopes, anticipations, and beliefs. Because faith isn't scientific, the outcomes can go against the strength of your beliefs. When that happens, a crisis of faith can result. This crisis has the potential to be a starting point for your faith deconstruction. In those moments, you find yourself questioning not only what you believe, but why you believe what you do. You need answers, and because you were focused on the outcomes of your desires, you're not prepared to face the reality of your disappointment.

Don't fret. It's not the end of the world. Disappointment is a natural companion to the faith journey — if and when it's allowed. Disappointment builds character and resolve. It helps you make meaning of what you believe, create space for setbacks, and become comfortable with setbacks. More than anything, disappointment strengthens your faith in yourself and the unknown.

Faith and struggle

Struggle is a natural occurrence, but no one wants to experience it. People avoid struggle like they do that one drunk uncle at the family gathering or that one annoying coworker who's always talking about something no one's interested in hearing another story about. Struggle isn't fun, glamourous, or sexy. And when it comes to faith, struggle is hard to process.

Religion has conditioned society to believe that struggle is the cause of an effect. Chapter 6 delves deeper into religion's role in faith and struggle. People struggle with struggle because they've been led to believe that if they live a certain way, do right, and have faith, they'll be immune to struggle and strife. Unfortunately, it doesn't work that way.

When it comes to faith, the task isn't to avoid struggle, but to have the tools necessary to face it head-on. Faith isn't the absence of struggle, but the tool by which you overcome struggle, survive it, and learn from it. In this way, you'll have the tools necessary to grow in your struggle and learn more about yourself the next time.

Chapter **6**

What Is Religion?

I n faith deconstruction, your relationship to your faith changes. It has to. To deconstruct your faith effectively, you must do the hard work of deprogramming your religious beliefs and the role they play in your life. That's why it's important to distinguish faith from religion. Although the two share some overlap, they also have distinct differences.

Being clear of the similarities and differences helps in understanding what exactly you're deconstructing, how, and why. Because the previous chapter spent some time defining faith, it's necessary to do the same with religion. This chapter explores religion: its relationship to faith, its origins, how it's different from faith, and what has made it problematic.

Trying to Define Religion

Most people assume that faith and religion are the same. But they're more like first or maybe even second cousins. They're related and have a good amount of overlap, but they aren't the same.

Faith, as defined in the previous chapter, can be understood as trust, assurance, and confidence in God. It's believing something is true and then committing your life to it. It's also confidence or trust in a person, thing, or concept. So then, what is religion? Religion, according to Merriam-Webster, has a few definitions:

>> A personal set or institutionalized system of religious attitudes, beliefs, and practices

>> The service and worship of God or the supernatural

>> A cause, principle, or system of beliefs held to with ardor and faith

In simplest of descriptions, religion is a system of beliefs and practices by which a community with the same shared beliefs lives, seeks understanding, and makes meaning. And with any religion or religious system, those beliefs and practices usually involve the following:

>> Belief in a higher power(s) or deity(ies)

>> Sacred texts and teachings

>> Some kind of ritual or ceremonial practice

>> Community roots

>> Some form of ethic and ethics

Although you may call it faith deconstruction, realistically you're deconstructing your relationship to faith by challenging the systems that have informed that faith — religion. The next section discusses what makes faith and religion similar and what makes them different.

A deeper dive into the similarities

As previously stated, deconstructing your faith involves deprogramming the influence that religion has on your beliefs and choices. That's why deciphering faith and religion is pertinent. Now that you have a working definition of faith and religion, this chapter digs deeper into their similarities.

Faith and religion have what could be described as a cogent relationship. In other words, the two share some things that make them relatable. Religion typically lays the foundation for faith. Religion provides purpose to your faith, explanations to your inquiries, and structure to your wondering. But — and this may be a doozy, so brace yourself — you can have faith without having a religion or being involved in a religious practice.

So what makes faith and religion similar? Well, both are rooted in a belief or beliefs of something greater. Sometimes that something greater is God, a group of deities, or the influence of divine spirits walking among the world. And both are useful in helping to give meaning to life or seeking after your purpose. This can involve questions such as whether to start a business, make a move, or chase after a dream. Both also provide hope and comfort in moments of uncertainty, struggle, and despair. Examples of this can include tragedies that arise unexpectedly and emergencies that can be life shattering.

TIP

Put another way, faith and religion are companions to one another. Both provide moral guidance, inspire action, and fulfill emotional and spiritual needs. Religion, when used effectively, offers faith support in moments when faith may be weak. Religion bestows tools by which you can expand your faith. Faith and religion are two sides of the same coin.

A look at the differences

Although they're related, faith and religion are also different. Faith is more individualistic than religion. It's personal and born out of your experiences. Faith is also more of an internal practice.

Religion, on the other hand, is much less personal and individualistic than faith. Religion is rooted in community and governed by its commitment to creating homogeneity within its community. To some degree, understanding, purpose, perspective, and intent are shared within religious communities collectively. Religion is the space where the mysteries of faith are investigated, whereas with faith, the mysteries are afforded the freedom to simply be mysteries. Faith has no obsession for clarity.

Put another way, faith is the outcome, and religion is the product.

REMEMBER

Faith is often the personal, internal aspect of belief, and religion is the organized, communal framework through which faith is expressed and practiced. Together, the two shape how people understand the world, themselves, and their place in the world.

The Origins of Religion

Attempting to understand where religion begins is like attempting to decipher the origins of mankind. For as long as society has existed, to some extent, religion or belief systems have been in existence. There are more religions than can be counted. Some are more well known or widely acknowledged than others.

Some religions are monotheistic, meaning there is only one God. Others are polytheistic and have many gods. Some worship nature, whereas others celebrate the stars. And some are indigenous in nature and stretch as far back as the beginning of time. But pinpointing the genesis of religion is next to impossible — even though many have tried.

Instead of trying to answer the impossible question, the next section focuses more on another aspect of the origins of religion — how, when, and where religion is present daily.

MORE ON WHERE RELIGIONS COME FROM

Some experts suggest the existence of as many as 10,000-plus religious practices in the world. But where, when, and how religion was created and developed is a mystery. The origin of religion falls into two camps. One camp believes religion was created as a tool to create order within societies. In some of these instances, the order was meant to unify the community on one purpose, one cause, and one identity. Another camp, however, believes that as humanity evolved, so did a need within the communities for understanding. To make sense of the mysteries they faced, communities began making meaning out of their questions. And their answers came by way of intervention by entities beyond them — divine beings.

Where religion begins for you

As with faith, your relationship to religion likely began locally. You were introduced to religion by the world around you. Maybe you learned about religion from one of these places:

>> Your home life or family

>> Church

>> Synagogues or other religious/faith-based institutions

>> School, friends, or the community around you

Perhaps you were born into a community of faith informed by a religious system. Whether it was Mormon, Seventh Day Adventist, Methodist, Presbyterian, Southern Baptist, Muslim, Reformed Jewish, Buddhist, Hindu, or some other form of religious belief all together, religion was part of your beginning. Even if your family wasn't religious or didn't explicitly identify as such, your home life was influenced and informed by some tenet of religion. Religion is and has always been all around you.

The influence of religion is baked into society. This is discussed further in the next section.

Maybe you attended a weekly worship experience or meeting. Or you attended some kind of event at your place of worship three to four times a week. These might have been special programs and assemblies, dedications and community rituals, naming ceremonies, rite of passage parties, prayers at specific hours every day, or other practices that were foundational to you and your identity. You celebrated religious holidays every year — sometimes having no clue why or what they meant. And those took place in community. All these things were just part of your life. Perhaps you assumed that everyone — from your friends and neighbors to the people you didn't know in other parts of the world — lived the same way.

But the impact of religion isn't and hasn't just been exclusive to communities. Religion has had other impacts on everyday life.

Religion in everyday life

The previous chapter discussed how faith shows up in daily practices. Such practices, from ritualistic prayers to moments of meditation, are informed by the religious entities you're connected to or hold membership in. But religion and its influence aren't just showing up in daily or weekly rituals or worship experiences. Religion is found in almost every aspect of this world and society.

Religious influence has an impact daily and historically. During the Civil Rights Movement, the "fight for justice" was rooted deeply in Christian theology. The same is true in places of work. Ethics policies that govern workplaces are informed by religious values like honesty, integrity, and fairness. Many foundational life moments, including wedding ceremonies and baby dedications, are informed by religious practices. And much art and literature has religious undertones or influences. Religion is all around.

Another example of how religion informs or impacts everyday life is through the political systems. In the United States alone, religion has a chokehold. Many of the laws that govern societies are informed, to some extent, by the tenets of religious thought and practice. Countless laws that are designed to ensure safety or encourage law and order have at their core some connection to religion. But some laws and political agendas are rooted in misunderstandings and misinterpretations of sacred texts and scripture. These laws are often credited with protecting the sanctity of religious beliefs, teachings, or practices. Examples include laws about marriage equality in the United States; blasphemy laws in Pakistan segregation; anti-LGBTQ+ legislation in African countries, Iran, and Russia; and apostasy laws that make it illegal to abandon your faith in parts of the world. In each case, the laws are developed, supported, and parroted by the religious stances of whichever political leader has the bullhorn at the time.

As discussed in Chapter 3, the influence of religion — which is often categorized as faith — may have promising implications. But the ramifications aren't always promising for certain sectors of the population. In some instances, such as the Mormons, entire communities are governed almost exclusively by their religious beliefs. From family structure to health practices to how they engage with communities beyond their own, everything is informed by the tenets of their religious beliefs and practices. They've historically isolated themselves from society-at-large as a means of preserving their community and identity.

Chapter 7 delves deeper into specific religious practices, their history, and how they appear in society today.

The Benefits of Religion

Although the deconstruction process calls for reevaluating and, in some instances, abandoning religious systems of origin all together, not all religion is bad. Not everyone uses religion as a means of homogeneous control. Some religious practices are deeply rooted in the culture of the community they're practiced in. This tie connects the community's history, legacy, and sustenance for the community's future. This is especially true in many indigenous communities and faiths. Chapter 13 digs deeper into some of these communities.

REMEMBER

The manner in which religion is used in some communities and in society-at-large is problematic. But many have reaped great benefits from religion and benefits from their ties to the communities of their origin.

The next section offers some examples of where, how, and when religion has helped and been useful throughout history.

When religion has helped within society

It may be farfetched to suggest that Former President Jimmy Carter was the first major political figure to deconstruct his faith publicly. But it's not too far out of reason to suggest that he may have been one of the more influential deconstructors. When Carter passed away in December 2024, many commented on how his faith had influenced decisions he made during his time in the White House and after leaving it in the early 1980s. Carter himself spoke often and publicly about how his faith and religious beliefs had influenced many of his decisions, not just politically but communally.

Carter wasn't perfect, of course, and he never claimed to be a faith deconstructionist. But if you've done faith deconstruction in the past or are doing it now, you may see some parallels between your questioning and Carter's growth in his faith. One example is how he broke from the evangelical church on his stances regarding civil rights and the LGBTQ+ community. He eventually ended his affiliation with the Southern Baptist Convention in 2000 because of the shift in his beliefs. He often challenged the scriptural interpretations of the evangelical church and their positions on issues such as women being subjugated to their husbands and the role of women in the church. He believed the Bible saw all as equal in the eyes of God.

Of course, religion has helped society in other ways too. The Civil Rights Movement harnessed scriptural lessons about love and justice to change history. Mahatma Gandhi and Mother Teresa are other examples. Gandhi drew on the principles of Hinduism to fight for independence of the people of India against British colonialism. Mother Teresa devoted herself to fighting for the poor and sick in India, informed and influenced by her Roman Catholic beliefs. From the abolition of slavery to Indigenous groups trying to educate on global warming and the importance of Earth care, religion has had great significance in society.

MORE ON PRESIDENT CARTER

Jimmy Carter served as president of the United States from 1978 to 1981. Born in the small town of Plains, Georgia, Carter also served as governor of Georgia from 1971 to 1975. It's said that Carter was the first self-proclaimed, evangelical Christian to occupy the White House. Until 2000, Carter was known to be affiliated with the Southern Baptist Convention, considered the most conservation Christian denomination in the United States. Although he might have been rather unpopular when he left the White House, he saw an impressive uptick in popularity in later years, due in large part to the causes he supported and the way he exercised his faith post-presidency. He taught Bible Study well into his 90s at his local church, volunteered his time and attention toward causes like helping build houses for Habitat for Humanity, and served globally through the Carter Center. When he died at 100 years old, he was the oldest living president in US history.

When religion is useful

The religious motivations of Jimmy Carter, Mahatma Gandhi, and Mother Teresa are also good examples of how religion can be useful.

Do a Google search for "ways religion is useful" or ask ChatGPT for examples, and you'll see a fair number of responses. But four truly encapsulate the usefulness of religion:

>> Providing meaning and purpose

>> Fostering community and belonging

>> Offering comfort and support

>> Providing guidance in times of conflict

To some extent, much of this has already been covered. From Carter, Gandhi, and Mother Teresa to the average individual in any community across the globe, religion is foundational in development. It's also a tool for keeping culture and identity alive.

Faith can get you through some of your toughest moments. It can also offer a semblance of safety, respect, and consideration that play a major role in how you show up in society.

Religion can be the foundation to build your life and success upon. When it is, the pride you have for your community and your religious identity permeates the work you do in society. It can also help you understand yourself and the mysteries of life. It can be a useful, productive, and informative tool by which you live your life and how you relate to others within and around your local, regional, national, and global community.

Religion can be something to look toward, a semblance of foundation on which to place your faith. The beliefs within religion work within a set of parameters to provide stability, understanding, and purpose. Whereas religion offers something to look toward, faith offers something to hope for.

But religion isn't perfect. Or, better yet, how people have used religion hasn't always been perfect.

The Problem(s) with Religion: An Overview

Religion itself isn't inherently harmful. In fact, it's one of the most useful and effective enterprises in the world today. The problem with it is humanity. Human beings make religion problematic. Religious problems can show up in the form of conflict, discrimination, and limits on freedom.

One example of this is rooted in the history of the Church of England. King Henry VIII initiated a break from the Roman Catholic Church to divorce his wife, Catharine of Aragon. He was deeply concerned about the future of the monarchy, and because she was unable to produce for him a male heir, he wanted the marriage annulled. However, Pope Clement VII refused. Therefore, the king passed the Act of Supremacy in 1534, making himself the head of the church of England. It was an act rooted in control, and it kicked off the English Reformation.

Countless other examples are available of religion being used to assert power over others. In many of these instances, religion was used as a ruse to justify efforts in the name of God. The Crusades from 1095 to 1291 is a perfect example. Christians felt it was their destiny to reclaim the Holy Land from Muslim control.

Within most religious practices is what can be considered the Golden Rule principle: Do unto others as you would have them do unto you. Variations of the Golden Rule can be found in these religions:

>> Christianity

>> Judaism

>> Islam

>> Buddhism

>> Hinduism

>> Confucianism

The Golden Rule has at least three themes:

>> **Empathy:** The ability to understand the realities and experiences of others

>> **Reciprocity:** The ability to exercise mutual benefit through exchange with others

>> **Universality:** The ability and practice of involving and including all

However, many leaders, whether in politics or in places of worship, have abandoned these concepts almost entirely. That's why deconstruction, when done effectively, is an important enterprise.

Chapter 3 discusses the influences that can contribute to deconstruction. Many of those motivations have to do with the problem(s) of religion and their utilization as a tool of harm, exclusion, control, and limitation.

MORE ABOUT THE GOLDEN RULE

It's difficult to pinpoint who may have originated the Golden Rule principle, but what's clear is that many great thinkers have incorporated the principle into their work. According to some historians, the earliest version of the Golden Rule is found in an Ancient Egypt text called *The Teaching of Ptahhotep*. Confucius is also credited with articulating a version of the Golden Rule in the *Analects*. The Hebrew Bible has it in the *Talmud*. Socrates and Plato are said to have explored the concept in their work. And within the sacred texts of Christianity are hints of the Golden Rule in the narrative of Jesus and his ministry found in the book of Matthew.

Chapter **7**

Abrahamic Faiths: The Big Three

P eople are often introduced to faith or religion by the communities that surround them. Many of those who are deconstructing are doing so by reevaluating their relationship with Judaism, Christianity, or Islam. These are considered the three major religions in the world. Despite their differences, these religions have a lot more in common than most people know or realize. This chapter provides a high-level look into the Big Three.

This chapter isn't an exhaustive recall of the history of Judaism, Christianity, or Islam. Anyone seeking a comprehensive historical analysis can look to Wiley's *Comparative Religion for Dummies* for that. This chapter seeks to offer a subtle overview of the religious systems through the lens of deconstruction.

A Look at the Big Three

Because of conditioning, it's easy to assume or even expect that everyone is the same. Maybe in your own community as you were growing up, everyone looked like you. If you were involved in a church community, a temple, or a mosque, you may have rarely visited faith communities different from your own. When you did encounter others different from you, you had to be willing to learn and change your perceptions. There's comfort in those who are like you.

The Big Three — Judaism, Christianity, and Islam — are considered the major religions because they have, historically, had the greatest impact on society. They also have the greatest number of followers globally. It's a common misconception that they're vastly different from each other. Although they have some glaring and obvious points of departure, they share some distinct similarities. One is their origin. Judaism, Christianity, and Islam are referred to as Abrahamic faiths because they're believed to be descendants of Abraham, a shepherd believed to have lived 4,000 years ago. Yes, relations between Judaism, Christianity, and Islam are plagued with turmoil, opposition, and conflict, historically — and even today — but, according to their own sacred texts, they're more like siblings than enemies. And if you know anything about siblings, sometimes they can be each other's mortal enemies. The story of Jacob and Esau in Genesis is a good example. That may be why they fight so much.

REMEMBER

Is Abraham an authentic historic figure? That's unclear. What is clear, however, is that his name appears in countless ancient texts, leaving many to believe he did exist and the Big Three to claim him as their patriarch. Why is this important to know? The faith deconstruction journey requires learning as well as unlearning.

Religious conditioning is usually done in opposition to others. Some within Christianity were taught to believe that Jesus is the only true prophet of God and the only way to God. This conditioning is called Christocentric. It makes accepting other belief systems close to impossible. But what's lost on many is that Muslims also believe in Jesus. For them, Jesus is the precursor to their messenger, the prophet Muhammad.

It's also worth noting that although many identify as Jewish (Judaism), Christian (Christianity), and Muslim (Islam), the communities within each belief system are diverse. No community is a monolith, regardless of what anyone says. As these religions have grown and expanded, factions have developed within each that have resulted in branches, or in some instances denominations. The following sections provide a brief overview of each belief system, as well as their branches or denominations.

Defining Judaism

Contrary to popular belief, Judaism — whose original name is believed to be Hebrew, loosely translated as "from across the river" — didn't start out as a faith system. The religion was born out of necessity by a people seeking to unite their community and organize their identity.

Like many religions, Judaism developed over generations and served as a tool for preservation. Jews believe themselves to be God's chosen people due to the covenant made between God and Abraham. However, it's believed that Judaism didn't originate as a monotheistic religion. In the early days of the religion, Judaism was influenced greatly by the world around it. Within that world were communities who worshipped other gods. Over time, the Jewish people began to see their God as supreme, resulting in the other gods no longer being accepted or allowed within the community.

Today, Jews number more than 14 million, mostly within the United States and Israel. Even though they're a monotheistic faith, they're not a monolith. Judaism has at least four sects in the United States. In other parts of the world, Jewish people simply identify as Jewish. The sects were created primarily due to their differing views, understandings, and interpretations of Jewish traditions and laws. The following section provides a brief overview of the sects — Orthodox, Reform, Conservative, and Reconstructionist — and what makes each unique.

Orthodox

Orthodox Judaism is commonly considered the most traditional of all sects. Orthodox Jews are said to be the most intentional in preserving not only the written law of the Jews, but also the oral laws and traditions.

If you've ever seen a group of Jewish men dressed in black suits and wide-brim black hats and women in long skirts and head coverings, they are more than likely Orthodox Jews. Within this group are Haredi Jews and a subsect of Haredi known as Hasidic, which you're probably most familiar with. Haredi are known to be ultra-Orthodox and more traditional in nature, emphasizing the observance of traditional laws and rituals. Hasidic Jews, on the other hand, are more open to emotional expression in their worship practices.

Of the sects, Orthodox Jews are usually the ones to honor the Sabbath, which occurs on Saturdays. They won't work on the Sabbath or perform duties considered to be work, including driving. They also refrain from turning on lights. Another traditional practice they honor is wearing a prayer shawl, called a *tallis*, during prayer. This practice is usually reserved for men exclusively unless the rabbi is a woman. Men and women are segregated in worship services.

Reform

Reform Jews are usually more liberal in nature. They're often dressed more casually during their worship services. And men and women aren't relegated to sitting separately during worship. For Reform Jews, following the Sabbath is optional, as are dietary restrictions. Reform Jews also differ in their view of the oral and written traditions. They believe the Torah is divinely inspired, but it's the product of human hands and written in the language of the time.

Conservative

Don't be fooled by the name. This isn't your conservative Christian in Jewish clothing. Conservative Judaism is somewhere between Orthodox and Reform Judaism. Conservatives follow many of the traditions as practiced in Orthodox Judaism but allow space for modernization. For them, like Reform Jews, no work on the Sabbath is optional. Also like Reform, men and women are allowed to sit together during worship. Women are allowed to be rabbis, and Conservative Jews may drive to worship on the Sabbath. They do, however, follow many of the dietary restrictions, like Orthodox Jews, and they believe in the authority of the Torah as divine.

Reconstructionist

Some debate whether Reconstructionist Judaism is one of the major sects within Judaism. Of the sects, it's potentially the most progressive. Reconstructionist Judaism is less concerned with being a religious practice and more invested in being seen as a form of modern civilization. Reconstructionists seek to mix scientific inquiry with spirituality and, according to some, reject that the Jews are God's chosen people. They see Judaism as a creation of humans rather than as divine revelation.

Defining Christianity

Although Jesus has been credited as the founder of Christianity, crediting the creation of the faith to him may be a misrepresentation. It's no secret that Jesus was Jewish. After his death, Christianity began as a movement within Judaism, with followers adopting his teachings as their directive for survival and how to live in community.

TIP

Jesus as the Messiah isn't exclusive to Christianity. The Quran, the sacred text of Islam, also records Jesus as the Messiah.

What sets Christianity apart from Judaism then and even today is the declaration of Jesus as the Messiah. For most Jews, Jesus doesn't fulfill the messianic prophecies found within their sacred texts. For them, he isn't the Messiah they believe will come to bring about an era of peace and love.

TIP

The Christian Bible includes the same sacred Jewish texts, known as the Torah (in Hebrew) or Pentateuch (in Greek); however, the order is different in the Christian Bible than in the Torah.

Like Judaism, Christianity isn't a monolith. Christianity has several branches that represent differences in perspective, especially as it pertains to Biblical translation, the authority of the Bible, tradition, identity, and understanding. Catholicism and Protestantism are just two. Within those traditions are several movements and denominations that make up Christianity as a whole.

The following section is an overview of the denominations considered to be the main seven. It also covers several other denominations that have a familiar and impactful history or have gained popularity in recent years.

Roman Catholic

Roman Catholicism, also known as the Catholic Church, is quite possibly the behemoth of Christianity. It's the largest in number, cultural influence, and historical impact. Led by the pope, the Catholic Church traces its history to Jesus and his disciples.

It may be hard to fathom the meager origins of the Catholic Church, especially when the institution claims nearly 1.5 billion believers today. Despite the sixteenth century Reformation that led to the development of Protestantism, the Catholic Church continues to hold great influence around the world. In addition, it's probably the most diverse Christian denomination in the world, with followers on six of the seven continents:

>> Europe

>> Africa

>> South America

>> Asia

>> North America

>> Australia

Catholics look to the pope as the prime authority on how to live out their faith. They venerate the Virgin Mary, believed to be the mother of Jesus. They also believe in *transubstantiation*, meaning that the bread and wine are changed into the body and blood of Jesus. Catholics also emphasize the importance of scripture and tradition.

Methodist

Methodism isn't the oldest form of Christianity, but it's one of the most impactful denominations. Its origins date back to eighteenth-century England. John Wesley, a theologian, is considered the originator of the movement, which gets its name from his methodical approach to religion.

During the Reformation of the Church of England, Wesley wanted to help people in their quest for understanding and purposeful living in faith. He and his colleagues found fault with the Church of England on several topics, including the role of bishops. They felt the church had become corrupt and was failing in its mission and purpose.

The exact number of Methodist-affiliated groups is hard to pinpoint, but it may be close to 100. The United States alone has numerous branches of Methodism. Until 2022, the major ones included the following:

>> African Methodist Episcopal Church (AME)

>> African Methodist Episcopal Zion Church (AMEZ)

>> Christian Methodist Episcopal Church (CME)

>> Church of the Nazarene

>> Free Methodist Church

>> Wesleyan Church

>> United Methodist Church (UMC)

In 2022, the Methodist Church experienced what's believed to be the greatest and largest denominational split since the Civil War. The rift was caused in part to the incapability of the church to find common ground on what it considered to be the issue of LGBTQ+ marriage and clergy. The more conservative Methodists are now the Global Methodist Church.

Methodists are led by bishops and conferences via a connectional system. They also believe in the authority of scripture and tradition and practice infant baptism.

Baptist

Anyone slightly familiar with the Baptist church would assume, possibly, one of two things. The first assumption is that Baptists are extremely conservative in nature, meaning they're against equality, justice, and anything else considered progressive. The other possible assumption is that they're only Baptist in name. Baptist churches are stereotypically autonomous congregations. What that means is that the local church, or that precise and specific congregation, is the governing body. They don't report and aren't governed by an organized body outside of the church. However, several congregations hold membership within a governing body. It all depends on the affiliation.

The Baptist tradition has a long history that stems as far back as the Protestant Reformation. What set Baptists apart from other Protestant movements in the early days of their founding in the 1600s included a belief that only adults could consciously profess their faith in Jesus Christ; therefore, baptism should be reserved for those of a certain spiritual maturity level and understanding. Baptists are also highly vocal about their responsibility to spread the message of Jesus through evangelism. They also emphasize *sola scriptura*, meaning that scripture is the sole authority in faith.

The United States has several branches within the Baptist tradition. Some of them include the following:

>> Southern Baptist

>> Missionary Baptist

>> Independent Baptist

>> American Baptist Association

>> American Baptist Churches USA

>> Cooperative Baptist Fellowship

>> Full Gospel Baptist Fellowship

>> Primitive Baptist

Presbyterian

The Presbyterian Church today has the unfortunate reputation of being known as the "frozen chosen." Designed to mock the tradition for their reserved and stoic worship style, the nickname also references the central theme of Presbyterianism — *predestination.*

Informed by the work of John Calvin and his system of theology known as Calvinism, predestination suggests that God only chooses some for salvation. Their selection is informed solely by God's sovereign will, which also means that God's choice isn't informed by anything the chosen do or don't do.

In addition to God's sovereignty, the Presbyterian tradition is credited with providing for the Protestant Christian movement an authentic and clear understanding of the importance of scripture due to their reverence for it. With the first Presbyterian Church being founded in Scotland in 1560, Presbyterianism today has two branches: Presbyterian USA, which is believed to be the largest of the two; and the more evangelical branch, Presbyterian Church in America.

Anglican/Episcopal

The Anglican/Episcopal tradition is, in a lot of ways, like the Conservative branch in Judaism. Although the tradition is theologically Protestant, meaning its perception of God and scripture aligns more with traditions like the Presbyterian and Methodist churches, in practice they're more Catholic in nature. In other words, they may dress like or worship like the Catholics, but when they open their mouth, they sound an awful lot like the Protestants.

In the United States, Episcopalians are part of the wider global Anglican tradition. And like many of the other Protestant movements, they consider scripture and tradition as equal authorities. Their roots are tied to the Church of England but also led by bishops. And although they have such traditional leanings, they prioritize social responsibility and advocate for marginalized communities.

The Anglican Church has several denominations, including these:

>> American Anglican Church

>> Anglican Catholic Church

>> Anglican Church in America

>> Anglican Episcopal Church

>> Anglican Mission in the Americas

>> Anglican Province of America

Lutheran

In the same way that the work and teachings of Wesley informed the creation of the Methodist movement during the Church of England Reformation, seeking to reform the Catholic Church, Martin Luther challenged many of the practices of the Roman Catholic Church. As a result, the Lutheran Church was born.

Like the Baptists, Lutheran ministries are autonomous in nature. According to the Lutheran World Federation. Lutherans number anywhere between 75 and 78 million believers across the globe, with some 150 Lutheran churches. However, factors like scriptural authority, culture, and organizational structure have resulted in the creation of several factions, or branches, within the denomination.

In the United States, some of these branches include the following:

>> Evangelical Lutheran Church in America (ELCA)

>> Lutheran Church — Missouri Synod (LCMS)

>> Wisconsin Evangelical Lutheran Synod (WELS)

>> American Association of Lutheran Churches

Internationally, you can find these branches:

>> Lutheran World Federation

>> International Lutheran Council

Like Presbyterians, Lutherans believe in the authority of scripture. They also value tradition and, like the Catholic Church, believe Jesus is present in the Eucharist.

Pentecostalism

Pentecostalism is known, mostly, for one or two reasons — the charismatic nature of its preachers and worship, or its expression of baptism by the Holy Spirit (also known and understood as speaking in tongues or prophetic utterances). Many describe the rise and popularity of Pentecostalism as sudden or explosive. Of the Christian traditions considered to be the majors, Pentecostalism is easily described as the youngest.

Some trace Pentecostalism's founding to the Azusa Street Revival, a series of revivals that took place in California from 1906 to 1915. Others suggest that Pentecostalism is an offshoot of the rise of Methodism and its influence on what's known as the Holiness Movement. Regardless, what's clear is that some Christians felt they wanted and needed a greater and deeper experience with the Holy Spirit and sought to re-create what they imagined existed in the early church as recounted in the New Testament scriptures.

Like many of the other denominations, Pentecostals believe in the authority of scripture. However, they take their relationship to scripture much further. In many other Protestant denominations, scripture's authority is housed in how it's interpreted. For Pentecostals, scripture is believed to be the inspired word of God.

The Assemblies of God is considered the largest Pentecostal denomination. Following are some others:

>> Apostolic Church

>> Church of God in Christ

>> Church of Our Lord Jesus Christ

>> Foursquare Church

>> Church of God

Other Christian denominations

If the preceding list tells you anything, it's that being a Christian or understanding Christianity can take many forms. In the same way that you can find diverse communities across the globe, you can find diverse communities within Christian religious expression.

This chapter highlights the more mainstream denominations and movements within Christianity, but countless others have influenced society or created space for the expansive "body of Christ." Those like the Moravian Church, Quakers (Religious Society of Friends), Mormons (Church of Jesus Christ of Latter-day Saints), Jehovah's Witnesses, Seventh-day Adventists, United Church of Christ, and Metropolitan Community Churches are distinctly Christian but with unique beliefs and practices that differentiate them from the mainstream. And some communities, like Unitarian Universalist, aren't Christian, but many of their members have Christian roots and have interfaith practices that are informed by Christian tenets.

Within some of these movements, most specifically Mormonism and Jehovah's Witness, many of the tenets seen as restrictive, isolating, and controlling have led and/or are leading many to deconstruct from the community. Jehovah's Witnesses believe that Jehovah is the only true God and that Jesus is Jehovah's first creation. Mormons believe in Jesus but also believe that God, Jesus, and the Holy Spirit are three separate entities. Both faiths are anti-LGBTQ+ and forbid premarital sex, drinking alcohol, and many other acts considered as worldly. Violation of church laws and rules can result in excommunication, as discussed in Chapters 8 and 15. Chapter 3 also discusses how women are not allowed to preach within Mormonism.

REMEMBER

Now that you have some idea of denomination history and origin as well as the communities they serve, you're probably wondering what sets them apart from one another. It's simple. Their interpretations of scripture and how they worship are the two main factors that set them apart.

BLACK CHURCH AND AFFIRMING MINISTRIES

Within most of the denominations listed in this chapter are communities "exclusive" to the Black diaspora in America and around the world. Within the Methodist tradition is the African Methodist Episcopal Church, the African Methodist Episcopal Zion Church, and the Christian Methodist Episcopal Church. Within the Baptist tradition are several churches that are predominantly Black, but also in existence are the National Baptist Convention and the National Missionary Baptist Convention. In many urban cities you can find predominantly Black Catholic Churches, but you can also find the Church of God in Christ.

These spaces have served historically as safe havens for African Americans at the height of some of society's most painful moments, including the Civil Rights Movement. And today, for many, the Black Church continues to serve as the center of the African American community, where people go for community and encouragement.

These churches have also resulted in the creation of spaces of safety and acceptance for others within the African American community — most specifically the LGBTQ+ community. These churches are often referred to as Affirming Ministries and serve to support Black and queer Christians. The Fellowship of Affirming Ministries and the United Progressive Pentecostal Churches are just two denominations born out of this need.

Defining Islam

It's important to clear up a few misconceptions about Islam. Many understand Islam based on roots in the narratives that have been fed to society. The average person might assume that all Muslims, those who practice Islam, are terrorists. You might be thinking the same thing. The truth, however, is that most Muslims are committed to peace, community, and unity. Their commitment to justice, compassion, and humility is informed by a profound sense of responsibility to God and to humanity.

What is it that sets Islam apart from Judaism and Christianity? This chapter has already established Islam's understanding of Jesus and his role in the faith. And, like the other two religions, Islam is monotheistic in nature. But in the way that Christianity believes in a Triune God — one God in three persons: the Son, the Father, and the Holy Ghost — Islam believes in only one God, Allah. For Muslims, God has no other entities or partners. Also, in addition to Jesus, Muslims believe in many prophets, including Moses and Ishmael (the son of Abraham and Hagar). Muhammad, Islam's founder, is the last and final prophet.

Islam also has many branches. It has some main sects or denominations, including Sunni and Shia. The following section offers a brief overview of the two main branches of Islam, what makes them similar, and what makes them distinct. It also points out some details about some of the other denominations.

Sunni and Shia

It's safe to suggest that of the many sects of Islam, Sunnis are considered the more mainstream. They're also considered to be more conservative in some ways. Following the death of Muhammad, the Islamic movement split into Sunnis and Shias over a dispute regarding who should lead them. Sunnis believed that anyone could be selected, whereas Shias believed that their leader should be a descendant of Muhammad. They believed Muhammad's cousin, Ali, to be the rightful leader.

Sunnis get their name from the Arabic word *sunna*, which means tradition or way. Shias derive their name from their stance on succession. The name stems from the Arabic phrase *shi'atu Ali*, which means partisans of Ali.

What they're called and who should lead them aren't the only other differences between these two groups. Some of the other differences include these:

>> Sunnis believe the religious leaders are fallible, whereas Shias believe their leaders are divinely appointed and infallible.

>> With Shias believing their leaders to be divinely appointed, Sunnis support the election of their leaders.

> ❯❯ All Muslims are known to pray five times a day, but in some instances, Shias may combine their midday and afternoon prayers, as well as their sunset and nighttime prayers.

What's also worth mentioning is that Sunnis make up the majority population of Muslims around the world. Shias account for roughly 10 to 15% of the global Muslim population.

Other forms of Islam

As with all other religious groups and movements, it's expected that some won't fit into the mainstream sects of Islam. In addition to Sunni and Shia, a quick internet search names at least six others: Sufism, Ahmadiyya, Zaidiyyah, Ismaili, Alawites, and Kharijites. Some of them share some overlap with Sunni and Shia but differ in distinct ways. One group is more mystic than the others, and one rejects the stances that Shias and Sunnis have on how leaders are chosen. A third is known to strictly believe in the literal translation of the Quran, Islam's sacred text. But all share the same commitment to God and a belief in their responsibility to humankind.

Beyond the Big Three

As discussed in Chapter 3, faith deconstruction happens for all sorts of reasons. Maybe you've experienced a life-altering moment causing you to reevaluate the communities you once considered sacred. Or maybe you've simply begun to ask pertinent questions as you witness the state of the world around you. Whatever the reason, it's possible to hold some form of membership or affiliation with one of the "Big Three." But because of your deconstructing, you may find yourself weighing the validity and viability of the very community that was once, and quite possibly might still be, sacred.

Deconstruction, like faith, is personal. And each religious community has pros and cons. Not a single one is perfect, regardless of the expectations of its believers. Deconstruction also has pros and cons. Some people deconstruct and continue their affiliation with the religion they were given at birth. Others embrace a completely different religious group altogether, experimenting and adopting an appreciation for just one or for several religious communities.

TIP

Chapters 13 and 14 cover some of the options available from other religious communities. Some may divorce themselves from religion completely. Chapter 11 highlights some testimonies.

Whatever the outcome, the choice is yours. As you investigate where you are, what you desire, and what's most fitting, I hope the information in this chapter has provided you with insight to make your journey smooth, manageable, and effective.

NOTEWORTHY PRACTITIONERS

Chapter 19 lists ten individuals from history and contemporary times who have used their faith to impact and influence society. But they aren't the only ones. From celebrities to faith leaders to political leaders, many of the people we celebrate and cherish represent some of the faith practices mentioned in this chapter. Here are just a few of them:

- Mahershala Ali, Muslim

- Muhammad Ali, Muslim

- Kareem Abdul Jabbar, Muslim

- Daveed Diggs, Jewish

- Albert Einstein, Jewish

- Elie Wiesel, Jewish

3

The Nuts and Bolts of Faith Deconstruction

Learn what questions to ask.

Navigate deconstruction at your own pace.

Examine what you believe about heaven, hell, sin, and other religious concepts.

Chapter **8**

Taking a Closer Look at What You Believe

et me say loud and clear that religion isn't all bad. However, one of the problems with religion is that it can limit its members. One benefit of deconstruction is that it's an opportunity to ask questions, consider, ponder, and evaluate. Deconstruction lets you choose for yourself. You get to investigate what you believe and why and determine your own relationship to faith and religion.

This chapter highlights the benefits of investigating what you believe, as well as the challenges you may face once you accept that you're in a state of faith deconstruction. This chapter also touches on some problems with religion on a fundamental level and its relationship to control versus skill and life building.

Revisiting the Cause(s) of Your Faith Deconstruction

One Sunday morning in the summer of 2009, I had a revelation that was the impetus for my deconstruction journey. The day before, I visited a Saturday afternoon/evening worship experience. Someone I was getting to know invited me to attend the service with them, and I obliged. While I was familiar with the pastor of the church, I'd never heard him preach. I went thinking this would be an opportunity to become more aware of the person so many others adore and respected.

I don't remember everything that happened during the service, but I do remember the preacher talking about being more like Jesus. He paired the auditing process commonly used by the Internal Revenue Service to being self-aware. He suggested, to be more like Jesus, it's necessary — paramount even — to do an internal audit of yourself and your life.

The entire time he spoke, I struggled. Actually, *struggled* isn't the most accurate word. I literally fidgeted in my seat. I didn't know why at the time, but I vehemently disagreed. The preacher focused all his attention and every point on being more perfect, more divine, more righteous. As far as he was concerned, everyone's goal should be to abandon everything that makes us human to be more divine like Jesus. But what if Jesus wasn't perfect? That was one question I pondered. Another question for me centered on the whole concept of God, Jesus, and the Holy Spirit. Mostly, if it's true that God made the choice to come to the world in human form, why would God then want people to negate everything about themselves that's human?

Something was missing. "What about his humanity?" I remember asking myself.

The next day, as I was sitting through a new members' class at the church I'd recently joined, the instructor asked, "What is the most important thing about Jesus?" After others in the room shared their perspectives, from Jesus being the son of God in the flesh, to Jesus dying on the cross for everyone's sins, I stated hesitantly, "his humanity!" Immediately after class, the instructor suggested I go to seminary.

If you've deconstructed or are deconstructing now, there's a moment that triggers a revelation so impactful and enormous that it creates a crack in your foundation. That's what that moment was for me. It led me to consider all sorts of things that were counter to what I'd been conditioned to believe. From that moment of cracking, I developed a lot of questions. What was missing from the sacred record as it pertained to Jesus and his life? Why was only a snippet of Jesus's life and ministry available? Why does the account to Jesus' life and ministry only cover his birth and then skip to his baptism at 33 years of age? What about the years between his time of hiding in Egypt to his time in the wilderness? Why are those parts missing?

I began to wonder if so much of his story was missing because of control. I began to wonder what was in the record that they didn't want people to see or know, and why? It caused me to consider all the ways in my life that a loved one — maybe a parent or authority — omitted some information I felt may have been important because, in their own words, they thought they were protecting me. It made me wonder if the same thing happened with the Bible or the life of Jesus.

Oftentimes, there's a moment that causes you to question, to be curious about what you know and what you don't know. What was that moment for you? What happened that has led you to question and deconstruct?

It's natural to have questions. If, and when, someone tells you to not ask questions or that you shouldn't, they're trying to limit you or, better yet, they're trying to control you, your process, your understanding, your very being.

As Chapter 3 discusses, the deconstruction journey is a process. The faith deconstruction journey is a long and, to some extent, arduous process that takes a lot of negotiating, processing, imagining, testing, questioning, and, at some point, acceptance. For many, the faith deconstruction journey is a lifelong experience.

No one deconstructs overnight. Rarely does it happen for anyone overnight.

Take my example, for instance. When deconstruction started, I was simply questioning because something I heard didn't align with me internally. Contradictions were at play, but it also took me being aware enough to consider that maybe what was being said had flaws. To some extent, the question may not have been the beginning of my deconstruction. But it pointed to me being in a full-blown deconstruction posture.

It would be years before I realized that I'd been on a deconstruction journey. Years. But once I made the connection, I needed to make decisions. The questioning was an important stage in my journey. But I needed to take a few other steps before I was in a full-on faith deconstruction posture. To some extent, I'm still deconstructing. But there have been moments along the way where I consciously made determinations that have influenced where I am now. Deciding to deconstruct and accepting that you're deconstructing are two very important stages of the deconstruction journey.

Deciding to deconstruct

Throughout this book, I talk about the concept of *cognitive dissonance*. Cognitive dissonance happens when your beliefs and values no longer align. You can find examples of cognitive dissonance in Chapters 3 and 4 for greater clarity. But, let me be careful not to oversimplify this. It's not just that your beliefs and values no longer align, but that the revelation of such becomes challenging.

So, what do you do with that? This moment can be painful for a lot of different reasons. You may experience a level of heartache as you begin to deconstruct. You may experience some form of grief. And rightfully so. Everything you thought you knew and believed has been utterly altered. To some extent, this change alters your entire identity. Who you thought you were in the world and how you related to the world becomes forever modified.

Perhaps, like me, your cognitive dissonance experience creates another feeling altogether. It might create fear, loneliness, and uncertainty, all of which I discuss in later chapters. There's a pain that comes with not knowing what to believe or how others will accept or embrace the changes you're experiencing in your deconstruction journey. It's scary.

Therefore, you must make the decision of whether you want to deconstruct. If you do, what does that look like? And, who then becomes your community? Will you be accepted, supported, and loved/embraced by the people who knew you prior to your deconstruction? Choosing to deconstruct isn't a decision you take or make lightly. Far too many things are at stake for you and for those around you. But once you do, the possibilities are endless.

WARNING

Be aware that in some societies and communities, deconstructing your faith is perceived as "denouncing" what you once believed. Doing so could result in the community that you once considered sacred ostracizing you, excommunicating you, or abandoning you completely. Some examples of this are seen in communities like the Amish, Jehovah's Witnesses, and the Mormon Church, as well as fundamentalist-leaning religious communities.

WHAT IS EXCOMMUNICATION?

Excommunication, also known to or referred to as disfellowship, is the process by which members can be removed from the religious community they were either born into and raised within or join at some point. But it's not just that you're removed. In some groups, any person disfellowshipped or excommunicated is fully and totally removed from the community. What that means for some is, not only do they lose their religious community, but they can lose access to and relationship with their entire family.

A person, or persons, can be disfellowshipped for various reasons. In some communities, like the Mormon Church, a person can be excommunicated for acts anyone outside of the community would obviously consider heinous, like murder and maybe even adultery. But a person can also be disfellowshipped for acts more commonly accepted in society, like homosexuality, apostasy, or even abortion. In the Jehovah's Witness Church, a person can be excommunicated

(continued)

(continued)

for sinning without remorse and not making the effort to repent. Someone can also be excommunicated for disagreeing with the church's teaching openly.

Excommunication is found in other world religions, too, but it's not as prevalent as it is in Christian faiths. Also, excommunication may not be as permanent or final outside Christianity. In some instances, excommunication is designed to lead an individual or individuals to *repentance* — the expression of regret or remorse. As a matter of fact, excommunication is meant to maintain order and adherence to the teaching of that group's religious tenets, not total separation.

Accepting your deconstruction

Deciding to deconstruct — making a clear and conscious decision to reexamine, question, and reelevate what you once believed and held dear — is just one part of the faith deconstruction process. Making the decision to question and challenge everything you've learned, been taught, practiced, and lived fully takes much more than just saying, "I'm deconstructing."

You also must accept that you're deconstructing.

Why? Because deconstructing isn't something you do in passing or haphazardly. It's not something you do halfway. (There's another phrase I wanted to use here, but you get the point.) Deconstructing your faith may be one of the hardest things you've ever done in your life.

REMEMBER

Deconstructing your faith takes intention. To do it, and to do it effectively — meaning in a way that's beneficial to you in the long run — you must be fully committed to the process. It's the only way to get the most out of the experience and be able to truly learn not only more about faith and religion, but about yourself and your relationship to whatever divine entity or entities you choose along your path.

I'm not suggesting that you'll completely abandon everything you once believed. Deconstructing your faith might actually make you feel closer to God. It could also lead you back to the very faith and religious system you grew up in. Because of your deconstruction, you may feel that you have a greater grasp on who God is and what God intends for your life. Chapter 11 shares some of those stories. As a result of your deconstruction journey, you may feel better versed, better aware, and better equipped to walk in your faith confidently.

But maybe as you've deconstructed your faith, you've realized that the systems made popular in Western culture no longer serve you. Perhaps you've ventured into more Indigenous faith practices, which are discussed in Chapter 13. Or you've leaned into spiritual practices prevalent throughout the continent of Africa (Chapter 13). Another possibility is leaning into atheism or agnosticism, discussed in Chapter 14, or some form of Humanism (also Chapter 14). Or maybe you've developed faith practices that intertwine with several religious and faith practices.

You can do these things because you accepted or, put another way, surrendered, fully to the process of faith deconstruction, allowing yourself to embrace the experience completely. As a result, you've found joy in the process of exploration, approaching the experience and learning and relearning with joy, excitement, and curiosity.

Pondering the Problems with Religion

I'm about to say something controversial. Ready? Here it goes.

Most religions are performative in nature.

Now, I know you may be wondering what I mean by that. It's simple; there is more emphasis placed on the presentation of religion than there is on how one lives out their faith in their everyday lives. Many people who profess to be members of a specific religious or faith tradition care more about the perception of being religious than they do about what truly makes religion effective and useful.

It's apparent almost every day in our political and cultural spheres. People wear their religion like a badge of honor. But more often than not, people are more concerned with how they're perceived than they are with doing anything meaningful for the larger society. They're plagued by individualism and ignore more religious movements' calls for collectivism. They use religion, religious language, and religious symbols to push agendas that are usually harmful to the very communities they claim to care about.

Historians will argue that the purpose of religion, at its core, is to do two things. First, when done right, religion can provide community by which to practice faith. Second, because of the community building, religion was meant to provide clarity on the things understood, or believed, to be mysteries. Questions might be: How did we as a people come to be? Where did we originate? What is our (as in community as a whole) purpose? Who are supposed to be? These are all questions that religion, historically, attempted to answer while building a thriving and healthy community of people.

Religion has gotten a bit off course with either of those intended goals, hasn't it?

One big problem with religion today is how it breeds. Whether it's competition, exclusion, and in some instances harm, religion has veered off incredibly from what most historians believe it was intended to do. But what if it's doing exactly what it was meant to?

That's a question for another time.

While religion, according to some historians, was meant to help communities or to build community, religion has historically broken communities, and in some instances, governments have wiped out entire civilizations under the name of "Big G" God. The following sections delve deeper into two problematic areas of religion: abuse and control and their relationship to faith investigation in deconstruction.

Recognizing religious abuse

"Do no harm" is a concept often found in religious groups and movements. The concept refers to communal care. It emphasizes avoiding any action that could potentially hurt another — most specifically, anyone within your own community or homogenous group. But it can also refer to caring for nature and everything within nature, as well as members of a familiar group.

However, as I mention in Chapter 3, victims of religious abuse are usually members of the same community they hold affiliation with.

Religious abuse occurs when religion is used as a tool of inappropriate influence. Condemnation and exclusion are two forms discussed in Chapter 3. Entire communities, like those who identify as gay, bisexual, lesbian, transgender, or same gender loving (which is how many Black men in the community identify), have become disconnected from their entire families because of religious abuse. In some instances, they've embraced concepts like internalized homophobia, also known as self-hatred. The scars of that abuse can be felt throughout the entirety of a person's lifetime.

Understanding these realities as a form of abuse should cause you pause. You don't have to be able to relate to the pain of the abuse to know that it doesn't align with what you've been taught about community and community care. In addition, it's worth doing your own inquiry, interrogating the lessons you received regarding who is and who isn't welcome, and the history of those exclusions. Speaking from the Christian perspective, there are a vast number of contradictions that the average person should have questions about.

Religion and control versus God and control

Most religious groups have at their core a commitment to community. They also have at their core ideals around personal responsibility. What has made them problematic, however, is the manner to which many in certain religious groups have used these concepts as tools of control.

You can find an example of this in the work and writings of religious scholars and leaders, like Kelly Brown Douglas. Douglas has written extensively about the impact majority culture (in other words, white culture) continues to have on the Black community. She points out how concepts of piety and the perception that members of the Black community are hardwired for deviance has stripped the Black community of its identity and pride in its heritage and culture. This is especially true as it pertains to issues of sexuality and sexual expression. According to Douglas, as a result, the Black community adopted a posture of shame — the very shame that has been used throughout the Black community to shun, exclude, and oppress those who also identify as LGBTQIA+.

Of course, examples like sexism and purity culture (both discussed in Chapter 3), blasphemy laws, and anti-LGBTQ legislation show up in other parts of the world too. As a means of maintaining order, as perceived by the powers that be, religion being used to dictate the actions and lives of others has become a common occurrence. And the "powers that be" have taken their direction from the community's sacred texts. Is it faith or indoctrination being taught?

What then does God have to say about all of this? It depends on who you ask quite honestly. Some suggest that God's position is clear on certain issues that plague contemporary society today. As a result, their actions are dictated by those directives. However, others suggest that, depending on what religious community you hold membership in, the sacred texts God has provided are clear that community care and support, and of course love, are the only true and meaningful directives that God has provided. They're found in frameworks like The Greatest Commandment Theology. (See the nearby sidebar for more.)

They suggest that God is love and love is for everyone. They suggest that what God wants of everyone is to live fully and to care for others. And as someone who's seeking to deconstruct, part of your task is dissecting what you've been taught about these concepts and how they align with what you believe God intends of you and those you're in community with. If they don't align, which more than likely they don't or you wouldn't be reading this book, you have an enlightening journey ahead of you.

MORE ON GREATEST COMMANDMENT THEOLOGY

The Greatest Commandment Theology has been made popular by pastor and theologian Kristian A. Smith, lead pastor of The Faith Community (TFC) and cohost of the Holy Smokes Cigars and Spirituality Podcast. It's the framework of Smith's work on deconstructing harmful theology and building community, taken from Christian scripture, Matthew 22:36-40 (NIV): "Love the Lord your God with all your heart and with all your soul and with all your mind. This is the first and greatest commandment. And the second is like it: 'Love your neighbor as yourself.' All the Law and the Prophets hang on these two commandments."

Smith and TFC's greatest commandment framework provide a fresh take on the scripture that has been used for generations to suggest that the commandment's intent is centered exclusively on Godly obedience and authentic relationship with God. The framework highlights that love of God is only one part of the equation, positioning love of self and love of others alongside Godly love and affection. It suggests that loving God also requires self-love and the love of others. How you love others and self is also apparent in how you love God.

Chapter 9

Unpacking Heaven, Hell, and Sacred Texts

What does it look like to deconstruct? Are there five or ten steps, and does the order matter? How do I know if I'm doing things right? When do I know I've successfully deconstructed? These are probably some of the questions, or some version of them, that you have. And they're valid and appropriate. You've probably operated in spaces, communities, and environments where you were taught that there are always answers to your questions. So, this moment isn't unlike any other. You're seeking answers and guidance. Why else would you have purchased this book, right?

I hate to break it to you, but the faith deconstruction journey has no clear pathway. No manual can provide all the answers you're seeking. When it comes to deconstruction, there are things to do and things to know, but it's ultimately a personal process that's unique to every person.

Deconstruction is a lot like grieving. You were taught the stages of grief — anger, bargaining, acceptance, and so on — to be aware and mindful of. But grief isn't linear, and neither is deconstruction. So, what *should* you look for, expect, or even do while deconstructing?

All hope isn't lost.

While it's next to impossible to provide you with a specific order, what I can do is provide you with some guidance on what to consider and how to consider it when it comes to many of the items and concepts that are often considered sacred. My goal in this chapter is — borrowing from my friend and technical editor of this project, Kristian A. Smith — to help you in your untethering. How? This chapter, in relation to Chapter 8 and Chapter 10, delves deeper into the nuts and bolts of deconstruction by pinpointing familiar and not-so-familiar concepts worth deconstructing, including the concepts of heaven and hell and how you view your religion's sacred texts.

Thinking About the Validity of Sacred Texts

One day while listening to one of the many podcasts I'm subscribed to, I was captured by something a guest said. The podcast was *Honoring the Journey* hosted by Leslie Nease. I can't remember what episode or who the guest was, but I do remember his words. Christians, he said, didn't have a Bible for at least the first 100 years and were still considered Christians. And he's right. Before sacred text was written, Christians had their stories. Even before being named Christians, it's believed, they had their stories. In my first year of seminary, a professor referred to Christianity as a once-oral tradition. (Oral tradition can be understood as how a group's stories and history are preserved, generation after generation, through the practice of telling and hearing.)

Over time, the stories are expanded, one teller adding details another may have omitted, forgotten, or been unaware of. Eventually, those stories were organized, compiled, and canonized.

They were immortalized. But what would Christianity be today without its sacred text? For that matter, what would any religious system be without its sacred text? Would they still be what their followers know and believe and understand them to be, or would they be something else? And what should followers' relationship to sacred texts be?

Part of the faith deconstruction journey requires asking these questions, as well as evaluating and reevaluating your relationship to the things you once considered sacred. Sacred texts are no exception. The following sections dig deeper into the impact that deconstructing can and should have on understanding sacred texts and their validity in your religious life.

Biblical literalism versus allegory

To this day, I've yet to read the Christian Bible in its entirety, from cover to cover. I did get as far as the book of Ruth during my first attempt. I told myself I'd give it another try later, but that never happened. During my time in seminary, I was successful at reading a good portion of it. I've read the gospels of the New Testament in their entirety, along with the book of Acts, Revelation, Ezekiel, Job, Proverbs, and Psalms.

As a writer/journalist/budding theologian, I realized in my reading that what I enjoyed then, and still enjoy today, isn't the messages found in the Christian Bible or the inspiration gleaned from reading it. No, what I continue to enjoy about the Christian Bible is the literature. This is especially true for the Old Testament. I often describe the Christian Bible as a collection of writings written or compiled, during a specific time in history, by people who were attempting to make sense of things that happened in their life and share their understanding of God's role in it all. At one point, I described the Christian Bible as a library.

Well, this is my perspective regarding the Old Testament. My perspective of the New Testament is slightly different — at least at this point in my journey. Due in large part to what I've learned about the New Testament, I view it and its many narratives as a legal brief. In other words, I experience the New Testament as a coordinated effort to prove that Jesus was the promised Messiah intentionally referenced throughout some of the Old Testament in the Christian Bible.

What set Christianity apart from Judaism then, and even today, is the declaration of Jesus as the Messiah. For most Jews, Jesus doesn't fulfill the messianic prophecies found within their sacred texts. Therefore, for them, he isn't the Messiah they believe will come to bring about an era of peace and love.

But Jews aren't the only group that questions the identity of Jesus. Faith leaders, atheists, and even deconstructionists question whether Jesus is a historical figure. Renowned New Testament scholar, Dr. Bart D. Ehrman, James A. Gray distinguished professor at the University of North Carolina at Chapel Hill, has written extensively about the historical Jesus. A proclaimed agnostic atheist, Ehrman has made the argument that Jesus is an actual historical figure. However, he doesn't believe Jesus to be the son of God.

The belief that Jesus was the son of God and the many narratives about his life and ministry can be understood as examples of biblical literalism. So, then, what is biblical literalism? *Biblical literalism* is the belief or understanding that the events of the Bible, as well as the characters and moments, are straightforward and exact. In other words, it's the belief that everything in the Bible happened exactly as it's written. The stories are taken at face value and, for some biblical literalists, aren't to be questioned, altered, or translated in any way beyond as they're written.

But reading and understanding the biblical text literally and explicitly is problematic. The Christian Bible contradicts itself throughout. Within the first book of the Christian Bible, Genesis, there are discrepancies and inconsistencies in the first two chapters. Genesis 1 and Genesis 2 are best known as the creation stories. In the first chapter, the order by which God performs creation is different from the order found in the second chapter.

Critics and opponents of the biblical text argue that the stories and lessons found in the Bible, whether the New or Old Testament, aren't to be taken literally. They see the messages and stories within the sacred text *allegorically.* They believe the messages within the text are deeper and possess hidden truths that must be interpreted to be understood.

Take the final book of the Christian Bible, Revelation. Known as an apocalyptic text, proponents of biblical literalism argue that

Revelation is a warning for what's to come in the final days of society and civilization. They believe the writer tells the story of what he saw and experienced as a prophetic warning to God's people. However, opponents of this argument consider the writing to be nothing more than a dream induced by some form of psychedelic — more along the lines of a fever dream.

While biblical literalists consider the Christian Bible to be, without a doubt, a historical document, nonliteralists, or better yet biblical criticists, believe that truly understanding and best utilizing it requires an analytical approach. They believe that studying the texts for form, style, message, and structure is the better approach to biblical interpretation and understanding.

Literalism isn't exclusive to Christianity. Most, if not all, religious groups/systems that possess sacred writings have some form of literalism at play.

When it comes to sacred texts, an important question for you to ask during your faith deconstruction is what value the texts have for you in your life and faith journey. Does it matter? If so, why? If not, why? What weight have you placed on the accuracy of the texts?

An important part of faith deconstruction and dissecting your faith is understanding what you believe. Are the stories found in the sacred text actual events, or are they examples that are meant to provide inspiration for your life? How you answer that question helps you in understanding what value and weight you give to the texts that are sacred in your tradition. Having an answer for the question also helps you in evaluating what is and is not sacred.

In some practices, because they believe the Bible to be literal (and to some extent infallible, which I discuss later in this section), it is sacred. In other practices, like humanism, the writing of secular artists such Audre Lorde or the poetry of historical greats like Maya Angelou are considered just as sacred as the writings in the Bible because humanists see the stories in the Bible as allegorical. (See the nearby sidebar for more on these writers.)

ABOUT AUDRE LORDE AND MAYA ANGELOU

Audre Lorde and Maya Angelou are often considered two of the most important Black women writers of a generation. Lorde is often described as a writer, philosopher, Black lesbian feminist, and socialist warrior. Her 1980s collection of essays, *Sister Outsider,* is one of her most beloved and popular pieces of writing. Writer, poet, actress, and activist, Maya Angelou, is the author of the critically acclaimed, *I Know Why the Caged Bird Sings,* which was her 1969 autobiography of her early life and experiences, including becoming mute after being sexually assaulted as a child. Both women wrote extensively about the black experience through the lens of Black women during their time. Their works and writings still resonate today and are quoted and highlighted in works of art as well as in academic offerings.

Your understanding of sacred is expanded and your relationship to religious sacred texts is shifted.

TIP

The things that possess value in your life are that way because of you. You assign value. Whether it's your work/career, your family and loved ones, the things you own and possess, or the items you consider sacred, they're of value because you decided they were. An important part of the faith deconstruction journey is determining the value of the texts.

I remember a time in seminary when a classmate was upset about the Christian Bible translation that was required. They were brought up on the King James (KJV) translation of the Bible. However, the school required the New Revised Standard Version (NRSV) because they believed it was a more accurate translation of the original texts. "You will not reduce my Jesus to a wind," I remember the classmate once saying at the start of a lecture. The value they placed on the text was connected to how they felt about Jesus. The simple change of one word between translations wasn't acceptable, even if it was possible that the NRSV was closer or more accurate to the true translation. As far as they were concerned, the description was of Jesus, literally, not some wind.

THE PROBLEM OF BIBLICAL ILLITERACY

Another problem worth mentioning is the sheer amount of biblical *illiteracy* present in society. Most people have no true grasp of what's in scripture or have no grasp of the historicity and context within the stories individually. Some may be able to rattle off some scripture from memory, but they lack awareness of the world and context of the scripture, also known as *exegesis* — the critical explanation or interpretation of a text.

Others know what they know because of what they've been told. Their level of biblical illiteracy is formed by what they've been granted permission to engage in. What they know is what they've been told for generations either by the pastors of the church where they were raised or in the home of that extremely religious parent who knows what they know from the pastor. They've never been granted permission to investigate for themselves. When they have, they've been told they were wrong. Or they were told not to question God or scripture, which is also a dangerous problem and component to both biblical illiteracy and literalism. Biblical inerrancy and infallibility

Just as biblical literalists believe that the Christian Bible is God's word and that it should be taken literally, they believe that the Christian Bible is *infallible*. Sometimes they have also used the phrase Biblical inerrancy. You've probably heard one or both said a time or two throughout your life if you grew up in a staunchly evangelical Christian environment. But what is meant by such declarations?

While many folks may use the words *inerrancy* and *infallibility* interchangeably, they don't exactly mean the same thing.

>> *Inerrant* is best defined as without error. It means that no fault is present in any way. To some extent, *inerrant* almost suggests that scripture is perfect in look, presentation, and structure.

>> *Infallible*, on the other hand, suggests capability. It's defined as unerring. Put another way, something is infallible when it's incapable of wrong, wrongdoing, or error. So, it's not just that error is missing or wrong is missing. Error or wrong isn't possible in any capacity. Not only is scripture without error — inerrant — but scripture is incapable of being wrong. It's perfect now and will always be right and perfect.

Consider, again, the discrepancies found in Genesis 1 and Genesis 2. While some biblical critics suggest that the differences and discrepancies found in the text are clear indicators that the Bible shouldn't be taken literally or considered inerrant and infallible, proponents argue that the differences mean nothing more than one version seeks to fill in the blanks missing in the other. The same is true for arguments regarding the differences found between the *synoptic gospels* of the New Testament: Matthew, Mark, and Luke. (*Note:* These gospels are often referred to as the synoptic gospels because of the similarities they share in the story, events, and descriptions of Jesus, his life, and his ministry.)

While there are overlapping similarities between the three books, there are also glaring differences. However, they are posited as authorities of the life and ministry of Jesus. When you add the Gospel of John, which is quite different from the others, it's worth investigating just how accurate and perfect they are and their weight as authorities. Each gospel has its own agenda that, for some biblical critics and deconstructionists, highlights clearly the reality of fallibility and errancy.

REMEMBER

As you deconstruct, you may find yourself wondering and questioning whether you believe the sacred texts are, or are not, infallible and inerrant. It's the same for inquiring whether you believe the Bible to be literal or allegorical. It is a question you can't ignore, and you shouldn't want to ignore. Having an answer will better serve you in your process and provide some clarity on what authority the sacred texts have in what you believe and why.

THE CHRISTIAN BIBLE VERSUS THE HEBREW BIBLE

In some academic spaces, what Christians know and understand as the Old Testament can and will be referred to as the Hebrew Bible. You might assume they mean the same thing, but they don't. While there are some core commonalities, there are also some differences. The Hebrew Bible, better understood as the Tanakh, refers to the 24 books of Hebrew scripture comprising the Torah, the Nevi'im, and the Ketuvim. The Torah, also known as the Pentateuch, encompasses the first five books — Genesis, Exodus, Leviticus, Numbers, and Deuteronomy. These books are also referred to as the Five Books of Moses. The Nevi'im is also referred to as the Books of the Prophets and is separated into two groups: the former prophets and the latter prophets. The Ketuvim, or the Writings, is the third section and includes the Psalms, Job, Lamentations, Proverbs, and seven other books.

The Hebrew Bible is set apart from the Christian Bible in a few ways. In addition to the Hebrew Bible having 15 fewer books, the order is different between the two. In the Christian Bible, the books on the prophets are at the end. Another main difference between the two is their function. The purpose of the Hebrew Bible is to portray the foundation of the Jewish faith and practices, while the Christian Bible's function is often seen as a foreshadowing of the coming of Jesus and his designation as the son of God.

Indoctrination

Notions of infallibility and inerrancy, along with literalism, create issues like indoctrination. As someone deconstructing, you can learn to recognize the signs and shed the influences.

When I was a kid, my parents sent me to summer camp at the local Young Men's Christian Association (YMCA). I loved it. No lie. I always looked forward to the weeks I would spend there. It was a pivotal time in my young life.

The highlight for me every day was morning devotion. As soon as the last kid arrived and was signed in, the camp leaders gathered us in the grand room and kicked off what I understand today as morning devotion. I can't remember what it was called then. One song we sang every morning was "Father Abraham":

Father Abraham had many sons

And many sons had Father Abraham

I am one of them and so are you

So, let's just praise the Lord

I now understand there are a few variations of the song known by many as a fun campfire song. But for me, it's always been sung this way and for the purpose of morning devotions.

Even though we sang several songs every morning, "Father Abraham" was, by far, my favorite and the one I remember the most vividly. A few times, the leaders and counselors let me and a few others lead the songs. I'd yell it at the top of my lungs, losing my voice by the time we were done. It was years later that I realized the Father Abraham we were singing about was the Abraham of the Bible. I can't say I knew or had any inkling that we were singing about someone specifically. We could have been singing about Abraham Lincoln for all I knew. It was just a fun, interactive, unifying moment for me and all the other kids.

That was probably my first experience of indoctrination. The leaders and counselors were laying the foundation. At the time, it was lost on me that I was going to a Christian camp. In my innocence and naivete, I just saw the camp experience as us having a good time, singing, expressing, and being a community — well before I knew what being a community meant. I was a kid having a good time, but I was also being conditioned. When I began truly being taught about the Bible, I already had some familiarity with the stories and some connection to the characters as one of Abraham's "sons."

Many years later, that connection to Abraham changed as I learned more about the text and context and did some identity work of my own. Many of my colleagues were taken aback when

I paralleled my journey into ministry with that of Hagar's in the wilderness. No longer was I a son of Abraham, but I digress.

Initially, I was going to name this section "Asking Yourself, Is This a Cult?" Of course, it would have been tongue-in-cheek. But indoctrination and cultist behavior aren't far off from one another. Ask anyone who has ever joined a cult unknowingly and eventually escaped it, and they'll tell you they never imagined themselves being the kind of person to join a cult. Yet, it happens more often than you think. Many of the tools that cult leaders use to recruit members can also be recognized in some of the most popular and successful religious groups — including Christianity. Religious indoctrination occurs when the beliefs of the group are taught in a manner that's seemingly coercive. Oftentimes, this is done authoritatively. When you're being indoctrinated, your own autonomy is restricted. You're limited in your ability to think critically for yourself and almost encouraged to share the beliefs of the community blindly. Some of the same manipulation, coercion, and limited critical thinking seen in religious indoctrination can also be recognized in cult recruitment.

TIP

Childhood religious education is usually one tactic of indoctrination.

When you hear or see the word *indoctrination*, immediate negative thoughts or feelings might arise. These feelings and thoughts are valid. To some extent, indoctrination is dangerous. But it isn't all bad or always bad. What makes religious indoctrination difficult, and to some extent dangerous, is the manner and practice of limiting someone's autonomy. This is when and how biblical literalism, infallibility, and inerrancy become effective. When someone has limited your ability to think critically and for yourself, you blindly accept ways of thinking, practices, methods, and perspectives that are harmful to you and others.

You accept traditions and rituals without investigating their meaning or reasoning. You adopt harmful theology instead of evaluating how some ways of thinking theologically as taught contradict other biblical lessons and thinking. And you act out these beliefs and perspectives without considering any other way.

REMEMBER

How do you deconstruct indoctrination? With patience. One important question to ask yourself is, "Why do I believe what I believe?" You must ask yourself that question before you can determine what you believe. Knowing the why is an important part of the deconstruction process because it gives you a big piece of your origin story. It becomes your point of reference for everything else.

Deconstructing indoctrination means being curious and courageous. It means not being afraid to be exposed to ways of thinking that may be uncomfortable. It means exploring the beliefs of others to see where you overlap and where you differ. Deconstruction in action also takes being open to all the possibilities and asking lots of questions.

The Heaven and Hell Debate

When I was younger, I was taught, quite simply, that Easter was celebrated to not only honor and celebrate the ultimate sacrifice Jesus made on the day he was crucified, but give thanks for his victory over death. As my 12- or 13-year-old brain understood it, Jesus's sacrifice — dying on the cross — paid the price for everyone's sins and the ultimate sin Adam and Eve committed in the garden. As part of the narrative, Jesus went into hell, took the keys, defeated death, and ascended into heaven.

Now that I'm older, I have a different perspective regarding the crucifixion, rooted more so in a belief that what Jesus died for was rooted in his anti-empire message and ministry. But that's another debate for another time.

As a young teenager, I accepted what was taught to me and took it at face value. I trusted those who were my teachers and guides. They were the authority on such matters, and I was their student. But over time, I had questions. I became curious out of confusion. If Jesus, as some of the more popular gospel songs proclaimed, had "paid it all," then what was the point of living a holy and righteous life? Hadn't all of that already been, as Olivia Pope would say in the hit television show *Scandal*, "handled?" I couldn't understand why it was that the narrative of living right and being righteous continued as a directive if Jesus's sacrifice had wiped the slate clean. How was it and why was it possible that choices I made in life could still lead to my being rejected from heaven and remanded to hell?

These were the questions my young mind, working through faith and understanding, had during that time — and still today, if I'm being honest. It just never really lined up for me. The problem, however, wasn't that I had the questions or that I asked them — even though there were times I felt as though my asking them was problematic. The problem that presented itself to me was that no one ever created space or allowance for my whys. The thought was that everything I needed to know, that I was taught, was right there in the Bible, and it was perfect and infallible and accurate.

Not only did these questions present for me the problem with the narrative regarding sin (discussed more in Chapter 10), but these questions created for me the problem with the concept of heaven and hell. These questions began, for me, a routine of seeing and reading contradictions in the text more clearly. As I found myself frustrated with the contradictions, I began to question piety, holiness, righteousness, long-suffering, theodicy, and the many other constructs that Christianity possesses.

The following sections continue the conversation regarding biblical literalism, inerrancy, infallibility, and indoctrination by discussing the constructs of heaven and hell, the problem with them as concepts, and the deconstruction of it all.

The real deal about heaven and hell

Are heaven and hell real? No real data is available to suggest whether they are or aren't, but it's safe to assume that the concepts of heaven and hell were developed in the same manner as religion in the first place.

REMEMBER

The origin of religion is believed to have two camps. One camp believes religion was created as a tool to create order within societies. In some of these instances, the order was meant to unify the community on one purpose, one cause, and one identity. The second camp believes that as humanity evolved, communities developed a need for understanding.

The belief in heaven and hell developed over time as a means of answering specific questions. One of those questions is where people go when they die. According to Joanne M. Pierce of Religion News Service, Jewish and Greek ideas influenced Christians' belief in the afterlife. Within the Hebrew Bible are references to a place in the afterlife, Sheol, where souls linger temporarily. Over time, it's believed that those souls have access to what Pierce describes as *bodily resurrection*.

Those that have roots in Catholicism may recognize this concept as purgatory. However, purgatory isn't believed to be an actual place, but a state of being or consciousness. It's between death and heaven, and it's meant to purify souls of their sins before they're granted access to heaven. If you're familiar with Greek mythology, you may recognize this at the underworld ruled by Zeus's brother, Hades.

Hell became understood, over time, as the final resting place for evil. Wrongdoers in life would be condemned to spend an eternity of suffering in the afterlife. Heaven, on the other hand, became the reward. It became understood that heaven is where God resided. Christianity adopted the concept of heaven from the same sources they adopted hell: Jewish and Greek thought. Heaven is where God sat on a throne, ruling over all humankind. Heaven is holy and righteous. And it's often considered to be the highest place.

In his book *Jesus Interrupted*, Bart Ehrman suggests that as apocalypticists, Jesus and his followers believed in what he calls *cosmic duality*. In other words, God ruled over all that was/is good and the Devil/Satan ruled over all things evil. It was believed that when the world came to an end, God would reign supreme, and a utopian kingdom would be born. However, Christians later began to change their tune because, as Ehrman surmises, things like the end of the world didn't happen as anticipated. As a result, Christians shifted to what Ehrman calls *vertical dualism* — the world below (hell) and the world above (heaven).

Whether or not heaven and hell are real is a question of faith. I think I've landed on hell *not* being real, but I'm not sure yet about heaven. Part of this is due in large part to my relationship to Romans 8:38-39 (NRSV): "For I am convinced that neither death, nor life, nor angels, nor rulers, nor things present, nor things to come, nor powers, nor height, nor depth, nor anything else in all creation will be able to separate us from the love of God in Christ Jesus our Lord." My position is also partly influenced by my ancestor veneration practices.

Some years after my maternal grandfather passed, I was lying down, asleep but also awake. I've struggled over the years to explain the experience. Initially, it felt like I was dreaming of myself standing on the platform of one of the public transportation train stations in downtown Atlanta. A woman was having some kind of distress experience, and I couldn't get to her. As I was struggling with what to do, I felt the presence of my grandfather at the foot of my bed. It felt like I was between two worlds: awake and asleep. But there my grandfather was, standing at the foot of my bed, touching my feet as if to ground me in the moment.

From that night forward, I began to accept that maybe, just maybe, loved ones are closer than anyone realizes after they pass on. And because of their proximity, I feel as though I have an answer regarding heaven and hell and where some go after they've passed on.

The question of theodicy

In the writing of this book, I came across a statement I'd never heard before: "Heaven is the carrot used by the wealthy to keep us working hard for the money." In my research, I found that these words may have been written by the German philosopher and writer Karl Marx. Known as an anti-capitalist and activist, among other things, Marx believed that the powerful and wealthy created the concept of heaven as a distraction. He believed the working class was less likely to challenge the status quo and fight against injustices if they were more focused on the afterlife. Heaven became, from his perspective, a mechanism of social control.

That concept recalls for me the phrase I used to hear a lot growing up: "heavenly bound and no earthly good." It was used as a critique of high and holy people. What it means is there are some people who are so concerned about the afterlife that they're completely absent from their present realities and responsibilities.

The idea of heaven as a means of social control is a valid argument. I've seen, firsthand, the way many around me have worked so hard in life to ensure that when their time comes, they'll be welcomed into the pearly gates of heaven with open arms. I've also witnessed people, at the end of life, fight death because of their fears regarding their soul salvation and where they'll go when they close their eyes and breathe their last breath. I believe that one of the reasons the construct of heaven and hell has been effective is because it's appealing to think that a person's actions and choices will result in a certain outcome. Society has been conditioned to live in such a manner that there's no denying the gift of the ultimate reward in death.

Taking into consideration Marx's argument, I can't help but consider how and why the concept of theodicy is effective in some respects. But there are still problems. *Theodicy* suggests that even though the world has evil and suffering, God is still omnipotent and powerful. It doesn't seek to explain away evil but to serve as a resolve. For me, it's mirky. I experience theodicy as an attempt at providing an answer to something that's unknown.

Borrowing from Ehrman's explanation of dualism, both good and bad exist in the world. Suffering and flourishment coexist too. In deconstructing, I find myself landing on the belief that systems in the world create inescapable binaries: rich and poor, charity and compassion, manipulation and coercion. People attempt to spiritualize as a means of explaining these binaries away and trying to avoid them.

If God exists, I align with what many scholars, like Marx, have argued. God isn't some divine being apart from humankind, hovering over society. God is ever present with everyone, right here and now, among, around, and within. Keeping God away and apart from society achieves greater manipulation and coercion to keep people chasing the carrot of the afterlife.

REMEMBER

Let me be clear. My intent isn't to sway anyone reading this book one way or the other. My goal isn't to turn anyone into an atheist or a nonbeliever or to make them anti-religious. The intent of this book is to provide information for consideration to help you not only become more aware and informed but assist in your process of discerning what's best for you in your faith and possible deconstruction journey. My intent is to help you get closer to your authentic and genuine self, recognizing and understanding that, to quote educator and content creator Conscious Lee, "Education is elevation."

Heaven and hell in other religions

Heaven and hell aren't concepts and constructs exclusive to Christianity. They're found throughout many religious systems. Because of the relationship between Christianity, Judaism, and Islam, you might assume a fair amount of overlap. But that isn't the case. Also, within other religious systems, there may be some similarities, but vast variations.

Following are a few brief descriptions of how heaven and hell appear in other faiths:

>> **Judaism:** Often referred to as Gehinnom, Judaism's concept of hell is more temporary in nature. Judaism strongly emphasizes ethics and the fulfillment of God's commandments but doesn't prescribe eternal damnation for failures or misdeeds. Damnation is rejected because Jews don't believe it to be consistent with God's mercy. Gehinnom is more widely seen as a process of purification, while heaven, often referred to as the Gan Eden, is believed to be a spiritual realm where the soul exists and reunites with God.

>> **Islam:** As in Christianity, hell is a literal and actual place for followers of Islam. Often referred to as Jahannam, those who don't follow God's commandments are punished to Jahannam. The same is also true for disbelievers. In Jahannam, one is believed to be spiritually and physically tormented for the sins they committed. Heaven, on the other hand, is known as Jannah and is believed to be garden-like in nature. In heaven, one is granted eternal happiness and bliss as a reward for living a righteous life.

>> **Buddhism:** While heaven and hell exist as fixed concepts in other religions, within Buddhism, they're states of existence. They're not permanent, but within the cycle of rebirth, understood as the samsara. The states are seen as temporary and believed to be determined by one's actions and karma from previous iterations of their previous lives. Heaven, also referred to as Sagga, is where people find enjoyment based on their past actions. Hell, also known as Niraya, is a temporary realm of pain and suffering informed by mistakes made in previous lives.

>> **Indigenous faiths and other beliefs:** Hinduism and many Indigenous faiths place their focus on the journey of one's spirit and soul in the afterlife. The spirit continues in existence, not necessarily traveling to a heaven or a hell. Some experience joy and reunion with other spirits that have gone on before them. In other instances, as in Hinduism, the spirit is reborn. Their reincarnation is informed by their karma.

Chapter **10**

Diving into Doctrine, Sin, God's Sovereignty, and Prayer

When I entered seminary, I was both excited and felt woefully unprepared. Many of the people who began that journey with me had either studied religion in undergrad or been in ministry for years. They already knew so much.

But I was there to learn. I knew how to soak up information, digest it, and regurgitate what I had heard, read, or observed. Plus, as a journalist, I understood the importance of simply reporting the facts. As a journalist, my job was to absorb the information being presented and dispense it clearly, comprehensibly, and intelligibly. I'd mastered that skill.

Having a perspective or opinion was forbidden.

Imagine my surprise, discomfort, and struggle when professors began asking what *I* thought about any given topic. And they weren't just asking as a means of conversation. In most instances, the assignments required having a perspective and communicating that perspective effectively. But I didn't know what I believed. I lacked self-confidence. I believed I didn't know enough to have an opinion on anything I was learning at the time. I also didn't feel as though I had any authority to have an opinion.

I didn't know it at the time, but the professors were building my confidence. Their pedagogical goal (their teaching approach) was to affirm my classmates and me, therefore building our self-confidence.

This chapter seeks to assist you in strengthening your awareness and self-confidence as you deconstruct. You get some help in your unpacking with thoughts on traditions and the symbols associated with them, the sovereignty of God, a critique on sin and how it's used as a tool, and a reimagining of prayer and its role in the faith walk.

REMEMBER

Perhaps, like me, you were conditioned what to believe. The default is to believe whatever your parents, your pastor, or your uber-religious aunt taught you to believe. The first stage of the deconstruction process is having the courage to question and reevaluate. The second is accepting that deconstruction is something you want to do and making a conscious decision to do so. Then, at some point, you can build your confidence and know that what you believe has value.

Reevaluating Doctrine, Traditions, Rituals, Iconography

With faith and religion, it's easy to do things on a regular basis without any idea as to why. Often, there's no connection to the origins of the things you've placed value on. You have no connection to the history and instances that birthed your doctrine, rituals, and traditions. You might perform these rituals and traditions blindly because, in keeping with the theme of this book, you've been taught and conditioned to do them without considering why.

Because of my time in seminary, I had the privilege of learning more than I'd been exposed to in church on Sunday mornings or while attending Vacation Bible School. The research gave me an insight into the history of Christianity that not only quenched my curiosity but birthed greater inquiry and considerations. I walked away with more questions than answers and with the confidence I needed to find fulfillment and enjoyment in asking questions.

Asking questions is paramount. Why are certain doctrines followed? Why are some traditions recognized by select groups and not others? How are rituals formed and adopted, and how have they changed over time? Why are some symbols iconographic? Why were some items and religious works of art retained while others were banned? These questions provide you, the believer (or questioner), with a greater understanding as well as an opportunity for authentic buy-in.

Doctrine

You probably don't need to know a whole lot about doctrine unless you're planning to go into ministry or lead a religious institution. But it's beneficial to have some idea of what doctrine is, what it means, and more than anything, what impact it's having or has had on your life and beliefs.

Doctrine is the set of beliefs that govern a community or group. Most often, a governing or organizing body develops the doctrines, and then a group agrees upon them. If you aren't familiar with the term *doctrine,* maybe you've heard one of these other words that mean the same thing:

>> Dogma

>> Creed

>> Credo

>> Articles of faith

>> Tenet

>> Teaching

>> Canon

>> Precept

Most religious groups or faith communities have a set of guiding principles that are either explicitly or implicitly understood as their doctrine. The concept of the Holy Trinity — God in three persons — is one example within Christianity. Within Catholicism is the doctrine of *transubstantiation*, or the belief that during the Eucharist (communion) the bread and wine not only represent the body and blood of Christ but become Jesus's body and blood. And within Buddhism, the Four Noble Truths are a doctrine. They are:

>> The truth of suffering: Suffering exists.

>> The truth of the case of suffering: It has a cause.

>> The truth of the end of suffering: It has an end.

>> The truth of the path that leads to the end of suffering: It has a cause to bring about its end.

Proponents suggest that doctrines' benefits far outweigh their problems. They suggest that doctrines provide a useful and necessary framework for an understanding of faith and how it's lived out. They suggest that through the guidance that doctrines provide, followers gain access to a greater relationship with themselves and the divine.

WARNING

But proponents often overlook the glaring problems with doctrines, such as how they can cause harm. This is especially true within faith systems like Christianity toward people who have historically been oppressed and marginalized. Inaccurate scriptural interpretations, proof-texting, and nationalist ideals often breed doctrines rooted in ideology that aren't authentic to the context or intent of the text. As a result, freedoms are stifled, and perspectives and interpretations that are more closely rooted in practical application are resisted.

The doctrine of *depravity*, which is the belief that humans are born inherently sinful (more on this concept later in the chapter), is one example of a problematic doctrine. This doctrine suggests that because of our sinful ways, given to us at birth, we are incapable of truly pleasing God. Such a belief creates a barrier between us and God through no fault of our own, causing many of to believe and accept that they're unloved by God.

Doctrines are beneficial when they're utilized effectively. In a perfect world, doctrines do exactly what their proponents suggest: They build community and commonality among members of a group. Doctrines are like a contract; they're an agreement among the members of a group to define their values, priorities, wants, and needs. However, all too often, the voice, perspectives, and agency of certain members are overlooked and neglected when the group has a disagreement or some differences.

REMEMBER

Doctrines become ineffective universally because of diversity. Rarely do people agree on everything. They have differences of opinion, needs, perspectives, and priorities. And in those instances, cracks in the foundation of the original intent of the doctrines form.

Tradition

This world and society are rooted in traditions: recognized holidays, family and community customs, and religious commemorations. Many attend yearly fairs and festivals from a sense of tradition.

Why do you participate in traditions? And what value do the traditions have in your life and the life of your loved ones?

To a certain extent, traditions are meant to represent lineage, culture, and value. They can preserve memories. Traditions keep the memory of a cherished family member and the time spent with them fresh in your heart and mind. You can keep the stories and memories of your heritage alive, and you can keep the history of your culture alive through your traditions. Traditions connect you to your past. For many, the reasons are much more important. The repetitive nature of traditions keeps your history connected to your future.

Biblical scholars suggest that many of the sacred texts found in the Christian Bible, and some other religious systems, aren't accurate accounts of the faith system. They suggest that the stories are born from the oral/aural tradition, passed down as communal stories, but not historical fact. As a result, there's been debate about these perspectives and what it means for the validity of faith systems.

Another problem is the limitations traditions can bring. They can be stifling.

I remember when I was working toward ordination. I won't name the denomination, but it's one of a few historically Black denominations across the globe. During one of my first meetings with the board of examiners, I was ridiculed and chastised for how I was dressed. At the time, I couldn't afford a black suit. I just had a black sport coat and some black pants. I was the only person of the half dozen who were meeting with the group that day who was close to having all the credentialing required for ordination. I had a bachelor's degree, and I was halfway finished with my master of divinity. None of the others even had a bachelor's degree. But my lack of a black suit was criticized more than the others' lack of the required education. That was part of my decision not to move forward with ordination.

WARNING

It's easy to get stuck in traditions. Traditions provide great beauty as well as danger. They have value and meaning, and advancing beyond them can be challenging. Pausing a tradition or not honoring one as often can make you fearful of losing your history. Or perhaps you fear not honoring a tradition can cause irreparable damage. These fears, which aren't just about cultural and communal traditions but also religious ones, interrupt the opportunity for new traditions, also of value, to be created. And they interrupt the validity of what someone may bring to the table. Being rigid about today's traditions hinders opportunities for current and future generations to find space for developing new traditions.

Ritual

You might assume that traditions and rituals are the same. Although the two overlap, traditions are rooted in customs and often passed down from generation to generation or community to community, while rituals are often more ceremonial in nature.

TIP

Some tradition is involved in ritual. And some rituals are traditional. But rituals are more prescribed and routine. Traditions, to an extent, are more organic and spontaneous in nature — at least starting out.

Rituals can show up in countless ways. Maybe it's a morning routine like grabbing a coffee at the corner store, stretching for 30 minutes before showering, or journaling or praying when you first wake up. Graduations, the national anthem before a game, weddings, and funerals are other examples of rituals.

In Christianity, baptism, communion, and the lighting of Advent candles during the Advent season are examples. Islamic rituals include daily prayer, fasting during Ramadan, and pilgrimage. Hinduism offers light to deities (aarti). Buddhism involves meditation and chanting sutras. Judaism has the lighting of the menorah during Hanukkah as well as coming-of-age ceremonies like bar and bat mitzvahs.

REMEMBER

Like traditions, rituals provide a sense of meaning. They can offer guidance to individuals seeking to obtain a greater connection to the things and communities by which they possess membership. They can create a sense of belonging and stability. But in some instances people lack a true understanding of the purpose and meaning of the rituals. They can build an emotional connection to a ritual without giving thought to the reasons behind it.

Take weddings, for instance. A wedding ceremony can be informed by dreams the couple has had about their wedding for much of their life. They might place more emphasis on their wedding day than on their marriage. Sadly, for many, rituals have become performative and obligatory.

Iconography

Prior to entering the seminary, I'd never heard of iconography. But as I learned more about it, I started to see how it shows up in everyday life.

If you're a Christian, that gold cross you wear around your neck is a form of religious iconography. That wooden cross you had hanging on your entry wall when you were young is another example. If you grew up in an African American household, that picture of the Rev. Dr. Martin Luther King, Jr. next to the picture of blond-haired, blue-eyed Jesus is iconography as well.

Calligraphy, totem poles, lotus flowers, the star of David, Buddha statues, the yin-yang symbol, and dreamcatchers are all examples of iconography. So, what then is iconography? Simply put, *iconography* refers to the symbols, images, and items used to represent or convey religious beliefs or purpose.

In some respects, iconography is widely accepted and represented in culture today, especially religiously. But my introduction to the concept was through a lecture on the history of iconography in Christianity and the Iconoclastic Controversy, which took place during the eighth and ninth centuries. The controversy sprung about because a group of people, the *iconoclasts*, opposed the use of religious images because they felt as though the practice went against scripture. They believed that because of the nature of God, God couldn't be depicted in images. They considered this version of veneration dangerous spiritually as well as theologically.

As a result, the controversy resulted in the destruction of countless paintings, manuscripts, icons of Christ and the Birgin Mary, and other pieces of art.

WARNING

While the controversy ended centuries ago, it's safe to suggest that iconography still creates quite a few dangers. Those who are deconstructing are aware of how some religious symbols have become idolized. As someone who's a fan of art, artistic expression, and making meaning through art, I'm a major proponent of art in all forms. However, as an example, the cross and the Bible in Christianity, which are forms of iconography, are being given more value than what they represent. Some are worshipping the symbols over the message, and people are being excluded simply because they don't value the symbols the same way others do.

Creating new rituals, traditions, and adopting new icons

It's quite possible that as a result of your faith deconstruction journey, you may abandon many of the traditions and rituals you once considered sacred. And there may become symbols (or icons) that replace the very symbols and icons you once held sacred as well. I know this was the case for me.

Before I began deconstructing my faith, I believed it was bad luck to go into the New Year without cleaning my entire house (or apartment) from top to bottom. Every dish had to be washed. Every floor had to be cleaned or vacuumed. Every bathroom had to be cleaned. And every item of clothing had to be washed. Nothing in the house could be dirty when midnight struck. And I had to make sure it was all done before I left for Watch Night Service — a worship service held on the last night of the year to bring in the New Year. Watch Night, usually recognized in Black Church communities, is understood as a holdover from slavery when the slaves watched over night for emancipation.

Eventually, I realized that, for me, it was absurd to continue in that tradition. Whether I had an unclean house or not, had no impact or influence on how God would or would not bless me in the New Year. I stopped excessively cleaning, and I stopped attending Watch Night Service. Now, I focus my energy on connecting and spending time with friends and family. Sometimes that has meant having friends get together for a game night or just some fellowship. A few times, we traveled to my husband's hometown and spent it with my in-laws. It has become a new tradition for us.

REMEMBER

As you deconstruct, you may also develop new traditions, rituals and adopt new icons. Or you may not. If you do, that's understandable. Sometimes there is a need to replace old habits with new ones. Or you may feel no such need. That's also equally understandable. Whatever you do, make sure the new is meaningful and adds value to you and your life in this deconstructed reality.

The Sovereignty of God

In the fall of 1994, gospel musician, artist, and organist James Hall released his debut album, *God Is in Control*, launching his music recording career. The project was a critical success in the gospel music industry and within Black churches around the globe. This success was due in large part to the project's first single by the same name, "God Is in Control!"

It was hard to avoid the song upon its release, depending on what areas of the world and communities you frequented. Not long after, most gospel choirs around the country made the song part of their repertoire.

The song was popular for two reasons: It sounded good, and it resonated. Theologically, the song was clear and emphasized what many had been taught to believe: God *is* in control. The song brought to life the truth of God's presence in everyday life. The song brought to life, for many, Psalm 46:1: "God is our refuge and strength, a very present help in times of trouble." This is the sovereignty of God — that God is all powerful, has all authority, and is therefore in control of all things.

Where do we get these messages? From our doctrines. Is God truly in control? Does it matter? The following section provides for you some considerations to help you in determining the question(s) for yourself.

Is God in control?

The thought of God being in control provides a level of comfort. Believing that something greater is the orchestrator of all things can help you embrace that you're not alone in the world, especially in times of struggle. But such a sentiment also presents a complicated dichotomy. If God is present and in control always, then God is in control when things are good *and* when things are bad.

For those deconstructing, the notion that God is in control creates a contradiction. Why? Because, realistically speaking, faith has no absolutes. It's messy and complicated, mysterious and uncertain. Faith works best when you surrender yourself to the reality that there really is no way of truly knowing. In many instances, things just are. That's the beauty of the mystery of faith.

REMEMBER

If God is in control, do you have any say at all? What about free will? If God is in control, why are some people poor and others rich? If God is in control, what about good and evil? If you're deconstructing, these are all valid questions. They're necessary questions that everyone should be asking but are rarely allowed to ask.

Spiritual bypassing

Whether you know it or not, the belief that God is in control is a form of spiritual bypassing. *Spiritual bypassing* can be understood as toxic positivity. It's believed that psychologist John Welwood coined the phrase in the 1980s. The Buddhist teacher and psychotherapist suggested that spiritual bypassing occurs when you attempt to avoid or deny the experiences of yourself and others — especially difficult and emotional moments — through the use of spiritual ideas and practices. In other words, spiritual bypassing is a quick fix.

Some deconstructionists consider spiritual bypassing to be lazy work. The most common instance of when spiritual bypassing is used is during a funeral of moment of grief. Statements like, "We loved them, but God wanted them more," "They're no longer in pain," and "To be absent from the body is to be with the Lord" are all examples of spiritual bypassing. I remember once during my time in seminary when I inadvertently used spiritual bypassing on a classmate after they shared a painful story about losing a friend when they were young.

"It makes sense," I said to them. "Their passing altered the trajectory of your life, causing you to end up here." Whether that was true or not didn't matter. I attempted to make light of their loss through a simple explanation.

It's natural to want to have the answer to whether God's in control. Society has been conditioned to have an answer to every life situation. People are taught to make sense of things that simply can't be explained, which results in spiritually bypassing others instead of just saying nothing at all.

A Critique of Sin: What Is It?

From a religious perspective, sinning means going against God, God's law, and God's creation. Within Christianity, sin is often presented in relationship to individual actions and personal piety. Anything you do that's believed to be against what God expects of you — or put another way, that the church expects and projects onto God — is considered sin. And when you act on your sins, you fail the all-powerful, all-knowing God and fall out of favor with God.

I don't know about you, but I have a complicated relationship with sin. As a word and as a concept, *sin* is triggering for me because of my upbringing. Most people are introduced to the concept of sin in church or another religious setting.

As I've pointed out in previous chapters, the faith deconstruction journey is a process commonly triggered or motivated by a moment or series of moments that causes questioning. Part of the reason I know and believe this to be the case is because of my own experiences with faith, organized religion, and many of the topics discussed so far. My identity as a Black man from the south is one motivating factor. But another is my experience as a Black man in the south who identifies as same gender loving.

For me, sin is a four-letter word.

There are mortal sins and forgivable sins. There are sins of commission (wrongdoing) and sins of omission (failures of obligations). Another sin, original sin, exists because humanity exists. Every sin has a category. And while in some groups it's believed that sin can lead to eternal separation from God, in other groups you can be forgiven for your sin if you repent (in the Catholic Church through the act of confession) or through your faith (in Christianity through the idea of faith in Jesus Christ).

Original sin: Sin in Christianity

Christianity teaches two important lessons:

>> **Everyone is born with a sinful nature.** Because of the disobedience of Adam and Eve in the Garden of Eden (you know, the story of the serpent and the apple), all humankind is born of sin. Adam and Eve's act of disobedience severed the original covenant with God.

>> **Jesus is without sin.** Even though Jesus was both fully human and fully divine, because he was born by the power of the Holy Spirit and of a virgin, he completely skipped the original sin as acted out by Adam. Therefore, he didn't inherit Adam's scar of sin.

Is original sin necessary? In the grand scheme of things, that's for you to determine for yourself. Within your deconstruction, you have the ability and opportunity to decipher whether original sin matters and whether Jesus being without sin matters.

If you look back to what's discussed in Chapter 7 and the belief that, for some Jews, Jesus doesn't fulfill the messianic prophecies found within their sacred texts, the narrative of Jesus's sinful nature (or the lack thereof) is an important literary tool. Human beings are going to have setbacks, hiccups, and moments of questionable decision-making. Do those moments happen because humans are innately sinful, or do they happen because life happens?

Sin in other faith practices

Sin is a central theme in Christianity. In Judaism, sin is understood and described as someone missing the mark. Islam views sin as a violation of religious law and Allah's command. In Hinduism, sin is perceived as acts born out of ignorance and desire. And in Buddhism, some assume that the concept of karma is related to sin. However, Buddhism doesn't exactly have a concept of sin, but the belief that someone can be out of harmony with nature. Greed, anger, and ignorance are to be avoided.

More on the problem with sin

The problem with sin is how society has been conditioned to understand it, perceive it, feel about it, and relate to it. Society has been taught to look at sin as a condition, the result of either forces beyond or things within that are out of control. Humans are taught to only understand sin through individual failures and perceived violations. But what does that say about oppression, abuse, and the mistreatment of those within communities at large?

If you take a cue from Chapter 8's discussion and the concept of doing no harm, you've limited sin and your relationship to it. Within most religious beliefs is a communal aspect of what to believe. There's an idea of people being in relationship with one another. People are responsible for the well-being of each other, and this responsibility is prescribed by God and God's law. However, communal care and justice are often omitted from the conversation. Isn't that a sin of omission? What do you say and do about that?

REMEMBER

For those deconstructing, it's necessary to shift not only your understanding of sin, but also your relationship to it as a concept and how it's utilized in society. Should you be concerned with personal responsibility, piety, and the limited, one-sided perspective of sin that, to some extent, is rooted in control? Sure, why not. But again, do no harm. If your actions aren't causing hurt, harm, or danger to others, why do you care so much?

In some regards, it's easier to spend time and energy proof-texting concepts and selectively prescribing them to others in society than to practically live out the tenets society claims to live by.

Should We Pray?

In the spring of 2025, while recovering from cancer surgery, I had an intriguing conversation with a colleague and friend via Facebook. I'd posted an image in my stories that popped up in one of my feeds. The image read: "If you think an all-knowing

God has a divine plan, yet prayer can change his mind . . . you might be indoctrinated." I didn't know this person, and to be honest, I didn't know what their actual intent of the image was. But it resonated with me, so I shared it.

The next day, the friend messaged me for greater clarification. Initially, I thought they were asking me to clarify the perspective of the person who shared the image. Unfortunately, I couldn't do that. I didn't know them and had never had a conversation with them. But I explained why the image resonated with me. And then they said, "The passage makes me ask, 'What's the point in praying?'" It's a valid question, and one I think everyone should be asking, regardless of whether deconstruction is something they're doing or not. Why do we pray?

The role and responsibility of prayer in religion

You've likely been taught to approach prayer in specific ways. Maybe it's part of your everyday ritual. As Chapter 5 points out, faith shows up in numerous ways. If you're Muslim, prayer is an integral part of your identity and culture. Five times a day, Muslims pray:

>> Fajr: Before dawn

>> Dhuhr: Noon

>> Asr: Late afternoon

>> Maghrib: Sunset

>> Isha: Nighttime

Growing up, it was paramount to learn the Lord's Prayer, found in the gospels Matthew (6:9-13) and Luke (11:2-4):

> "Our Father, which art in Heaven, Hallowed by thy name. Thy kingdom come, Thy will be done, on earth, as it is in heaven. Give us this day our daily bread. And for us our trespassers (debtors), as we forgive those who trespass against us (debts). And lead us not into temptation but deliver us from evil: For thine is the kingdom, and the power, and the glory, forever and ever. Amen"

Some faith practices have a posture of prayer. Some kneel. Some chant. Some meditate. Some faiths are more verbal and audible, while others are more silent and inward. Some groups pray in community, while others pray in private. In some Native American traditions, dance is a form of prayer. Prayer takes many forms, and no way is the one right way.

Is prayer a valid practice for all?

The answer to this question depends on what *you* perceive to be the purpose of prayer. Many are taught that prayer is how you communicate and commune with God. Through prayer, you can connect to God beyond and within. You tap in. You check in. You seek and cry and release when you pray. You celebrate and cherish and worship when you pray. For you, prayer might be an extension of your relationship with the divine and with yourself.

Perhaps you've been taught that prayer is rooted solely in petition — in wanting, needing, and expecting something from God. To borrow a phrase I heard somewhere years ago, maybe God has become your genie in a lamp, which makes the relationship solely transactional.

REMEMBER

It's for you to determine what you want the purpose of prayer to be. When I pray, I see prayer as an opportunity to be connected to God, to simply talk with God. That also means being quiet sometimes and listening, gleaning, and discerning. When I pray, it's a conversation I can have at any moment, at any time of the day or night, and in any instant. If your style of prayer is kneeling on the side of the bed before you call it a night, by all means do that. If your prayer means blessing your food before you eat, that's just as valid. If it's singing a song to the divine at the top of your lungs while tears stream down your face, you're allowed. Your reasons for how, whether, and when you pray are valid.

4

Discernment and Deconstruction

Hear what has helped others.

Explore other beliefs and practices.

Acquaint yourself with other faiths.

Learn what makes atheism, agnosticism, and humanism different.

Figure out where your support exists.

Chapter **11**

Learning from Others Who Have Deconstructed

'm a storyteller. It's a big part of my identity. But I haven't always known that about myself. You would think that I would have realized that about myself since I've spent much of my life writing and eventually venturing into preaching. But no, it took a while for me to come to this realization. The realization became clearer for me as I was transitioning out of full-time pulpit ministry. I had to discern who I was and who I was becoming since I didn't have a pulpit anymore. The experience brought me into view in ways I never could have imagined.

At the same time, I realized that I love hearing others' stories. Sharing your defining stories is powerful. They're a part of you and what makes you who you are. Those stories provide insight into what you've learned from your experiences, the things you've overcome, and the things that matter most to you. Storytelling is a way to learn about yourself and about others.

Everyone's story is different, as it should be. But there are also areas of overlap and similarities. More than anything, each person's story has lessons that can be useful to anyone reading this book who's considering deconstructing, struggling through deconstruction, or has gone through some form of deconstruction. My hope is that by reading these stories, you can glean some clarity or wisdom. If nothing else, you can see that you aren't or weren't alone in your deconstruction journey.

In Their Own Words

In this section, you hear from nine individuals. Some are faith leaders, while others are laypersons. Shared here are stories from artists, creatives, poets, and directors. Some grew up in conservative faith traditions; others found their way in spaces that were more progressive. Members of the LGBTQ+ community share in these next few pages. So do allies. You'll read the accounts of cisgender women and cisgender men. All are journeyers, thinkers, believers, and advocates for freedom, joy, and enlightenment.

I've encountered each of them along my journey of seeking, learning, and deconstructing. The nine storytellers featured here are as follows:

- >> Rev. Dr. Tony Lamair Burks II, New Thought Christian

- >> Lauren Murphy, Roman Catholic

- >> Jade Foster, Black Southern Baptist

- >> Danielle Taylor, Christian (inclusive gospel) with ancestral veneration

- >> Rev. Rachel Breyer Mulgrave, Presbyterian Church USA

- >> J. S., Progressive Pentecostal

- >> Synitta Delano, Nondenominational

- >> Bishop D. E. Paulk, Interfaith

- >> Verdell Anthony Wright, Zen Buddhist (more from him in Chapter 1)

REMEMBER

Stories of faith deconstruction typically begin with a moment, a spark, as Chapter 3 points out. Maybe it's a simple question. Maybe it's a realization that something doesn't line up or that everyone isn't welcome even though the leaders profess them to be. Everyone who has deconstructed has a moment. It may seem inconsequential, but the questions or queries or doubts eventually become so big, so loud, that ignoring them is impossible. Something has to change. For these few, something did.

Rev. Dr. Tony Lamair Burks II

For Rev. Dr. Tony Lamair Burks II, what changed was exposure. When he was maybe seven or eight years old, his paternal grandmother had him read Unity's *Daily Word* whenever she played hooky from Sunday morning worship. His grandfather was the senior pastor of the oldest African Methodist Episcopal Church in Dothan, Alabama. Burks comes from a long line of preachers and ministers on his paternal side, reaching as far back as his great-great-grandfather. But it was his grandmother who, possibly inadvertently, planted the early seeds of his deconstruction. "My grandmother, the First Lady, would say from time to time things like, 'Yeah, I'm not going to church today. I can get Jesus right here in the garden. I don't have to go to church [to get God].' I started to embrace a new thought approach to Christianity without having the language of new thought."

Lauren L. Murphy

For Lauren L. Murphy, deconstruction began during the sixth grade. A devout Catholic, thanks to her grandparents, God had never really been something she questioned. "Even with all the insanity in the world. That question of [if there is a God] doesn't exist for me. It just is." But there *were* some things worth questioning when a kid in her art class made a painful declaration. "He said, 'God can only be a man.' And I was like, 'Oh, wait, what if God's a woman?'" It wasn't anything Murphy had ever thought about before. But at that moment, it became a very real question for her.

And her questioning has continued.

Murphy didn't completely break from Catholicism. "I love the church, and I honor the church, but how I feel about the church does not have any negative bearing on my faith." Recognizing the fallibility of the church allowed her space to compartmentalize and acknowledge that her faith and her religious affiliation are two separate entities. "My faith is in God, Christ, spirit. My faith is not in this particular church. That's the container. And for me, I think it will always be the container." It's also worth mentioning that her husband is an atheist, and even though they may not completely understand each other's beliefs, or the lack thereof, they still have great love and respect for each other.

Jade Foster

Jade Foster began deconstructing her freshman year of college. "I had to deconstruct because I was gay." She found women attractive but was initially resistant to admit she might be gay. Once she got to the point of acceptance, she needed to reconcile what that meant for her religious identity. She believed her beloved leaders of the church wouldn't be able to embrace her in her truth, so she began exploring other faiths. "Because that's who I am. Prayer, spirit, study, it's my favorite thing to do. All of those things are my favorite things to do."

Foster started her exploration with Islam, wanting to be closer to her father, who was Muslim and died when she was young. She spent six months in Egypt. When she left Egypt, she traveled to Ghana and began studying African traditional religions. And even though the idea of the spirit world scared her a little bit, it was the first time she felt the most connected to her faith. She also visited a Buddhist temple a few times after moving to New York, but that experience wasn't the best fit either. Her godmother, who's Muslim, helped her to pivot. "She really cracked my forehead open." As a practicing Muslim, Foster's godmother integrated African spirituality, Indigenous/Native American faith, and Black American faith. Seeing her godmother's example and realizing she could be religious without letting go of ancestral influences set the tone that led her back to Christianity, but the Christianity that works for her.

Foster's deconstruction and subsequent integration empowered her. "It's just nice to have tools in your toolkit. The Bible is a tool, but so are baths, and so is meditation. So is sweating. So, I think it's empowered me to have tools in my toolkit and empowered me to tap into the spirit realm and to lean on my ancestors; lean on the folks looking after me." She didn't learn these things from her church home when she was younger despite being exposed to and interfacing with other forms of religious thought. Her deconstruction, exploration, and integration strengthened her beliefs and relationship to Jesus. She thinks back to something her pastor says often, "Religion is the vehicle. Faith is the destination."

Christianity and Black Southern Baptist practices, culturally, call out to her, but she isn't stuck there. She still integrates ancestor reverence into her practice as a Baptist. "Jesus is just a dope ancestor who did this thing. I like a good organ, good preacher that's not going to read my mind, a good Black Church experience with some pound cake and some fried chicken after service."

Danielle Taylor

Danielle Taylor's story begins similar to Foster's. During college, she began to recognize her same-sex attraction. But her deconstruction had begun much sooner. As a kid, she heard certain things during Sunday School that didn't quite line up for her. It didn't help that, in school, she was learning about dinosaurs and the Ice Age, but at church no one was talking about such things. "I'm a church kid. I was practically born on a pew." It led her to ask questions, which, she said, is the first step of deconstruction — interrogation. The older members of the church weren't receptive. "You can't start asking questions because, if you do, that means you don't trust what they know; you don't trust their interpretation. You don't trust what God has given them."

By the time she got to college and began interrogating her identity, it became difficult to continue believing the same things she was once taught to believe. To reconcile her faith with her feelings around her identity, she had to end her relationship with her beloved childhood church.

She started reading other translations of the Christian Bible. She was "raised on the King James Bible," but she couldn't reconcile how the same translation used to oppress entire communities could also encourage her to live a life of liberty and freedom in her relationship with God. "I'm either going to love and live and be free and have liberty, or I'm going to be trapped in drinking the Kool-Aid and be in bondage and die hating myself. They can't exist in the same space."

She also had to reframe her understandings of who God is and who God isn't available to. She'd heard others talk about members of the LGBTQ+ community as perverse, but thanks to a family friend who represented God's love in the flesh, she couldn't accept what she'd always been told. She calls him Uncle Tony. "Uncle Tony had this beautiful bond with God. We would sit, we would pray, we would talk about our concerns, whatever was going on during the day, and he would say, 'Let's go to God about that.'" It taught her that God was present in non-straight spaces. The lesson was a game changer for her.

Taylor's deconstruction journey also made her relationship with God stronger. As she dissected what she'd been taught, she used the tools from her upbringing to obtain more clarity. "I definitely did the deep dive. I looked up the definitions of words like *truth* in other languages." She also did her own Bible studies, looking at texts like Jeremiah, which talks about the potter making a vessel on the wheel. "In the story, it talks about how the clay was marred in the potter's hand. And then the text goes on to talk about how God is talking to the house of Israel."

She wasn't sure where she sat with God. She thought back to what her grandmother used to tell her, that God "don't make no junk," and remembered that her relationship with God was never lost. She also explored other faiths, including Buddhism. What she realized in her period of exploration is that God was still very much close to her. She had this revelation one day during a meditation exercise. "I was seeking a place to peacefully plant my thoughts. So, in my experience with looking into Buddhism, I'm doing my investigation, and my thoughts would still go back to God. I'd be sitting, meditating, doing this quiet thing. And I said to myself, 'I've been doing this all my life. I've been sitting with you all my life.'"

Rev. Rachel Breyer Mulgrave

Rev. Rachel Breyer Mulgrave also began deconstructing in college. Her process started in a History of Christianity class at a community college in Mesa, Arizona. The class was taught by an ex-Lutheran pastor whom she believed was deconstructing himself. She was already questioning the validity of things she was taught growing up in church. "I just had a deep sense that there was a lot of propaganda in a lot of the things I was being told." But, because her teacher wasn't a Christian authority figure anymore, she wondered how much she could trust what he was teaching. "I was contemplating what he would say in his lectures."

Eventually, she ended up at Azusa Pacific University and realized that maybe her suspicions were accurate. While taking a systematic theology course, she realized she was being given more propaganda than gospel teaching. She also began to realize something else: "I didn't have to stay Christian at all."

Realizing that she didn't have to be the kind of Christian she was taught to be, or that she didn't have to continue with Christianity if she didn't want to, was one lesson Mulgrave learned from her deconstruction. The realization was a big help and motivator. From it she became ruthless in questioning everything. "My only true desire, at the end of the day, was to feel close to whatever I thought God was. If I found that God was something figurative that represented my own ego or my own psyche, or that God was something deeply innate in me, then fine I want to be close to that."

In her quest, Mulgrave realized that God isn't apart from us, but an entity deeply concerned with the interconnectedness of everyone and everything. If she had to walk away from Christianity to get close to that God, she was fine with that. "So, I don't think of my Christianity as superior or ethically moral or anything like that. But I do think God is calling me to Christianity. That doesn't make it better. It just means the people I'm supposed to love and care about and help open their hearts are probably people within Christianity."

J. S.

While his questioning began when he was a kid, the defining moment of deconstruction percolated for J. S. while he was in high school. He and his family were heavily active in church activities for much of his childhood. His mother is active in their church, and his father is a church musician. His siblings and an aunt sang in every choir. He even provided support in several capacities over the years. His participation was, for all intents and purposes, expected and almost required.

Through it all, he had some questions regarding what it meant to believe in God. His questions became louder when, after receiving high marks for a school project, his parents advised that he "praise God" for the accomplishment in a public forum. The instruction confused him. "Why should I be praising God when I did all the work? From that point I wondered, if I am praising God because my parents told me to, what's the point?" From his parents' perspective, however, he said his questions felt like a lack of respect of their beliefs.

He thinks back to previous church experiences and how sheltered he was. The fact that the preachers and pastors he heard growing up recycled the same four or five texts throughout the year left him woefully restricted. He talked about how refreshing it was to attend other churches when he got older, where the preachers and pastors engaged the Bible beyond what he'd been used to. He wishes he'd been made aware of this kind of preaching and these kinds of preachers well before he began deconstructing. It may have had a useful impact on his approach to deconstruction.

Synitta Delano

Synitta Delano's deconstruction began simply as research when she was 12. As she read a book published by the Jehovah's Witness organization called *Mankind's Search for God*, she became curious. The book provided what she calls a "sprinkling" of different religions and what they believed in contrast to their practices and beliefs. It wasn't enough to cause anyone to "veer off" into other faith practices, but it was just enough to pique her curiosity. The question she began asking herself was, "If the

Jehovah's Witness faith got its start in the late 1800s, how and why are they the authority on all of these older religions?"

She spent years researching many religions, but Hinduism and Buddhism were the most interesting. She never practiced them — or any others for that matter. She liked some of what Hindis believed, as well as Buddhism. "It's very peaceful, and I liked that, right? But I'm not really a pacifist."

Deconstruction helped Delano realize that she didn't have to prescribe to, or pretend to follow, any manmade rules to be free. She subscribes to the rules of the universe. Instead of going back to Jehovah's Witnesses or Christianity and talking to other deconstructionists, Delano decided it was best to abandon religion completely, adopting spirituality as her foundation. "My spiritual beliefs are fluid. I recognize that there are greater things and entities than myself, but I don't agree that another human has the right to govern me or my spirituality." She chooses to be her own spiritual guide, having experienced far too many instances of toxic spiritual leadership.

Faith, for her, is a lifelong journey of discovery. When people suggest that she's agnostic, she pushes back. She doesn't believe she can truly embrace that moniker. "I'm not saying I don't know if there's a God or not. I think there is something greater than me." She also understands that people use labels for their own understanding. "They'll be like, 'So, you believe in source?' No, that's what *you* believe!" When she says something "greater than" her, she means beyond even that which can be comprehended. "In my mind it isn't fair to take something so vast and amazing and box it into something to simply say this is what I understand."

Bishop D. E. Paulk

Bishop D. E. Paulk found himself not only deconstructing the Bible, but also Jesus. It began with him deconstructing his understanding of the Bible as the inspired word of God. He first deconstructed what *inspiration* meant. What he found was that, in its historical context, the word isn't used in scripture. It's a Greco-Roman word to talk about living.

Then he questioned the identity of the Apostle Paul. After that, he began to question blood sacrifice, atonement theology. "Does God demand blood? Not saying Jesus didn't give it, but did he have to do it? And do we worship a God who can only be satisfied beating the hell out of his son? Is Jesus the Son of God? Did he become the son of God through certain Constantinian and Augustinian ritual? And what does that mean? Is this about hierarchy? Is this about trying to dominate the Greco Roman divine councils? I began to deconstruct all that stuff."

By the end of it, Paulk came out of it loving Jesus more than he'd ever loved Jesus before. Not as God or the son of God, born of a virgin, but as a Palestinian justice worker who just said too much and got in trouble for it.

Verdell Wright

As discussed in Chapter 1, most people deconstruct from evangelical or conservative fundamentalist influences in their religion. That wasn't the case for Verdell Wright. "I think my situation is unique, because when people hear me say I'm not a believer anymore, they automatically assume I was some conservative, super Christian." But in fact, he was progressive — so progressive that people felt he wasn't Christian enough.

Wright's shift began when he realized that progressive spaces that marketed themselves as safe and inclusive were also capable of being harmful. "This is where I escaped to still practice my Christianity. And the things we are asking them to do for other people, they won't do for us. I went there for God. I left where I was because I thought God was here. And it's not even that."

Thinking back to his childhood and his introduction to faith and religion by way of Christianity, Wright believes what would have been helpful to him is to have seen a tapestry of ways to navigate life. He wasn't forced to go to church, but Christianity was given to him as a child to explain the ugliness of childhood. "I walked into what I thought I was supposed to be walking into. It was the only road I saw."

Making the connection that his relationship to religion was conducive to conditioning gave him permission to choose for himself. "I just immediately stopped. I was never given the chance to figure out who I want to be on my own. Having the tools to determine things for yourself helps you get to self-actualization, self-awareness, and self-acceptance. That's the song that I've been singing and will keep singing it."

Wright isn't bothered or turned off by anyone who identifies as a Christian. Using a similar example as Foster, everyone has their own vehicle to get to their destination. "If your Christianity is the vehicle that gets you to feed the poor and to stand up against empire and to help the sick, if that's the vehicle that gets you there, great." He believes that everyone is destined to get to the same destination even though they may take differing paths and avenues to get there.

Revelations (From Their Journey)

Each of these people started at a different point and took differing paths. At the root of their process was inquiry and study. Some of them, like Paulk, searched for books on the topics that interested them. Paulk also sought community mentors, like Bishop Carlton Pearson, who helped him in his quest but also served as a conversation and accountability partner.

Taylor interrogated, but she also benefitted from community in the form of her Uncle Tony, who embodied what she was taught at a young age. His embodiment countered the narratives she'd been told.

As discussed in Chapter 9, faith deconstruction has no linear pathway. It usually has a starting point, and sometimes it has an endpoint (albeit temporary for most), but the space in between is full of twists and turns, starts and stops. It's like a maze; to get from point A to point B, you'll make right and wrong turns that may lead you to a dead end if you're not careful. (I'm not suggesting that the faith deconstruction process will lead you to dead ends, but it may lead you to walls you didn't expect to run into).

TIP

However, when it's over, what you may realize is that the maze was more like a labyrinth. A series of paths will lead you to reflect and meditate along the way.

Some common threads

The common thread for the individuals featured in this chapter is that they each had a revelation that what they were once conditioned to believe about faith, or better yet religion, had flaws.

Their revelations provided clarity for them. Some were inspired to pivot their approaches. For others, their revelations created freedom and comfort. Mulgrave is an example of the latter. When she realized she didn't have to be the kind of Christian she was conditioned to be, she felt immense freedom.

Reflections on their deconstruction

Those featured in this chapter are still on their journey to some extent. They've come to know a lot, but there's also a lot they didn't know in the midst of their journey. It's important to highlight not only their successes but also their challenges.

They have thoughts about what would have been helpful.

If you do abandon your faith, it's only to make room for what can be. Foster is the perfect example of that. Taking a cue from her Muslim godmother, she figured out how to integrate the experiences of her exploration with her return to Christianity. What she returned to was always there; she just needed to explore to find it. "I returned to the God in myself."

REMEMBER

As stated earlier in this chapter, the hope in sharing these stories is that it will offer your deconstruction some clarity, some confidence, and some resolve. Deconstruction can be a lonely and isolating enterprise. It's also one of the most confusing, disorienting, and unorganized journeys you can take because, again, it has no clear pathway.

Taylor and Murphy wish they'd known of others questioning in the same way they were. It would have been helpful, said Taylor, to have people around who were God lovers and understood the process of fusing identity with faith. Having competent and willing people around would have made her process much easier. She also wishes there was a community space to go and figure things out. "I don't know. Maybe a Starbucks. A Dunkin Donuts. Maybe we meet on Tuesdays, and we talk for 90 minutes. Maybe we read a text from the Bible, and we talk about what it means, what is this speaking to you, and how do you connect it to where you are with God? I would have loved to have that because I had to fight to find it in my own life. I had to fight to find it all my life."

Murphy shares Taylor's sentiment. She thinks it would have been helpful to know there were other people going through the same questioning. Deconstruction can cause anyone experiencing it to carry shame, even though it isn't shameful. "And we think that because we're doing it alone and people don't talk about it." People tiptoe around countless structures for safety and security. It's lifesaving for people to know they aren't alone and that there's a community available to them. "I think we have a lot of the problems we have because people have been silent. So yeah, I think I'm a good person. I think I'm not racist. I think I'm pro-LGBTQ+. But if nobody hears me saying these things, they don't have a clue."

The same is true for deconstruction, your faith journey, and your religious journey. When you talk about those things, you're capable of finding judgment-free zones that help, enlighten, and inform.

As you can see, everyone has a unique experience, which speaks to the vastness of deconstruction. Steve Jobs stated in a Stanford commencement address, "You can't connect the dots looking forward; you can only connect them looking backward. So, you have to trust that the dots will somehow connect in your future." Others' connections of dots can be useful for you as you process, consider, and journey through your own deconstruction. Such awareness and considerations can offer you a well-rounded experience.

Chapter **12**

Making a Decision About Your Faith Through Exploration

A s stated in the book's introduction, the intent of this book isn't to take your faith from you. I have no hidden agenda to convert you or to cause you to turn your back on God or your faith community. Instead, I've written this book to provide information and perspective, as you seek to obtain insight into the questions you have about your faith. Part of that process, as stated in Chapter 1, is to explore.

In Chapter 11, you heard from a few individuals who, as they questioned their faith and what they believed, sought answers through exploration. By exploring, they found parallels they didn't know existed. By exploring, they connected to the divine within. This chapter seeks to delve more deeply into what it takes to explore in your faith and why exploration can be helpful to your deconstruction journey. You can think of it as a bridge to Chapter 13, where you find out more about some of the other faith communities and their practices.

Seeing the Value in Exploration

At this point, I may come off like a broken record, but I don't know any other way to say it: You owe it to yourself to test your faith by exposing yourself to other ways of thinking and believing. I'm not saying join another faith community. Not at all. I am saying, it is worth examining through exploration.

You may never be courageous enough or willing enough to explore this way, and that's okay. I'm not suggesting that if you don't explore you won't grow. That's a point for someone else to make. But examining what you believe against other ways of thinking and believing affords you the opportunity to expand your understanding, and maybe even your connection and relationships with others. As a result, you may achieve greater faith than if you'd never take the time to research or expose yourself to the beliefs, thoughts, and practices of others.

REMEMBER

Exploring and expanding what you believe is valuable. And as you can see in Chapter 11, the faith deconstruction journey can take you in an interesting direction. This section explores what's possible when you explore your faith. It defines what that means and offers some insight on what options are available if you're curious about taking your faith further.

Experimenting with your faith

Curiosity is beneficial to everyone. This is especially true in the faith deconstruction journey because curiosity is a big part of deconstruction and is absolutely necessary.

When I say *exploration* or even *experimentation* for that matter, what I'm getting at is the process of journeying. It's like shopping: You don't know for sure if that shirt or those pants or shoes will fit until you try them on.

TIP

Exploration in faith is quite similar and doesn't have to be the same for everyone. Try it out.

What does faith experimentation look like? Chapter 11 has a few stories of what some people have done. From engulfing themselves into other faith communities and cultures as a means of learning firsthand, to doing extensive research on word origins and looking at sacred texts contextually, the approaches are diverse and unique. In Chapter 13, I share a little of my own story and what exposed me to diverse faith practices. The exposure gave me perspectives that informed how I related to others in spaces I frequented often.

I think of the time, some years ago, when I used to attend a spring break-esque event with my husband. It was a popular, well-attended, weekend vacation celebration for Black, gay, plus-size men. The weekend concluded with a Sunday morning worship experience. The benefit of this experience was to create space for those who didn't have the privilege of being able to worship God freely in their respective cities or communities. I became involved in this worship experience and, eventually, became the regular speaker/preacher for the services. One year, it was brought to my attention that the service wasn't inclusive of everyone who attended. The service was too Christian, I was told, and didn't consider the diversity of faith practices and identities within the community.

That experience motivated me to become more aware of the implicit religious biases I possessed. If the point of the entire weekend was to create a safe, welcoming, and inclusive environment for Black, gay men of a certain size and background, there was a blind spot in the faith component of the weekend. The feedback I received led me to explore not only from a personal perspective, but from a ministerial perspective. It also taught me an important lesson in what it means to be authentic community as someone who identified as Christian at the time — and the responsibility that comes with it.

As a friend of mine pointed out in a Facebook post in July of 2025, "The journey itself is its own reward." I appreciate this sentiment because I think it's true. The journey of faith deconstruction is rewarding because of what you learn in the process of doing.

Faith deconstruction is like math. You learn math by doing math. You can't figure out the answer without working through the problem or working to solve the problem. The purpose is not solely to get to the answer, but what you learn in the process of getting to the answer. It's the exercise of figuring out that teaches you the lesson. Now, I admit this analogy has a slight problem. Not everything in life can be solved or at least not solved easily. Looking back, I learned this lesson thanks to the calculus and trigonometry courses I took in high school, as well as the hit television show *The Big Bang Theory*. Not every problem is solvable or has a solution. That's why scientists and mathematicians spend their entire lives and careers chasing after discovery — in some respects, working on the same equation repeatedly.

Deconstruction is the same way. Yes, you may come away with more questions than you did before, but in some respects if you continue to explore you'll keep learning and potentially become comfortable with the unknown.

REMEMBER

What happens when you explore? Exploration and experimentation make you more aware. They've made me mindful of my baggage and allowed me the opportunity to genuinely connect with others — especially people I love and adore. These relationships have challenged me in ways that were fruitful. I'd venture to suggest that the same is true for many others who have explored their faith through deconstruction. God is big enough to be more than what you or I have claimed God to be. We've placed God in a box for our own comfort.

Faith deconstruction and the strange loop cycle

If you've never seen it before, *A Strange Loop* is one of the most thought-provoking and blatantly honest live theater productions I've ever seen. Part of the reason I wanted to see it is because it had been marketed as a show that shines a light on a specific kind of Black gay experience. The main character is a Black, gay, plus-size man who's a creative and wants love, acceptance, and success. I can relate to that story.

One of the initial taglines I saw when I first heard about *A Strange Loop* is that it's a musical about a playwright, writing a musical about a playwright, writing a musical. But it's about so much more than just that. What I got from seeing the show is a young man seeking. The main character, Usher, is an aspiring musical theater writer. But what's seemingly important to him is the acceptance of family and true, unconditional, love — romantic and familial.

I'd wondered why the playwright, Michael R. Jackson, named the musical *A Strange Loop*. A few moments into the show, I got my first clue. But it wasn't until the end of the show that the title became abundantly clear. Usher's description of a strange loop sounded a lot like the journey of faith deconstruction

TIP

If you're unfamiliar with the term *strange loop,* it's basically the process of cycling through an exercise only to return to where you started, but as more aware and enlightened.

In the play, Usher has a moment where he starts to feel as though the things he wants to escape may be inescapable. He's committed to writing a musical that's informed by and represents real life. He's trying to work through some of his own trauma in the process. Through the entire exercise of seeking and searching for not only the right direction of his play, but his life, he wonders, "What's the point?" He wants better, all the way around, but he doesn't feel any closer to that sense of better because of factors within and outside of his control. At some point, he feels like the hamster wheel, the cycle is endless and he's back where he started.

If I've learned anything, it's that life is made up of a series of cycles, some better than others. In some instances, the cycles may resemble the overall theme of the movie *Groundhog Day*. We wake up, repeat and cycle a series of events, over and over and over again, with seemingly no end in sight. The process becomes repetitive and, to some extent, torturously boring. But other cycles create the opportunity for revelation. They are the ones that teach, develop skills, and advance capabilities.

TIP

Some cycles are necessary for growth and development.

It goes back to the concept of the journey in the previous section. On the other side of the experience, or at some point in the journey, you realize that things have changed or are at least different. You may return to something familiar, but you aren't returning as the same person you were when you started. It may feel strange, but it's a necessary loop. You may not have all the answers, and you may walk away with more questions than answers. But there are things you come to understand because you journeyed through it.

Deciding Whether to Remain or Abandon Your Prior Beliefs

Is the faith you were introduced to in your upbringing still working for you? Are you getting everything you believe you need and want to get out of it for your own good? Is that faith beneficial to your life and identity? Do you feel that this faith is helping you see the God within, resulting in your feeling closer to the God within and beyond?

If it is, that's great. But if you're here and you've purchased this book, more than likely you have some doubts. More than likely, you have some questions — maybe a lot of questions. Your curiosity has gotten the best of you, and you're trying to discern whether you are where you're supposed to be spiritually, religiously, emotionally, and mentally. Because let me be clear: Faith has an impact on not only your spiritual well-being, but your emotional and mental well-being.

REMEMBER

A major part of the faith deconstruction journey, as you can see in the personal stories in Chapter 11, is the decision that you make to stay or go. At the root of that decision are several things, but it mostly boils down to the determination that what you once had and once believed is no longer serving you.

This section engages some of that decision-making for you. What's here is only meant to be food for thought. Again, at the end of the day, the decision is yours.

What are you seeking from your faith and/or religion?

Chapters 5 and 6 provide perspectives to consider regarding faith, religion, how they differ, and how they overlap.

REMEMBER

Faith can be understood as trust, assurance, and confidence in God; believing something is true, and then committing your life to it; or confidence or trust in a person, thing, or concept. Religion, on the other hand, is a system of beliefs and practices by which a community with the same shared beliefs lives, seeks understanding, and makes meaning.

When exploring your faith and experimenting with what you believe, it's worth thinking about what matters most to you in your deconstruction. In other words, what are you seeking, or what do you need from your faith or from religion?

As it pertains to your faith, what are you looking for? Are you seeking greater connection to God or greater understanding of your purpose? As it pertains to religion or your religious affiliations, are you seeking guidance for life in general, or are you looking for a community to support you when you need it most? These are questions worth considering. They're necessary because they can offer guidance in your deconstruction. The direction these questions provide is useful in managing and maneuvering through the evaluation aspect of your deconstruction.

During a biannual gathering I attended in the summer of 2025, I heard a preacher say, "We need to think about getting away from white supremacy theology and really consider 'what do our communities need from us to authentically be themselves?'" He then went on to say, "This room right here is the Black Church!" The point he was making is that far too often churches get so caught up in the religion of things that they lose sight of the heart of the matter. If the church is meant to be the place where people become free, where they're able to temporarily escape the ills of society, where they can be empowered and encouraged, but instead they walk into the doors of the church and are greeted with the same oppressive talking points they hear every day recapped from the current political environment, the church has lost sight of its purpose.

Listening to that preacher, I thought back to the period of virtual church during the COVID-19 shutdown. I was leading a small church at the time. Instead of taking a normal worship service and attempting to translate it to Zoom, our church decided to do a series of talks. The talks were sort of like Bible studies, but more like virtual panel discussions. One Sunday a guest at one of our talks shared a similar sentiment as the preacher from the conference, and it rattled me. This was well before I'd consciously determined that I was deconstructing my faith. But I remember listening to that person talk that day and feeling like the scales had fallen from my eyes. Even though I'd done all sorts of research on Black religiosity, including the conversion of enslaved Africans to Christianity during my time in seminary and since, I don't think the influence of colonialism (which is discussed in Chapter 1) had ever been that clear to me before.

I couldn't see before what I was being shown in that moment. And I was reminded of that moment during that gathering in the summer of 2025. It was a reminder for me of that work I'd done to evaluate whether I was interested in faith, religion, or something else entirely. I'm still figuring out that "something else" to some extent.

You may find that faith is what matters most to you, but you still crave the benefits of being in religious community. That means you no longer seek theological enlightenment from religious spaces. You can do that part on your own or find other spaces to do them, like some of those mentioned in Chapter 15. Some parts of religious spaces might continue to be thirst quenchers for you. Maybe it's the music department. Maybe it's connected to the hugs the church mother gives out every Sunday or the word of encouragement the head usher provides simply in passing.

It could just be the routine you're used to performing every Sunday morning or Saturday afternoon. Maybe it's just that being in religious spaces is familiar, or you see some validity in what they provide to others, and you want to be a part of that. Perhaps it's that you feel your responsibility is to be in the space and ensure that the same toxic theology you received growing up doesn't infiltrate the hearts, minds, and spirits of others, especially the young people. So, your presence there is about service and purpose.

Or you've decided to abandon the community completely and find other avenues of awareness, support, and enlightenment. Some people do that as well. They decide that their faith isn't predicated on the influences of tradition, or even affirming for that matter, religious communities. Maybe what you need is yoga on Sunday mornings, followed by a brisk jog through the park. Or maybe you've decided to abandon all of it, leaning into something else spiritual, but not religious. You might also want to seek mindfulness and meditation. Or perhaps spiritual direction, discussed in Chapter 17.

It's really for to you to decide.

Do you have to decide?

No, you don't have to decide. Whatever you decide is for you and you alone. But it would behoove you to make some sort of declaration, not for anyone publicly, but for yourself.

REMEMBER

Whether you decide to lean into a more faith-filled life sans any kind of religious affiliation, or you feel it's important to retain an affiliation with a religious community, your questions about your faith won't stop. They never stop if you're programmed to be curious or to think critically about anything and everything. And why should they stop? You're better served when you ask questions about the things you encounter.

Plus, your desires may change at some point. You may feel the need to abandon religious affiliation completely at this juncture, but five years from now you may feel it's necessary to be connected to something or someone. It's all valid. When I stepped down as senior pastor of the church I led for almost two years, I declared that I would never have another pastor again in life. To some extent, I still believe that. But I also see the validity in being connected to something. Having grown up African Methodist Episcopal, I'm familiar with a connectional system, the connectional church, and its benefits. (See the nearby sidebar "More on Connectional Church" for details on what it means to be a connectional church and how a connectional church differs from a congregational one.)

TIP

Having a choice is beautiful. Again, some will try to tell you that the best choice is to choose God — whoever their God is. And that's fair. I understand that, for some, what they know about life and faith is connected to their experience. For them, they are where they are in life because of their faith in God and the benefits of the community they hold membership in. All they know is the God of their understanding. That's the beauty of diversity and the beauty of deciding for yourself. If you still believe in God, having a personal relationship with the God you believe in is priority over anyone else's opinion or perspective.

(It's also not lost on me that, throughout this book, I've constantly referred to God, big G. That isn't a political or theological choice. It's just a habit.)

MORE ON CONNECTIONAL CHURCH

What is the connectional church, and what does it do? The connectional church is best defined as the network by which a group of churches are connected. Local churches become closely affiliated with other churches in their area, or district, of the same denomination. The local churches are also accountable to a larger body within the system. This is seen through the involvement of bishops and other governing leaders. In contrast, congregationalist churches are more individual; they're also understood as autonomous. Their decision-making is determined by a governing body within the church, often understood as the trustees or deacons of the church.

Most Methodist denominations, including the United Methodist Church, African Methodist Episcopal Church, African Methodist Episcopal Zion Church, and Christian Methodist Church are connectional entities. The Catholic Church, as well as Episcopal and Presbyterian Churches, also operates via a connectional system. Many Baptists Churches are congregational in nature. The United Church of Christ is one denomination that toes the line between congregational and connectional. There's a national structure, but most churches are encouraged to be autonomous in their decision-making.

Beyond the governance nature of connectional churches, what makes them beneficial is rooted in the name. By being a connectional church, members are afforded the ability to link with members in other parts of their area. Through regional and district meetings, retreats, and other forms of programming, members are granted the opportunity to collaborate with others across boundaries. Such a setup orchestrates community building that informs a person's religious and personal development.

What are the options in remaining or abandoning?

If you do choose, you have options. Maybe you'll decide you want something more spiritually based without the influence of a religious system and its expectations, beliefs, and practices. Maybe, like Jade Foster in Chapter 11, you want to try out a few groups to determine the best fit for you. Maybe you want to try out the practices of another faith system but stay close to the one you know is true to your core. You're free to explore in whatever way you want.

I didn't exactly try out any other faith system. As I share in Chapter 13, I was exposed to other groups and partook in some of the ritualistic practices of others as a means of understanding more deeply, but I can't say that I ever truly ventured very far from Christianity in my process. At this point in my deconstruction journey, as I'm discerning what makes the most sense for me and my faith identity, Christianity is the one I'm *choosing* to affiliate with. Jesus is my point of departure because of what he taught, based on what's found in the sacred text known as the Christian Bible. That's a choice I'm making as I discern if I'm truly some form of agnostic or polytheistic humanist.

I see and can see God in all of it.

What about your options? They're vast. Some of them are covered in Chapter 13. The intent of that chapter is to offer you just enough that you can weigh what matters to you as you discern. The chapter that follows, Chapter 14, provides greater insight into other options that may not be religious in nature but are also worth considering. At the end of the day, the intent is to give you useful information so that you can decide for yourself.

Chapter **13**

Getting Acquainted with Other World Religions

During my final years of undergrad, I had the privilege of taking a class called Sociology of Religion. Having wrestled quietly with questions regarding what I was conditioned to believe about God and the concept of monotheism, I was curious about what clarity the class would provide for me beyond religious indoctrination. I wanted a look behind the curtain. Little did I know the class would be as transformative for me as it was.

Over the course of that one semester, I visited a Hindu temple, attended what I understood as Buddhist worship, sat in on a Wiccan meeting, and went to a Mormon sacrament meeting. The experience didn't make me a nonbeliever in God or Christianity but rather expanded my imagination about God. By the end of the semester, I was left with one deafening question: *What if I've been wrong about everything I've thought, have taught, or was taught to believe?* What if every leader, prophet, and founder of these other religions tried to teach everyone the same thing, but what they taught was authentic to their specific community/audience? Taking it even further, what if all of them were pointing to the same God or gods, and I, or everyone else, was the one deciding they were different?

One of the gifts of faith is the power and ability to imagine. One of the problems of religion is almost the total opposite. Religion, in many ways, creates a hostile environment for imagining anything and everything beyond what's rendered acceptable. When deconstructing your faith, the practice of investigating and reevaluating your beliefs makes room for imagining in ways you've never been given permission to explore before. As you explore, you get the chance to test things to see what does and doesn't fit.

This chapter provides an introduction to just a couple of the more familiar faith systems that are considered world religions: Hinduism and Buddhism. In addition, it attempts to define African spirituality and shine a light on the Indigenous faith practices in the United States that have existed for generations.

The Many Options for Faith Exploration

The world and society are diverse. How much of that diversity are you familiar with? You may have coworkers with unique backgrounds. And you may interact with people daily who are from another county. But do you really know them? Do you know their story, anything about their background, anything about their faith? Usually, the answer is a firm no.

People tend to live and operate in homogeneous communities, with or without the influence of movements like Christian and American nationalism. By design, communities are built out of familiarity and comfort. It's rare to build strong relationships with people outside of those immediate identities. The downside? Missing out on creating meaningful relationships with people who are different from us and missing out on opportunities to experience the diversity of the world. This is especially true when it comes to faith and religious communities.

TIP

Learning about other belief systems is one of the most effective ways to strengthen your own. How are you capable of truly knowing what you believe if you haven't afforded yourself the opportunity to weigh your beliefs against others? Faith is developed most effectively in discovery. Discovery is one of the greatest outcomes of exploration, and exploration is one of the most effective forms of learning.

Most Christians believe that Jesus is the *only* way to God. This belief is hinged upon John 14:6:

> "Jesus said to him, 'I am the way and the truth and the life. No one comes to the Father except through me."

However, there is a lot of debate over how accurate the common translations are. Many Biblical scholars believe that instead of Jesus declaring himself as *the* way, meaning the only way, the accurate translation of the original text should read as Jesus saying he is **one** way to God. Not the *only* way. As a result of this misinterpretation, many Christians aren't inclusive of other religious communities. Within Islam, the Quran emphasizes the importance of not forcing their faith onto others, even though they believe Islam to be the one true religion. And even though Judaism doesn't recognize Jesus or Muhammad as prophets, it recognizes other religions and teaches its followers not to demean the faith practices of others.

TIP

If your beliefs are so fragile that they can be altered by simply learning about something else, then they were never truly firm in the first place. One of the best ways to sharpen what you believe is to learn what else is out there. The exposure allows you to assess and appraise all the things you value, especially with faith.

But what are some of these other religions? What do their followers believe? What do they practice? And what makes their communities unique?

Monotheism beyond the Big Three

Did you know that Judaism, Christianity, and Islam aren't the only monotheistic faiths? In the words of Jaqueline Follet in the *Devil Wears Prada*, "SUPRESE!" It's true: Several religions identify as *monotheistic* — the belief that there is only one God — outside of the major three. However, they're often overlooked or discredited because of the nature of monotheism. Due to their dogmatic perceptions, acting as though they have a monopoly on God and monotheism for that matter, some religious groups believe their God is the only true God. Therefore, they don't see or consider the other monotheistic faiths — or any faith beyond theirs — as true and authentic. Oftentimes, other monotheistic faiths are judged unfairly and treated harshly solely because they're perceived to worship, or serve, or recognize a god (lowercase g) they consider to be *other*.

Let's take a brief look at two other monotheistic religions: Sikhism and Baha'i. This chapter discusses another monotheistic religion, Rastafari, in the "African spirituality" section.

Defining Sikhism

The common misconception of Sikhism is that it's born out of, or an offshoot of, Islam or Hinduism. But according to many of its followers, that assumption can't be further from the truth. Believed to be the fifth largest religion in the world, with more than 25 million believers, Sikhism is one of the youngest global religions. At least three reasons account for the misconceptions.

>> First, the religion was founded nearly 500 years ago in the Punjab region of North India. At that time, Islam and Hinduism dominated the region.

>> Second, the founder of Sikhism, Guru Nanak, was born into a Hindu family. However, his motivation for Sikhism was heavily influenced by his exposure to multiple cultures and religions during his upbringing.

>> Third, a fair amount of culture overlap exists between Sikhism, Hinduism, and Islam. This is due, mostly, to Guru Nanak's teachings.

Another misconception may have something to do with assumptions made regarding how Sikhs dress. Men wear turbans to cover their uncut hair, have long beards, and are usually dressed in a loose shirt and pants, known as a kurta-pajama. Women also cover their heads, traditionally, opting for a scarf or chunni. Finally, women wear loose pants with a long tunic, known as a *salwar kameez*.

Sikh is loosely translated as disciple or seeker in Sanskrit. Sikhs believe that one God created the universe and that all people are equal before God. As proponents of social justice and charity, they're against the caste system, believe men and women have equal statue, seek to serve others, especially those who are less fortunate, and believe that all should live honorable, honest, and generous lives.

Like Islam, Sikhs believe in the Christian prophet Jesus. However, what they believe differs strongly from what Christians and even Muslims believe. Sikhs don't negate Jesus's existence. Neither do they negate that Jesus was a prophet. This understanding aligns with their belief in tolerance of all religions. However, they don't support the Christian idea that Jesus was God. For them, God can't be born. According to Sikhs, God is creation. In Sikhism, God is the creator of all things; because of that, they believe God can't have been born.

A few other facts about Sikhism:

>> Sikhs call their leader a *guru*.

>> The guru is charged with helping Sikhs connect with God.

>> Following the death of Guru Nanak were nine other gurus, believed to have been inhabited by a single spirit.

>> Following the death of the tenth human guru, Sikhs believe that spirit was transferred into the Guru Granth Sahib, the sacred scripture of Sikhism.

>> Hymns, prayers, and the teachings of the 10 human gurus are housed within the Guru Granth Sahib. Teachings from other faiths can also be found within the scripture's pages.

Defining Baha'i

Like most of the religions discussed in this book, the Baha'i faith has a difficult and complicated history. And it starts with none other than Islam. Baha'i is believed to be one of the fastest growing religions in the world, besides one of the youngest, yet many Muslims — most specifically Shias and Sunnis — consider the Baha'i faith to be heretical.

Why is there friction? Simply put, Baha'i is said to have emerged from Islam. Its founder, Bahá'u'lláh, is believed to be the successor of Báb, a Muslim who founded the Bábí movement within Islam. However, most Muslims considered Báb a false prophet. Whereas Muslims believe the Prophet Muhammad to be the last and final prophet, Baha'is believe that prophethood has continued and identify Bahá'u'lláh as the continuation.

Other things worth knowing about the Baha'i faith:

>> Baha'is believe in progressive revelation. This concept is also familiar in Christianity and suggests that over time God reveals truth. They suggest that God has done so over time through Moses, Jesus, and Muhammad.

>> Baha'is believe that all religions, including Judaism, Christianity, Islam, Hinduism, Buddhism, and others, are part of God's great plan, and each religion has contributed to the spiritual evolution of God's creation and people.

>> Baha'is support inclusion not only among religions, but also among humanity. They're proponents of unity overall, strongly support racial equality, and oppose any form of prejudice and exclusion.

One final point worth highlighting is the Baha'is' position on their sacred text. Like the Sikhs, the Baha'is believe their holy writings are a continuation of their prophet's teachings and a continuation of previous scriptures. However, they don't consider their holy book, called the Kitáb-i-Aqdas, to be the living embodiment of their former leaders.

Polytheistic belief systems

If you grew up with monotheism, you might have looked down upon any religion supporting polytheism. You probably considered it countercultural, maybe a little weird, and possibly even scary to some extent. I remember the first time I visited a Hindu temple. I felt anxious about what I would see, what I would experience, and what punishment God would reign upon me for even being in the building.

However, there was a time in human history when polytheism was common and shared broadly. So, what is polytheism exactly? Merriam-Webster defines it as a belief in or worship of more than one god. However, it's not as simple as that.

In polytheism, it's believed that each god governs a specific facet or a particular place, space, or situation. This means that one god reigns over the sun, one over the moon, one over the sea, and so on.

This section discusses one of the most known polytheistic religions: Hinduism. In addition, it discusses a religion often referred to as a pagan religion: Wicca. And no, this isn't the WB's *Charmed*, Disney's *Agatha All Along*, or even the Salem Witch Trials for that matter. But it's worth highlighting Wiccan's place in this conversation if you're considering venturing beyond one of the more well-known religious practices to find community during your deconstruction journey.

Defining Hinduism

What makes Hinduism fascinating as a religious concept is the way in which many understand and perceive the faith. There are those who suggest that Hinduism is polytheistic. This categorization is due in large part to the religion's emphasis on specific deities and their roles in the lives of the Hindus. However, Hinduism has at times been considered surface-level monotheistic.

Like some of the monotheistic faiths discussed thus far, Hinduism does believe in one supreme God. However, that God is represented by many deities. At the center of all creation for Hindis is Brahman. Brahman is the source of all creation for Hindis and beyond all understanding. Brahman is formless, infinite, eternal, and transcendent and has four main characteristics, also known as attributes:

>> Sat, which means existence

>> Chit, which means consciousness or awareness

>> Ananda, which means bliss or joy

>> Nurguna, which means without attributes, or formless

Each characteristic or attribute is meant to best convey Brahman's transcendent and infinite nature. Each highlights Brahman as the source of all but also suggests the goal for all within Hinduism. Through the practices of meditation, self-actualization, and oneness with self, you can experience the kind of spiritual realization that gets you closer to the source of all creation.

As *one* of the oldest, if not *the* oldest religion in the world (according to some scholars), Hinduism has no single founder. As a result, Hindis also don't have a governing body or single central leader. They're made up of a diverse collection of sects and may have a leader who influences a specific region or community. In addition, Hindis adhere to no main doctrine.

For a more comprehensive look into Hinduism, I suggest Wiley's *Hinduism For Dummies*. But following are a few other things to know about Hinduism:

>> A central belief in Hinduism is reincarnation.

>> The actions of your life today dictate your next life. This concept is also known as *karma*.

>> The sacred texts of Hinduism can be separated into two categories: that which is heard and that which is remembered.

>> Spiritual practice is highly important.

>> Hinduism has three main deities (Trimurti): Brahma, Vishnu, and Shiva.

>> The controversial caste system has major significance in Hindu society and culture.

Wicca

Some critics don't consider Wicca a true and authentic religion. The cause of this assertion is rooted in a great amount of misinformation about the Wiccan community and their practices.

Usually when someone hears the word *Wicca*, they assume that the practitioners are a group of weird outcasts who believe in magic, perform small animal sacrifices, consider themselves to be witches, and worship the moon like werewolves. Yes, some Wiccans dabble in the practice of drawing from the energy around them. And to some extent, they consider these practices magic. However, Wiccans are more than that. And, if I'm being honest, they may not fit comfortably into the category of polytheism. However, when you're looking at the definition of Wicca as defined by Merriam-Webster, you notice the components that make the religion polytheistic in nature.

Because Wicca focuses on multiple deities, it's generally considered polytheistic. Wiccans believe that the divine can be manifest and present in many forms, but most especially in nature. But not all Wiccans are polytheistic. Some believe in at least two supreme beings. Others believe in only one deity: the Mother Goddess.

As one of the youngest religions worldwide, Wicca got its start in England and is often classified as a pagan religion. But labeling something *pagan* is almost like labeling something *heretical*. Wicca is considered pagan because it isn't one of the Abrahamic faiths. Contrary to popular belief, Wiccans aren't satanists or devil worshipers. They don't include anything evil-based in their practices. As a matter of fact, the origins of Wicca are informed by pre-Christian beliefs and enlightened by the natural world.

Following are a few takeaways about Wiccans:

>> They believe in the spirit world.

>> They see magic as a tool for healing and shouldn't cause harm.

>> They emphasize self-empowerment.

>> They're ritualistic in nature and utilize crystals, incense, and tarot readings for guidance, care, and support.

In addition to the self and self-empowerment, Wiccans believe in caring for the world and nature, as well as neighborhoods and communities. They're informed by what they call the Rule of Three. As a guiding principle, the Rule of Three suggests that whatever energy you put out in the world, whether positive or negative, that same energy returns to you. When it returns, the energy returns three times. Sounds a lot like karma, doesn't it?

Nontheistic groups and practices

Before you panic (or get excited), no, this isn't the section on atheism. That topic is reserved for the next chapter. This section discusses the belief system known as nontheistic. What makes them nontheistic? They're not centered on a deity or deities. They're worldviews or belief systems that are rooted in community and focused on perspectives, philosophies, and experiences. What makes them religious in nature is tied to their practices. In other words, nontheistic religions are religions because they act as religions even though they're not rooted in the belief of a higher power.

Buddhism is probably one of the better-known nontheistic practices. Another one is Humanism, which is discussed more in Chapter 14. Unitarian Universalists are also considered nontheistic even though many within that community engage Christian tenets and themes. A moral framework is associated with most nontheistic groups. They perform rituals and practices in community, they share a commitment to community and identity as a group, and they have sacred texts and writings that govern their beliefs, stances, and practices within and beyond their community.

For an in-depth understanding of Buddhism, pick up Wiley's *Buddhism For Dummies*. For the sake of this conversation, consider a few principles mentioned here if you're deconstructing. Buddhism grew out of strife present in India during the dominance of Hinduism in its earlier carnations. Having grown up in the region, the founder of Buddhism, Siddhartha Gautama (also known as the Buddha), was impacted by the teachings of the time, informed by Hinduism. As a result, Buddhism and Hinduism share a few themes:

- >> A belief in the cycle of life: birth, death, and rebirth

- >> The concept of karma

- >> Meditation and self-discipline

As a spiritual tradition, Buddhism's central focus is guiding people to *enlightenment*, or investigating for themselves. Through enlightenment, a person can become more self-actualized and secure. Some would consider Buddhism to be a hyped-up version of self-help, but that's a gross misconception and interpretation. Liberation from suffering is the goal.

Unitarian Universalists fit within the category of nontheistic because they allow any and every person in their community to believe whatever they want about God, god, or a supreme entity. More liberal in nature, they believe in community building and that life is better and more meaningful when experienced and shared in community.

Like many of the religious communities discussed thus far in this chapter, Unitarian Universalists recognize the existence of the historical Jesus. They consider him to be a prophet and even the son of God, but they don't recognize Jesus as God or a god. They believe Jesus and God to be separate, singular beings. What makes them universalists is their belief in universal salvation. They consider God to be loving and incapable of sending anyone to hell. From their perspective, God saves all and makes heaven attainable to everyone.

African spirituality

Of the many religious communities often denigrated in society, African diasporic faith systems are usually the most disparaged. Colonialism and Eurocentric biases have played a major role in how African diasporic faiths, almost considered more broadly as African spirituality, are perceived not only within the United States, but across the globe. Even though the practices, rituals, and tenets of many religions practiced in Africa or originating in Africa share similarities with Christianity, because they're not practiced under the guise of Christianity, they're perceived as dark and anti-Christian.

Many Black Americans and members of the Black African diaspora have embraced African spirituality because of a need to "decolonize" their faith. Decolonizing their faith, specifically for members of the African diaspora, means acknowledging the impact colonialism has had on what you believe and dismantling those beliefs and influences. In some respects, much of our faith – especially within Christianity – is anti-Black. Some within the African diaspora have recognized how they have adopted anti-Black. As a result, they've felt the need to decolonize their faith, which is a form of deconstruction.

Members of the diaspora realize their faith — oftentimes Christianity — isn't serving them well as Black Americans or descendants of Africa because of how slavery has stripped them of their original identities and cultures. They've sought greater clarity and an authentic connection to their ancestry and their African roots. The faith of their upbringing no longer fits, which means evaluating what does. African spirituality has provided for many spaces to feel welcome, to be and feel seen, and to connect in ways that most mainstream religions, especially the Westernized ones, haven't allowed.

A plethora of African religious practices represent the diversity of thought, expression, and identities within and beyond the continent of Africa. Some of them are polytheistic in nature. Others are monotheistic.

These religious practices include the following:

>> Yoruba Religion (Orisha worship)

>> Vodun (commonly referred to as Voodoo)

>> Zulu Religion

>> Akan Religion

>> Igbo Religion

Yoruba and Vodun are two of the most familiar African spiritual religions. They're also commonly misunderstood.

Vodun

Those familiar with Vodun immediately imagine all the things that have become affiliated with Voodoo in pop culture. They think about Voodoo dolls being used to torture someone, or they imagine human sacrificial rituals. But Vodun, which is native to West Africa and the Caribbean but also found in Haiti and Louisiana, is deeply rooted in love, protection, health, and wisdom. Ancestral veneration is a central component to Vodun. Practitioners believe that their ancestors continue being in the world as guides and protectors. They believe Mawu to be the creator of the universe and their supreme god. They also believe spirit guides engage with them closely in their everyday lives.

Yoruba

Maintaining harmony and life balance is at the core of Yoruba, also a polytheistic religion. Olodumare is their supreme god and maker of all creation. But believers rely on other spirit guides, known as Orishas, to intercede on their behalf. Not only that, Orishas rule over specific domains and provide access and guidance in specific areas. How many Orishas are there? Some experts suggest 400 or more. Others report thousands.

Some of the common Orishas include these:

>> Eshu governs communication and is considered a trickster.

>> Ogún is considered to possess all technology, making him the god of war.

>> Oshosi is described as the hunter.

>> Obatalá owns the mind and is referred to as the father of not only the Orishas but of humanity.

>> Oyá rules the winds as well as the dead.

>> Oshún has dominion over the world's streams and rivers, as well as love and fertility.

>> Yemayá resides over the lakes and seas, as well as maternity.

>> Shangó is a warrior Orisha, ruling over lightning, thunder, fire, drums, and dance.

> » Divination and wisdom are held by the Orisha called
> Orunmila. This Orisha is the only one to have been allowed
> to witness the birth of the universe.

Yoruba is the religion of the Yoruba people in Western Africa. As a people, they're believed to be the third largest ethnic group in Nigeria. They're heavily ritualistic in practice and nature and keep not only their faith, but their culture alive through the Yoruba religion. But Yoruba's influence is vast, having made its way throughout the African diaspora, but also to Cuba, Haiti, and Benin. Yorubas also have a rich history of finding purpose in celebrating and preserving history and culture. Another thing that's unique about Yoruba is the way many people of other faiths can find space to practice Yoruba and meld it with the beliefs and practices of their religions of origin. For many Black Americans in the United States, Orisha worship is an invaluable way to enhance their cravings for spiritual guidance, stronger communal connection and belonging, and cultural affirmation.

Rastafari

Rastafari is another religion commonly associated with African spirituality. In some ways, distinctions are plentiful between Rastafari and other African religions — one of them being the incorporation of Christianity within the belief system — but many of the themes found in African spirituality are present in Rastafari. These themes include ancestral veneration (which it's safe to suggest is also present in Christianity), as well as a connection to nature, as seen in most African spiritual practices.

Hoodoo

Hoodoo is another form of African spirituality practiced almost exclusively by Black Americans. Those most familiar with Hoodoo suggest it's not a religion, but more so a practice, a thought, mindset, or way of living. They do not consider it a religion because of it lack of a deity or a theology.

Some have referred to Hoodoo as "folk magic" and define it as a tradition rooted in the supernatural. Core elements of hoodoo include ancestor veneration, rootwork (herbalism), and ritualistic practices like charms and spells.

Indigenous faith and practices

Quiet as it's kept, most of the religions of today were at some point in time an Indigenous faith. One of the main characteristics of Indigenous faiths is the practice of their being passed down from generation to generation. "Oral traditions" is another way of describing Indigenous faiths. The elders of the community maintained not just the stories of the community, but its history. And they did so through the practice of storytelling. Imagine, if you will, campfire story experiences.

Not only were the stories kept alive through these oral traditions, but so were their histories, cultures, rituals, and heritage. The elders held to what was familiar to them — keeping their history, their stories, and their ancestors alive by passing them down from generation to generation. And they didn't just tell their story; they connected it to their identity and their culture, teaching their young the importance of caring for the land, respecting nature, venerating their ancestors, and supporting each other. Their pride in themselves, their history, their community, and their culture were baked into their stories.

Over time, some communities began organizing those stories and creating the systems now known as religions. Both the Torah, the sacred text of Judaism, as well as the Christian Bible are believed to have their genesis in the practice of communal oration. Many of the religions today have ventured away from their Indigenous origins, but some communities have maintained the analog nature of their culture, history, identity, and tradition.

As you consider the practice of deconstruction, it's worth highlighting the existence and importance of these communities. Many Indigenous faith communities have suffered loss due to the practices of colonialism and assimilation. Many of them have lost access to lands that once served as locales of sacred spiritual importance. As they became marginalized, much of their history and story was forgotten. But all hasn't been lost. Recent years have seen an uptick in celebrating the people and culture native to the lands being occupied. As a result, they've been able to revitalize their history and culture, while teaching those within greater society who are willing to listen the importance of knowing their stories, histories, and heritage.

Faith throughout Native American culture

Native American religions are as diverse as the communities they represent. The culture is diverse. You probably recognize the names Cherokee Nation, Sauk People, Navajo, Sioux, and Cheyenne, but many other tribes exist. As many of them assimilated, they became known as the Five Civilized Tribes, which are as follows:

>> Cherokee

>> Choctaw

>> Chickasaw

>> Creek

>> Seminole

As expected, most tribes have their own religion or religious practices. The Navajo, Lakota, and Cherokee are three with unique spiritual practices of their own on record. *Animism*, or the belief that nature is alive with a soul, is one of their core beliefs. They also have a great reverence for what they consider to be the Great Spirit. And like most African Indigenous religions, they practice ancestor veneration. They believe that the ancestors continue to serve as guides and protectors after they've passed on.

Their spiritual leaders are called *shamans* and are the elders, healers, and medicine men of the tribe. As shamans, they possess the knowledge needed to support the tribe in healing, survival, and rituals. They do this as intermediaries between the spiritual realm and the natural world. As people of the land, they're interconnected with creation, which means they're responsible for maintaining harmony and balance in every facet of life.

Aboriginal faith in Australia

The Aboriginals of Australia and Native Americans share several commonalities. The first is their designation of being believed to be the first inhabitants of their native land. In addition, Aboriginals of Australia and Native Americans have similar relationships to nature in that they revere and honor the land. But there are, of course, also quite a few differences between Aboriginals of Australia and Native Americans.

When it comes to their faith and religion, Aboriginals, like Native Americans, have sustained their culture by passing their story and history down from generation to generation through oral transmission. In addition, Aboriginals practice ancestral veneration, believing that the spirit world exists alongside the natural world.

However, Aboriginals aren't a monolith. One example of this is the diverse relationship to what they call the Dreamtime. In some respects, the Dreamtime or the Dreaming is the Aboriginal origin story that tells how the world came to be. The Dreaming is the period when the ancestors created the world, the land, and the inhabitants of the land. Some of the ancestors are historical; others are mythological. But at its core, the Dreaming is meant to explain the origins of all creation and all living things, not just in the past but into the future. However, depending upon the region the community resides, one community's story could be different from another's.

Finding Greater Self-Awareness and Meaning

If I've learned anything in my faith deconstruction journey, it's this: I have more questions than I have answers. But the gift in the exercise is that I'm more self-aware today than I've ever been. Part of that is due to the process of exploring. Ever heard of the saying, "You don't know what you don't know"? Conditioning leads to developing perspectives, opinions, and judgments on groups that, when I really take the time to pay attention, have more in common with me than I ever knew.

It sometimes makes me wonder what would happen if people allowed themselves to consider, if only for a moment, something I've questioned for at least the past decade: Is it all God? Whether Baha'i or Hindi, Zulu or Cherokee, what would happen if people allowed themselves to believe that everyone's talking about the same thing but just in a different language, form, name, or understanding? This is the process of meaning-making. Within the deconstruction journey, the answers aren't what you find. It's the questions that provide more clarity because they're the motivation for the journey.

NOTEWORTHY PRACTITIONERS

Chapter 19 lists ten individuals from history and contemporary times who have used their faith to impact and influence society. But they aren't the only ones. From celebrities to faith leaders to political leaders, many of the people we celebrate and cherish represent some of the faith practices mentioned in this chapter. Here are just a few of them:

- Aunt Caroline Dye, a renounced Hoodoo woman
- Marie Laveau, the "Voodoo Queen" of New Orleans
- Alex and Maxine Sanders, Wicca
- Raymond Buckland, Wicca
- Steve Jobs, Buddhist
- Tiger Woods, Buddhist

Chapter **14**

Exploring Other Forms of Identity and Community

I enjoy having deep, thought-provoking conversations with people. Likewise, I relish when someone says something that makes me think about anything and everything. I'm especially moved by experiences where I walk away having learned something I didn't know or having been exposed to something I hadn't considered before. I always feel that way after I've had a chat with Dr. Jason Oliver Evans. He's a dear friend and one of the smartest people I know.

During a conversation with him on the topic of sin, he stated that faith deconstruction is something everyone should be doing. "You're finally applying your mind to thinking about your faith. Welcome to critical thinking. Welcome to the task of theology — applying your mind to what you actually believe." I hadn't thought of it like that.

True faith ignites thought. True faith, as Evans put it, causes you to reflect on what you believe concerning God and all things related to God. True faith also causes you to think about who you are in relation to God and things concerning your relationship to God. Maybe within that process, you're not only questioning and reevaluating your faith, but coming into an understanding of yourself — self-actualization. Faith deconstruction is intentional and personal discernment.

As you put what you believe to the task, deconstruction may change everything for you. How you identify religiously may have to change. You may continue to identify with the faith community you belonged to when you started this journey. You may try out several faiths and eventually create an identity amalgamation that you feel fits best for you. You may abandon religion completely and connect with a community that has no religious affiliation. All these possibilities are valid.

This chapter explores several other forms of expression that are often considered outside religion. What are they, and what do they stand for? What misconceptions do you have about some of them? Are they a good fit for where you are in your journey? Read on to find out.

Being Spiritual but Not Religious

Spiritual but not religious, also known as SBNR, can best be defined as a belief system that doesn't adhere to any organized religion or sets of rituals. It prioritizes personal spirituality, finding organized religion unnecessary. But SBNR does engage in many practices commonly found in some of the more popular religious expressions, like meditation (Buddhism), mindfulness (Hinduism), and communing with nature (Wiccan or Indigenous Practices).

The first mention of SBNR is believed to date as far back as the 1960s, when the phrase is believed to have appeared in a few scholarly anthropological journals. However, some reports speak of references as far back as 1926 in the description of the Rotary Club. The description became more widely known and popularized in the 2000s when, it's believed, online dating became more popular, and users were prompted to choose a religious affiliation. Whether that's the case has been debated, but it's undeniable that in the 2000s SBNR became the newest major headline.

One major critique of SBNR is its perceived emphasis on individualism. Wherein religious groups profess to be community based or communally focused, SBNR is often portrayed as explicitly individual. Many within religious communities see this individualism as problematic. However, what has drawn and continues to draw some to SBNR as a belief system is the idea of individual responsibility.

TIP Most people who identify as SBNR aren't without faith. They aren't atheist (which I discuss later in this chapter).

While SBNRs may not believe in a divine being or deity, they do believe in a higher being. Like some other forms of religious expression, SBNRs describe God as a state of heightened awareness or consciousness. Unlike other forms of religious expression, however, they don't subscribe to a perfect God who rules over all creation. But they do emphasize a desire and commitment to being connected with a higher power, especially as it pertains to finding and living into their purpose. In most instances, they reject the traditional beliefs and practices of the more well-known religions, are disillusioned with what they consider to be distractions and limits within other well-known religious communities, or have become curious about exploring other spiritual practices and have settled on SBNR as their identity.

Looking back on my own experiences, I went through what I would now call an "I'm spiritual but not religious" phase. Now, I'm not suggesting that anyone else who identifies as such is going through a phase. I'm not that dismissive, and I'm not one of those people who likes to throw around the "it's a phase" thing on others. I dealt with that enough when I was younger and learning to lean into my identity as a Black, same-gender-loving man, I know the harm that "it's a phase" can do. Your journey is your journey, whether you're in a phase or not. I'm clear it was a phase for me because of the intent behind the declaration.

Wounded from my experiences of coming out and feeling abandoned by "The Church," I began describing myself as SBNR.

I was being rebellious. I'd heard others refer to themselves as such and, because it sounded like something worth aspiring to, I decided I would be the same. It was a moment in time in my journey. Nothing more, nothing less. I had no idea at that point what it meant to be spiritual but not religious.

If you're exploring faith deconstruction, it makes sense for you to land on SBNR as your belief system. However, it's important to ask yourself "Why SBNR?" in the first place. What are your motivations? What are you seeking to explore? How does it align with who you are and who you believe yourself to be? What are the benefits?

Considering Christian spirituality

Now, before you say anything, I know. I KNOW. You're wondering why I'm including a section on Christian spirituality. Is that even necessary within this conversation and this chapter? Isn't it the same Christianity (i.e., traditional Christianity) that I've been talking about this entire time? Actually, no.

Yes, the two overlap. And yes, to some extent they're intertwined. But they're not the same thing. They have some differences that are worth pointing out, especially if you're deconstructing your faith and struggling to decipher what community and what identity is right for you. There are *so many* options that it's worth delineating as many as possible. Buckle up!

Traditional Christianity, as it's understood today, refers to the things that govern the religious system. That includes the doctrines, beliefs, practices, and institutions that make up the "faith" — using *faith* loosely, of course. These sources, as well as scripture itself, serve as the authority by which an individual, a member, relates to God and its system.

Christian spirituality, on the other hand, is or can be characterized as more individual in nature. The motivation and focus of Christian Spirituality is rooted in how one relates to God. It's about personal relationship with the divine — in this instance the Christian God — and the practices used to reach that goal. Prayer. Meditation. Contemplation. For anyone who identifies with Christian spirituality, the goal is to establish a deep and personal connection with God and an experience with the Divine.

In most instances, traditional Christianity is the underpinning for Christian spiritualty. Traditional Christianity offers the guidance and structure by which Christian spirituality is built upon. But once that foundation is developed, you can practice Christian spirituality independently of traditional Christianity. Some do practice it outside of the context of traditional spirituality. They often refer to themselves as "Lovers of Jesus, but not the church."

Is this group an official Christian community? It's hard to say, but some, as the result of their faith deconstruction journey, have chosen to consider themselves followers of the teachings of Jesus yet have no desire to be in relationship with "The Church" universal. This is their way of separating themselves from Western Christianity. They can, and oftentimes do, profess to be able to separate the teachings of Jesus from the structure of religion. They're committed to expanding their relationship with Jesus by prioritizing individual and personal development and community engagement over attending worship services on Sunday morning or volunteering their services to the institution of church. And they do so by spotlighting Jesus's instructions of love, justice, and empathy over adhering to doctrine.

Like many others who have journeyed through faith deconstruction, this group has experienced some form of hurt or disillusionment with the institution of church, which has motivated their focus on a more personal relationship with Jesus and his teachings.

TIP

In contrast, those who are traditional Christians understand the church as Jesus's bride. They're committed to the work of the church as an extension of their love and commitment to Jesus and his teachings.

Christian spirituality versus SBNR

Christian spirituality and SBNR aren't the same, but it's easy to assume a relationship between the two. For a while, if I'm honest, I made a similar assumption. Not wanting to be affiliated with the Christian church because of baggage and hurt, I wanted to have some connection to the space that I loved — the church — without having to be affiliated with it. I, like many others, assumed that Christian spirituality and SBNR were the same, or at least related.

But the only thing they really have in common is that both have *spiritual* in their name.

The other most obvious distinction, as pointed out in this chapter, is that Christian spirituality still has some connection to Christianity and, to some extent, the Christian church and its teachings. Those who identify as SBNR, on the other hand, may have had some historical connection to Christianity, but they're not affiliated with any religious system. And while both are individually based in nature and driven by a desire for personal connection with a higher being, SBNRs' understanding of that higher being is broader and more focused on enlightenment.

TIP

SBNR utilizes meditation, nature, and mysticism, while Christian spirituality draws on prayer, scripture, and in some instances regular church attendance. Both focus on a deeper sense of meaning, understanding, and purpose, but the manner and tools they utilize to get there are vastly different.

REMEMBER

For anyone seeking to deconstruct, it's helpful to have this understanding of both — Christian spirituality and SBNR — and what they represent. As you deconstruct, finding the right groups to provide the tools, perspectives, and practices to help you best identify your faith is necessary. That may mean test driving one or the other to see. Or it may mean building community with people who have already done the work to see how it helped them and then trying it for yourself. It's up to you to determine the best fit, if finding connection to a higher power is what you desire.

If you aren't interested in a connection to any higher power, read on. The next section has information and insight on other options available to you: atheism, agnosticism, and humanism.

MORE ON CHRISTIANITY VERSUS SBNR

I believe that other forms of expression, like SBNR, are looked down upon for two reasons. First, any form of expression that isn't Christian is disdained and relegated as wicked and lost. Second, groups like SBNR are commonly mislabeled as atheist, which is likely rooted in fear and control. Because these groups can be demeaned and discredited by the powers that be, those who show interest or attraction to the groups can be deflated.

Atheism, Agnosticism, and Humanism

There is this phrase I heard many years ago. I cannot remember if it was during my years in undergrad or before, but whenever I heard the phrase, it has stuck with me all these years. "Whoever controls the media, controls the mind." I've repeated the phrase countless times, always pointing out that I heard from a former teacher or professor. (I later learned that the teacher I'd credited for so long with the saying isn't the originator.)

What you believe is probably informed, and sometimes manipulated, by who told you and what they told you. What you know, or better yet what you think you believe about God, faith, and society at large, has been informed by those who controlled the narrative. Everything you think you believe about God, about Jesus, and about other religions is due in large part to the narratives you've accepted and adopted.

The same is true for how I judged anyone who identified as a humanist, how I understood atheism historically and, based on what others have told me about it, how I chose to understand agnosticism. This next section provides brief descriptions of atheism, agnosticism, and humanism, their connection — if any — to faith, and some insight to the role they've played in the faith deconstruction — and reconstruction — process of many.

Understanding atheism

Most people who have heard of atheism or have some familiarity with this identity believe atheists to simply be people who don't believe in God. While this description to some extent is true, there's more to it. I'm not an atheist, so some of what I'm about to say in this section is informed by what I've learned, heard, read, and gleaned from other sources about the belief system.

TIP

For an in-depth understanding and read of atheism, I suggest picking up *Atheism For Dummies*. Author Dale McGowan, PhD, provides a much more thorough explanation and background to atheism than I can in this short section.

While some suggest that atheism is a modern phenomenon, born out of one of many enlightenment eras, historians and scholars suggest that atheism stems as far back as ancient Greece. Atheism, they believe, existed in societies known and considered to be polytheistic. One book, written by Greek culture professor Tim Whitmarsh, suggests that truth during the time atheism thrived. Whitmarsh's work also challenges what's known as *religious universalism*, the assertion that human beings believe in gods because they're naturally predisposed of such beliefs.

Atheists aren't a monolith.

>> *Implicit atheists* don't believe in gods but haven't completely abandoned the possibility.

>> *Explicit atheists* not only actively reject the idea that gods exist but assert that none exist.

ATHEISM ON A SPECTRUM

Atheism, like many ideologies, exists on a spectrum. The following secondary labels include some insight into where one may fall on the spectrum of atheism:

- **Atheist:** One who doesn't believe in gods or supernatural beings.

- **Agnostic:** One who claims not to know whether supernatural beings exist and aren't convinced it's possible to know.

- **Freethinker:** One who utilizes independent reasoning to hold opinions outside of the influence and authority and tradition of others.

- **Skeptic:** One who waits for sufficient evidence before making a judgment.

- **Humanist:** One who prioritizes caring for and being concerned about what plagues the world, people, and society. They may sometimes believe in God or heaven, but they focus on the current realities of life.

- **Secular humanist:** One who takes humanism a step further to assert the nonexistence of gods.

How or why might someone become an atheist? It's different for everyone. Some lean into atheism because of a deconstruction journey. It may be the result of some harm they experienced from their faith community or organized religion at-large. Or their conversion into atheism may be the result of witnessing harm done to others, such as someone they love or are in community with.

McGowan shares in *Atheism For Dummies* that neither of these instances happened to him. He wasn't upset with the church or didn't have any kind of painful breakup with religion. As he journeyed through life, which also meant attending church with family and others, he had questions. He wondered about the things told and taught to him, so he chased after the questions. He studied the scriptures, asked other believers, and even studied the sciences. Eventually, he landed on the idea that society was infatuated with filling in the spaces that had holes as a means of control and comfort. He didn't need that. He was perfectly fine with accepting that their answers didn't have to be his. He also, quite comfortably, identifies with every label within atheism.

Acknowledging agnosticism

While it may be safe to suggest that agnosticism has some correlation and connection to atheism, there are some important distinctions:

>> Atheists don't believe that a supernatural god or any gods exist, with some asserting the nonexistence and their rejection.

>> Agnostics assert that the existence of supernatural gods is unknown and incapable of being known. This is probably one of the clearest distinctions between the two.

Like atheism, agnosticism dates as far back as ancient Greece. But it first received its name in 1869 when a man named Thomas Henry Huxley derived the word from two Greek words that mean "without knowledge." Huxley was believed to be among a group of scientists and thinkers who struggled with reconciling the science of evolution with the principle, and argument of fact, present in traditional religious belief. Knowledge and human understanding have limits; therefore, they believed that focusing on the world through observation and empirical evidence better served society and humanity.

Note: What I'm saying about agnostics isn't from my firsthand account. Instead, I'm approaching this understanding from the position of someone who's just as curious as anyone reading this book. I don't want anyone to be misled and think that what I'm sharing about this group comes from personal knowledge.

But I *am* curious, which is key in the faith deconstruction journey. Being actively and openly curious benefits you in whatever process you're exploring. If you're not curious and open, you won't learn.

Embracing humanism

Humanism prioritizes humanity and human value over the supernatural. Therefore, humanists not only believe in but also advocate for the values and principles of humanism. They reject supernaturalism and are committed to addressing human needs and wants in the world through reason and compassion. Every human being has dignity and should be treated as such.

Like atheism, there are types of humanism. The most common type is secular humanism, which emphasizes human rights, social justice, and ethics. Other types include:

» **Philosophical humanism:** Can be religious or nonreligious

» **Religious humanism:** Best found in Unitarian Universalism, but also in Christianity and Judaism

» **Scientific humanism:** Believes sciences can be used to best improve the lives of humanity.

REMEMBER

Something else that stands out to me about humanists and humanism is their focus on the now instead of God and the afterlife. Many Christians are conditioned to believe that if they live a good life, they'll receive a reward in heaven. This is especially true within Black religiosity — not just Black Christianity, but also other forms of Black religious expression.

In Chapter 9, I explain the phrase "heavenly bound but no earthly good." Heavenly bound but no earthly good people have tunnel vision; they have blinders on and can only see what they want to see right in front of them. The problem with "heavenly bound but no earthly good" is that it allows people who buy into this ideal to selectively do good. They claim to be committed to the work and the causes of their doctrines, but they easily overlook the realities and experiences of others living in what the church people like to call "the here and now." Heavenly bound but no earthly good people treat "salvation" like a competition.

But with humanism, the focus is on caring for humankind and society, without the air of ulterior motives or a concern that their actions and efforts will result in a divine being greeting them with praise and admiration, open arms, and a loving embrace at the pearly gates.

In recent years, I've heard more scholars and faith leaders embracing humanism than I can ever remember. My first introduction to humanism occurred while in seminary. I was introduced to the work and writings of professor and humanist Dr. Anthony Pinn. I would later interact with his work again in a class on the Book of Job during my Doctor of Ministry studies. By this time, I was slightly more familiar with humanism as a concept but still not all that versed.

MORE ABOUT ANTHONY PINN

Considered to be one of the leading scholars on African American humanism, Anthony Pinn teaches at Rice University, where he's the Agnes Cullen Arnold Distinguished Professor of Humanities. Growing up Methodist, Pinn became a humanist to answer the questions that plagued him. He noticed the failures of religion and how they never truly addressed the issues that afflicted the communities he grew up in and cared about. Believing that religion is humanity's effort to make meaning of life, Pinn offers humanism as a better option for African Americans, specifically. In addition to his work at Rice, he's the director of research for the Institute for Humanist Studies and has authored or edited over 35 books, including *The Black Church in the Post-Civil Rights Era* (2002); *Terror and Triumph: The Nature of Black Religion* (2003), and *Noise and Spirit: Rap Music's Religious and Spiritual Sensibilities* (2004).

For many years, there was only one person I knew personally who identified as a humanist. This was before I became familiar with Pinn. We know each other from our work in the metro Atlanta area. Because of my lack of understanding and ignorance, I dismissed their (not Pinn, the person I know in Atlanta) labelling themselves as a humanist. I assumed his choice was a response to whatever harm he experienced in the church. Now that I've become acquainted with several other humanists (including Pinn) — whether secular humanists, Christian humanists, or something else — I have a better understanding of the vastness and diversity.

The role of atheism and agnosticism in returning to faith

Some years ago, I heard someone say, "Atheists know the Bible better than most Christians." I didn't know their statement to be true, but their thesis intrigued me. It also shamed me.

If atheists don't believe in God or in anything divine, why would they know anything about the Christian Bible or any religion's sacred text? That was the question I asked myself after hearing the statement. It never dawned on me that maybe, just maybe, they knew the writings because they had either been staunch Christians at one time or, as is the case of McGowan, used and studied the texts to help them decipher and determine what they actually believed and how they actually identified.

It makes sense that atheism and agnosticism are viable options for some going through deconstruction. It's also feasible that, to an extent, some people will journey through one or both philosophies and find their way back to Christianity or another form of religious expression at some point.

The faith deconstruction journey affords you the space and privilege of experimenting with yourself, your faith, and your beliefs. It's not uncommon for someone, as their perspectives shift, to venture back. A few reasons may also include:

>> Spiritual longing

>> Community and belonging

>> A crisis or life-altering experience

>> Spiritual and emotional maturity

Again, I'm not suggesting that your journey through one of these philosophies is a phase. But I *am* suggesting that the faith deconstruction journey is a process of questioning and inquiry. You may encounter many of the same questions that have led others to one of these philosophies. It's common to wonder either privately or aloud whether God or gods truly exist. You may find yourself in a space of deciding that the question and the answer are too daunting, and the answer doesn't matter. Or you may find yourself saying that you can't prove any of it and yet choose to stay (or return) because it's familiar or provides a sense of belonging and identity.

REMEMBER

All your decisions and questioning are valid and permissible.

PHILOSOPHIES, NOT RELIGIONS

Atheism, agnosticism, and humanism aren't religions. And while they engage religious themes and understandings, they're not forms of religious thought. The best way to explain or describe them is that they're philosophies. They take a stance on religion, and in some capacities they have practices and values, but they don't operate in the same manner as religions or religious systems.

Why would anyone think they're religions? Quite simply because of how they function and what their impact is. In other words, in the same way that people use faith and religion to provide clarity, answer big life questions, and, to some extent, determine their purpose, some atheists, agnostics, and humanists look to these philosophies for the same. Atheism, agnosticism, and humanism also provide for some a sense of community and identity and emphasize (at least in the case of humanism) some level of ethical and moralistic inspiration.

That's why atheism, agnosticism, and humanism can *feel* like a religion. And if you consider Paul Tillich's definition of faith as the state of being ultimately concerned, then humanism is probably the one more closely religious, or faith-based-leaning. But they're *not* religions, and they don't profess or even attempt to operate as such. They have no doctrine, hierarchal authoritative body, or sacred text.

Chapter 15

Deconstructing in Community

The faith deconstruction journey is best served when it's done in community. Why? Because it's a lonely experience, or at least it can be. Not only that, to borrow from Proverbs 27:17, iron sharpens iron. But you can't be in community with anyone and everyone.

Not only does community provide a level of safety and comfort, it facilitates. Community is like an incubator. The right community supports your processing, questioning, and, in certain respects, reconstruction. The wrong community, however, may lead to feelings of shame, doubt, and insecurity.

This chapter offers guidance on community gauging and building. You find out how to determine if the communities with which you're already affiliated are ideal for your faith deconstruction incubation. If you find they're not, you discover how to curate communities that are beneficial and fruitful for your journey.

Looking to Family and Friends for Support in Your Journey

I don't often have regrets. I shifted my perspective on regrets around the same time I stopped making New Year's resolutions. It's easy to wish something would have turned out differently or that you could have made a different choice or decision, but I view everything in life as an opportunity. I don't know what I don't know until I experience it. That's why regret no longer sits right with me.

I must admit, some moments during my faith deconstruction journey I looked back and thought to myself, "I wish I'd . . ." or "What would have happened if . . .?" Deconstructing in a community is one of those things.

I was listening to one of my favorite podcasts, *Holy Smokes: Cigars and Spirituality*, one afternoon on my way home from work when I first heard about deconstructing in community. Immediately, I began reflecting on my own journey and the idea of how beneficial it might have been if I'd done the same.

While I realize now that I'd been on a faith deconstruction journey for quite some time, I didn't admit publicly that I was deconstructing my faith until the spring of 2023. I wrote an essay about the changes in my faith as part of the Collegeville Institute's Emerging Writers Mentorship Program. Prior to then, I didn't know that the questioning and dissecting I'd been experiencing was deconstruction. Not only did I not have the words, I had no clue that others were doing the same questioning and dissecting I'd been doing.

As I shared in the essay, my placing deconstruction and faith together was informed by the cooking competition shows where contestants would deconstruct a beloved classic meal or dessert. I related to the idea of taking the same ingredients and creating something different. That's what I'd done with my faith and religious practices for years.

But I deconstructed alone, at least in the beginning. I was surrounded by people who were heavily involved in ministries of their own and, as I saw it, staunch in their beliefs and understandings. I wasn't bold enough to admit that my beliefs weren't the same or were changing.

In addition, I was insecure about what I was experiencing. Therefore, I didn't trust that the people who were supposed to be my village would embrace the person I was becoming and be willing to journey with me. I'd heard of what happened to others who'd questioned what they believed publicly, like Bishop Carlton Pearson. (See the nearby sidebar for more on Bishop Pearson.) When he began questioning the theology of salvation, the people who once affirmed him and supported him publicly shunned him and abandoned him. Even though I was young in ministry, the idea of being shunned scared me.

I didn't want to be labeled a heretic. I felt isolated and afraid. But I didn't have to be. Since I've progressed in my faith deconstruction journey, I've begun to realize that I had the community I needed. Don't make the same mistake I made. Part of the process of finding support in your deconstruction journey is talking about it with others, starting perhaps with your friends and family. Some may not understand. Others will and might be struggling with the same questions you are. You might not be as alone as you think.

WHO IS BISHOP CARLTON PEARSON?

On the back of his book *The Gospel of Inclusion: Reaching Beyond Religious Fundamentalism to the True Love of God and Self,* Bishop Carlton D. Pearson (1953–2023) is described as an independent spiritual leader and successful gospel recording artist. Describing him in such simple terms may be a disservice to his work and legacy. At the height of his ministry, he had one of the largest evangelical

(continued)

(continued)

churches and ministries in Oklahoma. He's believed to be the first or one of the first Black televangelists and ignited the careers of some of the world's most well-known preachers and gospel music recording artists thanks to the annual Azusa Conference he produced.

When he began to shift his teachings to a gospel of inclusion, supporting the LGBTQ+ community, believing that everyone is granted entry into heaven and that hell doesn't exist, he was labeled a heretic and shunned by the greater evangelical Pentecostal church movement. In 2018, Netflix released a movie on Pearson's life called *Come Sunday*. Later in life and ministry, he mentored young preachers and teachers of New Thought Christianity, inclusion, and deconstruction.

Are your friends a safe space?

I should have talked to my friends more about what I was going through. But that's the thing about religion and the power of indoctrination. It's like that scene in the movie *Mean Girls,* when Karen tells Regina George, "You can't sit with us" because Regina breaks one of their rules: wearing sweatpants on the wrong day of the week. Religious indoctrination, as discussed in Chapter 9, can be cultish in nature. If you stray from the practices and beliefs that are held in high regard by the community, you can begin to feel like an outsider.

REMEMBER

As discussed in Chapter 5, some parts of the world have literal laws, called *apostasy laws*, that make it illegal for you to abandon your faith and faith community. And, as discussed in Chapter 8, you can be completely excommunicated or disfellowshipped from your family and community for disagreeing with what's taught and for disagreeing openly.

Try not to take the resistance you receive from friends personal. It's conditioning. Part of the conditioning that isn't openly talked about is the fear incorporated with the unknown. It's why religion works so well. People believe what they want because they're afraid of the alternative. Obviously, no one wants to spend an eternity in hell or suffer for the choices they've made. Nor do they want to lose favor with God or take their chances because, as everyone's been taught, the alternative is almost unbearable. It wasn't just that I was afraid to admit my deconstruction. That was part of the reason. But I was afraid of being ridiculed, abandoned, and further isolated. It was easier to keep quiet so that I could hold on to the relationships I considered dear than to open up and find myself alone. Abandonment issues are real and powerful.

But if true belonging provides the opportunity to create safe spaces where difference can be embraced, honored, and celebrated, shouldn't friendships and relationships be the ideal locale for effective deconstruction?

TIP

How do you go about knowing if your friends are safe for your deconstruction? Look for signs. Relationship experts suggest that, overall, the healthiest relationships are built on:

>> Mutual respect

>> Trust

>> Openness

>> Authenticity

>> Commitment

>> Healthy boundaries

This list isn't exhaustive, but it's at least a starting point to help you consider whether the people you call friends, your village, your chosen family, or your community are capable of supporting you during your faith deconstruction. If you aren't having difficult conversations, you can't know if your friends are safe for your deconstruction. Experience is one of the best teachers.

If the only thing you talk about with one friend is related to their most recent dating escapades or lack thereof, maybe they aren't someone who feels comfortable talking about faith and religion. But if you have a friend you've had incredibly in-depth, transparent, respectful conversations with, they might be open to talks of faith deconstruction.

You won't know if you don't try.

What purpose does friendship play in your life? Why are your friends your friends? What value do they bring to you and your life experiences? Do they hold you accountable or blindly cheer you on? Are they only good for club or bar hopping, or are you visiting museums, seeing shows, and creating adventures with them? Do they only call you when they want to vent about someone, or do they randomly call you every now and again just because they were thinking of you?

REMEMBER

These are things to consider when discerning your friendships and assessing whether they're safe spaces. You don't have to journey through deconstruction alone. People in your life may be capable of journeying alongside you as you explore your faith.

Is family a safe space?

I was 45 years old before I built up the courage to express, in front of my mother, how my faith and thoughts about Jesus had changed since graduating seminary. As I've shared, I came to an understanding within myself that I saw through lines in all religions. I began to see the religions as related, almost like cousins. As a result, I begun leaning more toward an interfaith expression within my religious identity. I was afraid my mother wouldn't understand the shift in my beliefs. Don't get me wrong; my mother's faith is one of the things I admire most about her. I don't know anyone in this world whose faith is as defined and harnessed as hers. But I wasn't sure how she would respond to my deconstruction and reworking of my beliefs.

FORTY. FIVE.

In the same way that I was unsure how my friends would react if I admitted what I believed to them, I was afraid to do the same with certain members of my family. At that point, I'd only really shared my morphing religious beliefs and faith to one of my half-sisters on my father's side.

Families are important. They're the first introduction to the world and society that you experience, and, much of what you believe is informed by the community you're born into — especially your family. Families can be both predictable and unpredictable. And depending on the kind of environment you were born into, sometimes family is a safe space, and sometimes it isn't.

It's natural to want to have the approval of your loved ones. It's nice to be celebrated by members of your community or people you work closely with. But that doesn't compare to knowing you have your family's love and support. It helps you to know that they see you and respect you. There's nothing quite like it.

There's also nothing quite like that feeling when you know you've let your family down or disappointed them. When they've been the source of your identity and beliefs for much of your life, the fear of losing their love and support — or even being excommunicated like within the Jehovah's Witness community or the Mormon Church — is debilitating. So, of course, you're hesitant to let them into your deconstruction journey. The idea that their knowing could lead to them not accepting you or your journey is frightening.

Determining whether your family is a safe space for your deconstruction is hard. Sometimes it comes down to the kind of relationship you have with them. If you've had the kind of relationship where nothing is off limits, everything is on the table, they welcome your inquiries and are open to alternative perspectives on all things considered, they sound pretty safe. Maybe one member of your family has always created a welcoming environment for your questions and didn't avoid your whys when it mattered most. Perhaps you've witnessed a parent or loved one embark upon their own journey, which in turn inspired your questioning and research.

WARNING

But — and this isn't an exact science — some topics *may* be off limits, and you just hadn't reached the limit until now. If you've tried to have hard conversations before and they reacted in a way that left you hesitant, resistant, and uncertain, I'd advise you not to invite them into your faith deconstruction journey until you're more confident within yourself about who you're becoming and what you believe. Then again, you may be surprised.

TIP

If a member of your family is incapable of supporting you in your deconstruction, it may not be because they *can't* support you. Maybe they don't understand.

If I've learned anything in my faith walk, seminary training, and faith deconstruction, it's that everyone's relationship to faith is individual and experiential. Because their faith works for them, they may be incapable of considering that the same may not be true for you. Some view their faith as the most consistent and beneficial aspect of their lives. They don't know anything else. Their faith, as this book discussed in Chapter 4, helped them survive the darkest and scariest moments of their lives. It's all they know and, because of that, it's potentially impossible for them to hear their same faith isn't working for you. God has sustained them, and they believe that the same God can and will do the same for you.

Is your family a safe space for your deconstruction? The one way you can know is to try them. That may mean having a specific kind of conversation with members of your family about what you believe. It takes courage. Just as it may be worth testing the waters with certain friends to decipher if they're a safe space, the same is true for family. It may mean having the courage to simply admit it aloud and let the chips fall where they may.

DECONSTRUCTING WITH OR WITHOUT YOUR PARTNER

Deconstructing your faith may have some impact on other relationships in your life. This is especially true if you married, partnered, or in a committed relationship.

As you determine whether deconstructing your faith is the path for you to take, it is possible that deconstructing your faith may either strengthen your relationship or cause strain. As you discern, be sure to also discuss what you are feeling and how your beliefs are changing to your partner. In some instances, like mine and others I know, your spouse (or partner) may support your deconstruction. Your journey may motivate them to deconstruct. Or they may refuse to deconstruct, holding to what they believe while they support you in your process.

In Chapter 11, I include the testimony of someone who identifies as Catholic but is married to an atheist. Through communication and unconditional love, they have found space to be open with each other about their beliefs without feeling challenged or feeling the need to persuade the other to change.

It's also possible that your partner may be incapable of supporting your deconstruction. I cannot suggest to you what to do in that instance, but keeping communication open and seeking the support of couples' counseling may provide you and your partner with the guidance needed.

Finding Community Elsewhere

If you don't have your family and you don't have your friends, where can you turn for support during your faith deconstruction? Don't fret. All hope is not lost. When I began my deconstruction journey, I did so quietly and privately. While part of my choice was informed by fear and anxiety, the other truth is that I didn't know where to turn.

I didn't even know what to call what I was doing.

But that was a different time. Due to the "popularity" of the topic, more spaces are available to you in your process and journey. Countless resources and options are available now. From online communities and professional deconstruction coaches to therapists who specialize in religious trauma, the options and resources are vast.

Chapter 17 focuses more on the role therapy can play in your faith deconstruction journey. In this section, I offer insight into determining whether the communities currently available are fitting for you and will list a few of them I've come across in my journey and research. This section also provides guidance and considerations for you as you seek out the community that fits you most effectively.

COMMUNITY ACCORDING TO BELL HOOKS

If you've never heard of bell hooks, you should look her up. bell hooks (1952–2021) is one of the foremost voices in American history and literature. Born Gloria Jean Watkins, she chose the name bell hooks in honor of her maternal great-grandmother, Bell Blair Hooks. Writing her name in lowercase was also a choice, intentionally intended to place the focus on the work and the messages within the work. She desired to center and highlight the experiences of the often neglected, oppressed, overlooked, and ignored in her writing.

Over the course of her career, the Black feminist, author, activist, and educator wrote somewhere near 40 books and countless scholarly articles. Each of them centered on issues pertaining to race, class, and gender. Many of her books are collections of essays and poems, but she also wrote five children's books. *All About Love: New Visions,* which was released in the fall of 1999, is arguably her most popular, beloved, and well-known collection of work.

In her book *Belonging: A Culture of Place,* hooks reflects on her upbringing in Kentucky and the lessons — both implicit and explicit — that have informed her life, her work, and her identity. Within the pages, made up of a series of essays that are one-part autobiographical and one-part cultural critical analysis, she weaves memory and revelation, moving between past and present. At the core of the book's message is the importance and power of community and belonging.

For hooks, belonging isn't just about the places you might connect to, the space(s) that you've chosen or that have meaning for you. It's also about the people within those communities. There's a spatial as well as spiritual connection to community and belonging. She believes these spaces and people are necessary for the mind, body, and soul to survive and excel. I couldn't agree with her more. While hooks isn't speaking specifically about faith deconstruction, there are parallels.

What to look for in community

What should you be looking for as you explore communities of support? It really depends on what you think you need. You may be looking for a space where you can get answers to your most basic questions (but hopefully you will find that in this book). You may be looking for a space to hear more closely what others have experienced in their deconstruction journey. Perhaps you're looking for a space where you can be exposed to thoughts and perspectives you hadn't already considered. Or a space where you don't know what you want or need, but you're open and willing. All of these wants, needs, and desires are valid.

I realized that what I wanted wasn't what I needed. Or, more precisely, what I needed wasn't exactly what I wanted. If I'm being honest, I didn't know what I wanted. But what I needed was a space where I could freely observe, process, and ponder. I needed a space where, when I had questions, I could ask them without fear of being chastised or made to feel ignorant and unaware. What I needed was a space for conversation and inquiry. What I wanted was a space to be affirmed, but not necessarily in the most mature or emotionally healthy way.

What I didn't want was a space where I could or would be challenged. I didn't feel as though I was ready for that. But that wouldn't have been the most effective environment for me to deconstruct within. I needed to be challenged, carefully and methodically of course, but I didn't want to be. As a result, I was looking for something soft to land, but that wasn't what I needed.

When looking for a community for your faith deconstruction, it's easier to determine what to look for when you have an idea of what you *aren't* looking for. The journey itself is unpredictable. You don't know what you don't know. But you may be able to determine what you need by determining what isn't a priority for you. Does this space affirm and challenge you? Does the space cause you to think and consider beyond what's most comfortable and familiar for you? Does the space stretch you and truly cause you to think about your whys? Are you made better because of the community you've found? These are the questions worth asking as you discern the best fit.

Exploring existing communities

As I've shared openly, my foray into deconstruction was clumsy. I didn't have the language, knowledge, awareness, or where-withal I needed to navigate it early on. Thankfully, I've been lucky enough to connect with impressive people doing the work of faith deconstruction in recent years. Much of what I know and believe now has been informed by conversations I've had with them or interactions with the content they've created. One of the things I appreciate most is their commitment to creating communities and resources for others.

In this section I include a few suggestions for communities worth exploring. Some I've engaged with personally and bene-fitted from them. Others I've come across in my own research but not explored personally. Take these suggestions with a grain of salt. This list isn't exhaustive or all-encompassing. But it provides a pinch of examples for you to research for yourself. These are simply suggestions worth considering as you search for yourself.

Unfit Christian is a digital faith community focused on "disman-tling the Christian Evangelical legacy of anti-Blackness, misog-yny, and colonialism" in spiritual practices and routines. It was founded by the best-selling author of *The Day God Saw Me as Black*, public theologian, and content creator Danyelle Thomas. In addition to the website, unfitchristian.com, it has an active, members-only Facebook group.

The Faith Community (as mentioned in Chapter 8) is led by the virtual community's founder and lead pastor, Kristian A. Smith. It's an intentional community, centered in the Black Church tra-dition (Baptist/Pentecostal), committed to supporting those who are unchurched or under-churched, and welcoming of all people from diverse backgrounds. Through its work, which extends beyond TFC into other initiatives like the *Holy Smokes: Cigars and Spirituality* podcast and their active, members-only Facebook group, it challenges damaging theology and religious indoctrination.

As they were seeking to discern their own deconstruction path, the creators of *The Sophia Society* decided to create a space where others who were journeying through deconstruction could find a safe space to engage their own queries. They founded a website, created a blog, developed the *Holy Heretics: Losing Religion and Finding Jesus* podcast, and published an e-book, *Deconstruction 101*. Their purpose is to support those deconstructing in finding new pathways to spiritual awareness.

Reclamation Collective is a 501c3 organization committed to survivors of religious trauma and spiritual abuse. They're also a virtual community and host support groups for "those navigating deconstruction and reclamation." In addition, they host workshops and house a database on their website, reclamation collective.com, where you can find a therapist in your area.

Created by Sarey Martin Concepcion and Dan Koch, *So You're Deconstructing* acts as a virtual one-stop shop for anyone deconstructing. Koch hosts the *You Have Permission* podcast, and Concepcion is a filmmaker and entrepreneur who cofounded TidyCo Creative. Visitors to the site can also find therapists in their area, information on yearly events, like the Wild Goose Festival, and a listing of other online deconstructing communities. I've never attended the Wild Goose Festival, but I know people who have attended and benefited from their experience. A four-day festival hosted in Harmony, North Carolina, the event incorporates "music, art, and justice," creating a space for inquirers, thinkers, artists, and activists to gather, connect, and build community.

Building and Curating a Community

It's possible that none of the communities mentioned in this chapter or others that you may find are the best fit for you. That's okay. Not all spaces are created equally, and due to the beauty of diversity in the world, every space can't meet every need. While groups generally attempt to be safe spaces for all, each of them is also fully aware that they have limits and can't speak to the lived experiences of all. It's also not lost on me that most of the communities I've mentioned lean heavily toward those deconstructing Christian evangelicalism and fundamentalism. Again, the faith deconstruction journey is individual and unique, and faith deconstruction isn't exclusive to Christianity.

If you can't find a community that's a good fit for you, it may be worth curating the kind of community you need, want, and desire. Sometimes creating your own is better.

TIP

One way to build and curate a community is to collect conversation partners. It takes having authentic conversations with people whom you trust. It's important to have people around you that you feel comfortable enough to be vulnerable with about what you're thinking, experiencing, and processing. You might be surprised to find out that they have the same questions you do.

How do you find these people? You may already have a community and not even know it.

Some people I've found as I've engaged other communities, and others I was affiliated with in the ministries I was involved with. Some came to me through other people; others I met randomly here and there, and we stuck to each other. Some may have commented on something I shared or responded to a comment I made on something on social media. The possibilities are endless. But it also took me letting down my guard. I had to be willing to share my thoughts more deeply to build community.

REMEMBER

Mine isn't an exact blueprint. As I've stated before, deconstruction is unique to everyone. But finding and curating communities should be both intentional and organic. There's a level of intention involved, but once the initial connection is made, it's like dating — it takes time. You're aligning yourself with people who will become your greatest advocates, conversation partners, and journeyers. Iron sharpens iron.

Some Important Takeaways Regarding Deconstruction and Community

Your community doesn't have to be made up of people just like you. They don't have to think like you, see the world exactly as you see it, or even completely agree with you. But they do have to be a safe space for you.

As you're exploring communities, don't be quick to jump on the first one you find. Again, treat it like dating. Spend a little time. Feel it out. Test it. You may realize that it's not the one for you, but you've become so invested that you're either disappointed or find it hard to break away from. I made this mistake many times during my days seeking a church community. I'd find a church to visit, and after the second or third visit I'd walk to the altar during the invitation to join their membership. I allowed my emotions to get the best of me.

I became so addicted to the "feel good" of the space that I wasn't efficiently discerning whether it was the right fit for me. But after that third or fourth visit, it never failed — I'd become heartbroken by something someone did or said from the pulpit. Usually, it was one of those fire and brimstone, anti-gay rants during the alleged preaching moment. Each time I felt defeated. Each time that would be my last day in attendance and, unfortunately, no one ever reached out to figure out what happened and why I didn't return.

Other things to keep in mind when finding or building your community:

>> **You don't have to be connected to just one community.** You're allowed to be connected to as many communities as you see fit. Just don't spread yourself too thin.

>> **Be curious and courageous.** Trust your experience and your perspective but be open and inquisitive.

>> **Take your time.** Your time and energy are valuable.

>> **The choice is yours.** Don't allow anyone to convince you otherwise.

>> **You have a voice.** Use it with confidence.

>> **Be honest with yourself and those you're in community with.** Be transparent with the people you love and be honest with yourself in the process.

Deconstructing takes courage. It also takes being calculated, emotionally mature, and patient with yourself. But it's your journey and up to you to get the most out of the process. So, get what you need and make it worth it.

5

Things to Consider When Consider When Deconstructing

Chapter **16**

The Personal Toll of Deconstruction

I've soaked up a lot of content regarding faith deconstruction: a few books, a couple essays via blogs, several podcasts, and countless social media reels. Yes, I've gone down the rabbit hole. What's been crystal clear from all the content I've digested is that loss is a big part of the deconstruction experience. Just about every personal story I've come across has involved some level of personal loss. As they've done the work of unlearning and relearning, the deconstructionists have personally lost something, from friendships to romantic or legal relationships, to employment, and even lifelong dreams. Every story has included some portrayal of the personal toll of faith deconstruction.

You can find countless stories of preachers, pastors, and other faith leaders who, after they began shifting their theology publicly — especially from the pulpit — had church member-ships suffer. You can read about Bishop Carlton Pearson in Chapter 15 and Bishop D. E. Paulk in Chapter 11 as just two examples.

Even I have some anxiety about this book because of my own fears about deconstructing and what I could lose. But the reality is, there will be losses. And that's okay.

This chapter highlights what I consider to be some of the challenges of deconstruction: from loneliness, to struggles finding community, to facing the questions and challenges from others as you deconstruct. The journey has associated costs. My hope is that this chapter will provide not only an inkling of what to expect, but some solace for the decision you're making to deconstruct. Deconstruction may be difficult, but it's not debilitating.

Deconstruction Loneliness

In 2023, the United States Surgeon General Dr. Vivek Murphy labeled loneliness an epidemic. In his advisory titled "Our Epidemic of Loneliness and Isolation," he declared that loneliness is also a major public health issue. At the time, many people credited the issue with the coronavirus pandemic. But Dr. Murphy pointed out that loneliness had plagued society for much longer than the pandemic.

The Harvard University Graduate School of Education took a cue from the surgeon general and did their own research. As part of their Making Caring Common project, in 2024, they released "Loneliness in America: Just the Tip of the Iceberg?" What they found is that many Americans between the ages of 30 and 60 were lonely, with many of them between the ages of 30 and 44 reporting that they felt lonely always or frequently.

What were some of the causes of their loneliness?

>> Technology

>> Insufficient time with family

>> Overworked or too busy

>> Mental health challenges

>> Living in an individualistic society

REMEMBER

There was another reason I was relieved to see in the report. About half of those who participated in the research project reported that their loneliness was due to a lack of a religious or spiritual life. Faith and faith communities are a large part of the human identity. And, as discussed in Chapters 4 and 5, many people's first meaningful communities — beyond their families growing up — were churches or faith communities/institutions.

When I saw faith, or the lack thereof, listed as a reason and cause for loneliness, I wasn't surprised. I would almost assume that faith deconstruction has something to do with their feeling of absence. It may be a stretch to suggest that this is the case for each respondent. But I would bet a few of them, if not half, have had some experience with faith deconstruction. It's impossible to know. But I think it's worth considering that deconstruction has had a role in people's feelings of lack and, as a result, their loneliness.

If people feel lack, it may be because a faith or spiritual life once existed for them. How else would they miss it, and how else would they be feeling lonely? At some point, they had an active religious and spiritual life, but that changed. Now that it's missing, they feel alone. Maybe it's missing because they deconstructed.

WARNING

The faith deconstruction experience is a lot like losing a loved one.

Human beings are said to be hardwired for connection. People are meant to be in relationship and community with each other. That's why it's easy to understand why loneliness (or feeling alone) is so debilitating. Sounds a lot like Maslow's hierarchy of needs (explained in the nearby sidebar).

Many do all they can to avoid any form of loneliness if they can help it. It's why so many chase after love and relationships. It's why people stay connected to family members and loved ones who are toxic and no good to be around. And it's why some retain their affiliation and memberships at religious spaces that are damaging or hold on to traditions that are harmful and limiting.

MASLOW'S HIERARCHY OF NEEDS

Ever heard of the concept, Maslow's hierarchy of needs? Developed by psychologist Abraham Maslow, the hierarchy of needs situated the needs of human beings into five levels, or a five-level pyramid. At the top of the pyramid is self-actualization, but to get there the other levels must be met.

At the bottom are physiological needs. These are the basic needs for survival: food, water, rest. The second level is safety. When physiological needs are met, one seeks security and stability. From there, one desires love and belonging. This is where social connection becomes a priority: friendships, intimacy, and so on. This is followed by the fourth level — esteem needs. Status, a sense of accomplishment, and recognition becomes the focus in the esteem level. And finally, at the top, is self-actualization. This level is where one becomes the best possible version of oneself. Here, you realize your full potential — creatively and/or personally.

It can be scary to let go, not knowing what will happen when you lose access to the spaces you once viewed as sacred. There's a fear you'll lose the connections that define your community, belonging, and purpose. It's debilitating to consider it. I experienced loneliness in my deconstruction because I felt like I was the sole survivor of a crash on a deserted island. I wanted space to be my authentic self in my identity and beliefs, but I didn't see anyone else on the island with me. Or I thought I was alone on the island, not realizing there may have been civilization on the other side.

So, how do you deal with the loneliness? Finding or curating communities is one way, as Chapter 15 discusses. Or, as I cover in Chapter 17, you can seek therapy or spiritual direction or even deconstruction coaching.

TIP

What's most important is understanding that you aren't as alone as you think. (Look at Chapter 11 if you haven't already.) Also know that feeling alone shouldn't hold you back from doing the necessary work of defining for yourself who you are and what you believe.

When finding community is challenging

In Chapter 15, I discuss how to curate community when it's difficult to find one that already exists. Here, I want to delve deeper into the challenge of finding community. There were moments I jumped from space to space in an effort to find the "right fit." Over time, I've realized that finding the right fit isn't always possible. No one is perfect, and the same is true for most communities and institutions.

The following list features a few communities and outlets that I've found particularly helpful over the years and that you may want to check out as well:

>> One of the things I appreciate most about online spaces like **Unfit Christian** and **The Faith Community** (highlighted in Chapter 15) is the maturity and humility present there. Differences are handled with grace, fairness, and maturity. People aren't tossing around insults or throwing fits because of disagreements or unintended offenses. The few times I have engaged both, I have appreciated the openness and thoughtfulness each member and the curators of the space have brought to the conversations and debates.

Occasionally, you might witness a moment or two of someone getting sassy in a response, but for the most part, the environment is curated so well that each participant understands their responsibility in the space.

>> *Holy Smokes: Cigars and Spirituality* **podcast** is another outlet that has become helpful to me in my deconstruction journey. At the beginning of every episode that I've listened to, they recite their one rule: Honor each person's lived experiences, and don't uplift theory over what someone has lived. They also point out that kindness is key. They've set a tone that's informed by the Greatest Commandment Theology discussed in Chapter 8. Setting that tone has helped to ensure that their space is healthy, mature, and effective.

>> *Honoring the Journey* **podcast**, hosted by Leslie Nease (highlighted in Chapter 9), is another space that has been helpful to me in my deconstruction journey as of late. Hearing the stories of others that have deconstructed their

faith, and the causes of their journeys has been revelatory. There's been a lot of common ground between my own experiences of questioning what I believe and what others have experienced as well. Hearing the stories of others has also helped me to feel as if I'm not so alone in this journey.

But honestly, much of what I've learned about faith deconstruction I've experienced by my own questioning, seeking, and dissecting.

REMEMBER

You may not find the kind of community you're seeking, and I'd be remiss if I didn't take some time to address that possibility. My hope is that you'll find somewhere to engage or support you as you deconstruct. But if you don't, it may impact how you work through your deconstruction.

TIP

What has helped me is engaging more than one space when necessary, including the ones mentioned above.

Growing up in religious communities, I was conditioned to believe that my membership in those spaces (in other words, churches) was exclusive. In other words, if I was a member of a church, I was only allowed to be a member of that church and that church alone. Over time, as I moved from congregation to congregation during my many years of discerning, I came up against people's commentary over my actions. I didn't just face this in traditional religious spaces. When I left communities that identified as "affirming," some members and leaders made me feel as though I'd abandoned them or was no longer welcome in their space because I left and joined another one.

My perspective around membership changed because of a dear friend, Billy Michael Honor, who had a concept of ministry partnership when he was pastoring. He believed that people weren't members of church, but partners in ministry. Therefore, the church he led at the time didn't have members — or that's how I understood it. The idea that churches didn't have a monopoly on the people began my process of rethinking church membership. That rethinking, along with what was a fledgling interfaith interest at the time, helped me process the freedom that everyone has in engaging more than one space for emotional, mental, and spiritual nourishment.

Engaging with more than one space may be useful in helping you navigate your deconstruction journey. For example:

» Listen to podcasts on the topic from *Holy Smokes* to *Honoring the Journey* with Leslie Nease to *The Progressive Christian Podcast.*

» Prioritize your health and well-being (discussed in Chapter 17).

» Don't sit in the funk and loneliness of faith deconstruction alone. Finding a therapist, spiritual director, or deconstruction coach can also provide the personal and emotional connection you're craving during deconstruction.

Be good to yourself. Kindness isn't only key when engaging with others. It's also key when prioritizing yourself. Be kind and patient with yourself throughout this process.

How others filled the void

I lost my father in the fall of 2021 when he was 88 years old. After he transitioned, I thought a lot about his life and how the world had changed before his eyes. I thought about all he witnessed. I thought about the moments in history he lived through. And I thought about how, at that time, he had no way of knowing the impact those moments would have on society. The day I realized my father was in his early 20s when Emmett Till was assassinated was a sobering moment for me.

Reflecting on my father's life, I was reminded of the power of resiliency, which is one of the few things I find myself in awe of about other people. Anyone's ability to face a moment and find the power and strength to overcome it is impressive. And through those challenges, some of the greatest inventions are birthed. I don't mean inventions in the sense of devices, but in the sense of creation. I think about how enslaved Africans survived by taking scraps and creating soul food. I think about how indigenous communities looked at the land and sought to create a legacy from it. I think about the creation of the blues from hardship.

Resilience is how you overcome. It's how you fill voids.

You must be resilient to survive faith deconstruction. Real wounds are associated with feeling abandoned. Abandonment creates scars of loneliness that are hard to overcome and make it hard to trust again. That's partly why issues like church hurt are so difficult. When seeking safe spaces, people look for specific signs. When they don't find those signs, they're hesitant. It's natural to look for some form of homogeneity in new spaces when you've left your sacred community due to deconstruction.

There's nothing wrong with seeking like-mindedness. The problem comes when you're unreasonably looking for exactness. Try to connect to people with differing views and perspectives.

As discussed in Chapter 9, some communities are created as a means of filling the void left or felt from the losses experienced in faith deconstruction. I think of the movement of affirming ministries, discussed in Chapter 7, and how they were formed as a means of overcoming the discrimination that members of the LGBTQ+ community felt. They followed in the footsteps of the "Black Church," born from the discrimination that enslaved and formerly enslaved Africans faced from mainstream, white, Christian churches. Today, some are creating communities, like The Faith Community and Unfit Christian, as a means of filling the void left by faith deconstruction.

And then there are others, like Rachel Mulgrave, discussed in Chapter 11. After deciding to continue her relationship to Christianity, she created space for the churched and unchurched, believers and nonbelievers, to gather in a local brewery and challenge assumptions, question, and be open. The effort is called Pints and Parables and is an extension of some of her previous deconstruction work following undergrad.

Filling the void is different for everyone. While some fill that void by creating new spaces and communities, others do something totally different. They create podcasts or go into social media content creation as a means of helping others or to test their curiosities. All in all, filling the void means being resilient, calculated, and thinking strategically.

One thing you don't want to do in faith deconstruction is create community out of desperation. The outcomes are never good or healthy for anyone.

Bracing for Others' Questions/ Lack of Understanding

If there's one thing I've learned in my own faith journey, it's this: You're allowed to believe whatever you want or need to believe. Possessing perspectives different from others isn't all bad. Yes, society has shared views, as it should. But turmoil results because of homogeneity and people being hellbent on forcing others to believe and live exactly as they think they should. Whatever happened to life, liberty, and the pursuit of happiness?

It's taken me a long time to get to this point, but experience is often a good teacher. As I advanced in my own faith deconstruction journey, I began to realize that I couldn't care less what someone believes unless it impedes on me and my life. Unfortunately, everyone wants to be right today, and if you disagree with them or think different than they do, you're wrong. That's a regular occurrence in the faith deconstruction journey.

The following section offers some insight and suggestions for how you can deal with others when deconstructing. Some who don't understand will question you. The more religious and conservative ones will suggest things and maybe even offer warnings. And at times people will say you're flat-out wrong. All that is to be expected.

Be patient: They're learning

I still remember the time that someone I loved dearly told me that they didn't believe my prayers made it to heaven. It was one of the most hurtful things someone has ever said to me. I harbored negative emotions for them for a long time afterward. Eventually, however, I let the negativity go. This person didn't know any better.

Their faith is all that some know and all they have. And because they believe it's working for them, they believe the same will and should be true for you.

Those who believe in it want to go to heaven. And because of what they've been taught about heaven and hell, discussed in Chapter 9, their reaction to your deconstruction can be rooted in selfishness. Not only do *they* want to go to heaven, they want *you* to be there with them. They can't imagine anything else. Your deciding to deconstruct, which is also rooted in their lack of knowledge about it, creates space for the possibility that you won't be granted the same reward as they'll be given. They mean well, but it's presumptuous.

TIP

Something I try to do whenever I encounter someone who's resistant to deconstruction is meet them with grace. You bought this book because you had questions. Those around you are as unaware, as ignorant, and as blind as you once were. Just because you've "seen the light" doesn't mean they have. It's worth being patient and gracious with them.

They may come around, or they may not. They may agree with your deconstruction, or they may not. Maybe they've never felt the need to question the things you're now questioning. What you're doing is as scary for them as it is for you. Whether they do or don't agree with it is a moot point, however. Yes, you want the people you love to be on the same page as you. Yes, you want them to embrace, accept, love, and support you. But it's possible that they won't. It's up to you to decipher how much their understanding or even acceptance matters to you.

Building confidence in deconstruction

I wasted a good amount of time struggling in my deconstruction with fear and doubt. If I'm being honest, I still do. I've had this ongoing question in the back of my mind even before I became aware of my deconstruction: What if I've been wrong about all of it? It's entirely possible that everything I know, believe, and say about God, faith, the church, Jesus, and the Bible is wrong.

So, how do you build confidence in deconstruction if all of it could be wrong? That depends on what you believe about faith and religion. What is their purpose and authority in your life? Are you deconstructing because you want to be right or proven right?

Or are you deconstructing because you're on a quest for clarity, understanding, and greater awareness of who you are and what you believe?

As discussed in Chapters 6 and 8, one of the many problems with religion is how it can rob you of your faith. The mysteries of God — if God is something you believe in — are intended to be just that: mysteries. Religion shouldn't steal your ability to imagine. It shouldn't have so many rules, restrictions, and hindrances to living. Religion isn't interested in mystery — not in the way that you've probably come to experience it in your life. And this isn't just true of conservative and fundamentalist religious spaces. Even some of the more liberal and progressive religious spaces have leaned into areas of problematic and toxic religion and religious practices.

Faith, at its core, is a heart thing. It affords access to freedom if you truly want it. Faith has no concrete answers but a genuine query, curiosity, and seeking. Faith deconstruction itself is a confidence-building exercise because it gives you courage to question and investigate, with the enjoyment and fulfillment of exploration. But this only happens when you're clear about your why.

MORE ABOUT THE GOSPEL OF INCLUSION

The gospel of inclusion concept was made popular by the late Bishop Carlton D. Pearson in his book *The Gospel of Inclusion: Reaching Beyond Religious Fundamentalism to the True Love of Self and God*. In the simplest of explanations and descriptions, the gospel of inclusions explores that everyone is granted access to heaven through Jesus, regardless of who they are, how they live and identify, and what they believe. This is also understood as universal salvation. The argument is that many of the ills of society are due, in large part, to religious dogma, which does more harm than good to society.

(continued)

(continued)

Many critics of Pearson's assertion have denounced his work. They argue that not only was Pearson suggesting that heaven is available to everyone, but his argument completely negates the existence of hell. They also believe that the gospel of inclusion waters down Jesus, almost placing the gods of other faiths on equal standing with Jesus. They believe and see Jesus as the one true and all-powerful God.

The gospel of inclusion is foundational to many faith deconstructionists and affirming ministry leaders. It lays the foundation for spaces where those often overlooked or considered to be outcast can see themselves as part of God's great design and beloved community.

Chapter **17**

Deconstruction and Mental Health

've actively been in some form of therapeutic support for much of my adult life. My first experience with therapy was as a preteen. It wasn't under the best circumstances, and the therapist at the time wasn't very effective. I still remember him falling asleep a few times during our sessions. That experience set the tone for me and therapy. Even though, looking back, I'm fully aware of the moments when therapy would have benefited me, that initial encounter at a young age hindered me from seeing the benefit.

But during my last year of undergraduate study at Kennesaw State University, a professor suggested I visit the school's counseling center. Eventually, I took his advice, and I'm glad I did. What was supposed to be only a few sessions over a few weeks turned into a yearlong relationship with a therapist who set me on a path of self-awareness and personal healing. She saved me.

Therapy, in general, is good practice. Everyone needs an ally, someone to assist in life's challenges. Therapy provides support, accountability, and safety. It helps you become the best you can be, at least emotionally and mentally. When it comes to faith deconstruction, therapists become the ideal community partners. They offer perspective, neutrality, and the stability needed as you process, shift, and shed. Therapy helps you keep your mind and emotions in order. But it's not the only tool or outlet available to you in your faith deconstruction journey. Spiritual direction is another useful tool that can help you find direction and clarity as you deconstruct.

This chapter points out some of the benefits to therapy while deconstructing. It also engages spiritual direction as an option to be used in tandem or apart from therapy. Finally, the chapter covers a little about the fast-growing enterprise of deconstruction coaching and how it can be useful to deconstruction.

Therapy and Deconstruction

Yes, I know. For some of you, therapy is a taboo topic. If you grew up in a conservative, evangelical, or fundamentalist Christian space, therapy was likely forbidden or at least looked down upon. Therapy has gotten a bad rap.

Even seeking therapy is sometimes looked at as an indictment of your faith. If you're seeking therapy, you might be led to believe that your faith is weak or that you've given up on God. You've heard the narratives:

>> Depression is an evil spirit that can only be eradicated with prayer.

>> Depression, loneliness, and sadness are the trick of the enemy.

>> You don't need therapy. You just need to get on your knees and petition God.

>> You're not sad; you're distracted.

>> The enemy just wants to throw you off track and keep you from fulfilling your purpose.

>> All you need is Psalm 121:1–2, "I will lift up mine eyes unto the hills, from whence cometh my help. My help cometh from the LORD, which made heaven and earth . . ."

Believe you me, I've heard them all or know someone who has.

Maybe you're afraid of the idea of telling a stranger your business. Maybe you're afraid of letting someone you don't know into the deepest and darkest crevices of your mind, heart, and soul. The idea of being transparent and vulnerable with someone you don't know and the repercussions of those actions is dauting and debilitating. It's all too much for you. Several people in my life aren't open to the idea of therapy. The very idea of it is too much for them to handle.

But therapy isn't as bad or scary as some imagine it to be. Now, there are some bad therapists out there, and therapy is a lot of work, but the benefits truly outweigh the downsides. When deconstructing, therapy can serve as the additional support you need when asking questions, changing your mind, and rethinking your relationship to the communities that were once integral to your identity. The following section highlights the role therapy plays in deconstruction and how it can be a much needed and beneficial outlet.

Brief overview of therapy

I'm convinced that much of the reason people are hesitant to partake in therapy is because they don't truly understand what therapy is and what its benefits are. Most people are informed by what they assume or what they've been told about it from others who have never had a therapist. And, again, there's the taboo of it.

Maybe when you think of therapy, you immediately imagine what you've seen on television and movies: the stereotypical office, with light and dark brown décor, a couch on one end, flanked by end tables and a lamp and bookshelves around the room. In front of the couch is one lone chair where the therapist sits. You, the patient, lie across the couch on your back and have one hand rubbing your forehead. You're talking to the therapist with despair in your voice, going on and on and on about life, how difficult it is, and your struggles to understand the point and purpose of it all.

>> What's my purpose in life?

>> What is all this for?

>> Am I wasting my time?

>> Why am I still single?

>> Why can't I find that perfect job?

Blah blah blah. In your mind, it's all very dramatic, but also very real.

There's a bit of truth to the stereotype. Therapy offices usually do have a couch and a chair. The show *Couples Therapy* has some validity to it. The therapist is sitting in the chair, jotting notes in their yellow notepad. They're listening, nodding a few times, and every now and again asking, "What do you think that means?" Or "How does that make you feel?" I've had a few experiences like this one. But it's not as dramatic as media portrays it to be. And thanks to modern technology and the pandemic, many therapists have abandoned the office space or even home office and are set up for virtual sessions. Tools like telehealth, doxy.me, and other versions of video conferencing have become more frequent and accessible.

So then, what is therapy, and what can you expect from it? What should you get out of the practice of regularly seeing a therapist and having check-ins? From a clinical perspective, *therapy* is medical treatment designed to help someone overcome a medical issue, illness, or disorder. Most therapy is informed by scientific research and methods, requires that the practitioner be licensed and trained, and involves providing strategies and developing goals. Therapy isn't necessarily focused solely on healing, but more on coping and learning.

Most partakers of therapy are looking for support to address one or a few to the following:

- Stress
- Anxiety
- Depression
- Grief
- Alcoholism
- Sexual abuse
- Physical abuse
- Verbal abuse
- Eating disorders
- Mental illness

When you hear the word *therapy*, you might assume that it's referring to talk therapy or psychotherapy, especially as it pertains to mental health. But therapy can take many forms. That's why it's important to point out specifically what kind of therapy you're referring to. Even within the more specific cognitive or psychotherapy are different forms. I won't go to deep in the woods about them, but they include:

- Cognitive behavioral therapy
- Dialectical behavior therapy
- Emotion-focused therapy
- Play therapy
- Group therapy
- Family therapy

A professional executes each of these forms of psychotherapy. BetterHelp.com lists several types of therapists:

- Counselors
- Social workers
- Psychologists
- Psychiatrists

At the core of talk therapy is talking, which is what makes most people uncomfortable. People don't like talking about their feelings or emotions. But therapy involves more than just talking. It's also about learning and processing and evaluating, all of which apply to deconstruction as well.

Therapy only works if you are committed and invested in the process. That means being vulnerable and honest about what you are dealing with and open to getting the help you desire.

Benefits of therapy in faith deconstruction

In her book *Spiritual Formation and Mental Health*, Melanie Miller, LPC, writes, "Our mental and emotional well-being directly influence our ability to make informed choices, discern biases, and navigate the complexities of our beliefs." This is why outlets, like talk therapy, are beneficial to the faith deconstruction journey. By having a licensed therapist as part of your community during the faith deconstruction journey, you're ensuring the strength of your mental health and well-being. As a result, you're better equipped to handle and face the difficulties and challenges you may encounter in your process.

Mental health isn't just about having joy, harnessing fulfilment, creating coping mechanisms that are avoidance tactics in disguise, and medicating yourself just to get by. Mental health ensures that your decision-making is strong, your awareness of yourself and doubts and triggers is developed, and you approach life (which includes deconstruction) as effectively as possible. Investing in your mental health, especially during deconstruction, ensures that you're better able to think clearly, process more effectively, and discern more clearly. As I've shared throughout this project, at times I've had to hold myself accountable as I deconstructed. Sometimes old biases presented themselves in the most unexpected and inopportune times.

During my most recent studies, there was a moment I didn't allow myself to be open to the experience. A friend invited me to a community grief ceremony being held by a group she's heavily involved with. As they began with some of their

Yoruba-informed rituals, I felt uncomfortable and uncertain. Eventually, I shut myself off from the entire experience and began, internally, judging. In an instant, my old religious baggage regarding African Spiritual practices reared its ugly head. But if not for the work I'd done in therapy to be mindful, I wouldn't have been able to course-correct. Once I realized what I was doing, which didn't take long, I was able to authentically be in the space and learn what I could about their practices and beliefs. It was one of the most enlightening and informative experiences that influenced a good amount of my research on grief at the time.

REMEMBER

You'll potentially meet similar moments. There can be and will be times when you believe you've advanced in your thinking and understanding only to realize that some of the unconscious biases are still within you. It's a trigger. But through therapy and forms of mental health care like it, you can better manage the trigger and govern yourself more effectively.

Therapy is a useful and helpful companion to deconstruction. It doesn't remove you from doing the work, but it does provide the tools, awareness, and maturity you need to effectively move through your journey as healthfully and intentionally as possible. One thing I've learned in my journey is that it takes courage and effort. Making psychotherapy a priority in your faith deconstruction only makes the deconstruction journey better.

Therapy and Spiritual Direction

If memory serves me correctly, my earliest recollection of spiritual direction as a practice was either during the summer of 2014 or 2015. I was working for a small seminary at the time that was either developing a certificate program or had recently launched the program. Initially, I related spiritual direction more closely to some other kind of therapy. But as I learned more about it, I remember almost discrediting the practice. Even though I considered myself to be liberal in my worldview and faith, part of me was still arrogantly Christian. In other words, spiritual direction felt spooky, almost hippie in nature to me. Because of that, I found it difficult to embrace.

But again, initially, I saw spiritual direction as another form of therapy. I assumed spiritual directors were like therapists or counselors. I didn't understand the nuanced differences between the two. I was so oblivious that I sought out a Christian therapist at one point to assist me in making some sense of where God was leading me in my life. I went into the experience thinking I had a grasp on the practice of spiritual direction, but I realized quickly I was way off. And I paid a price for my confusion. Hiring that Christian therapist was a big mistake. She spent more time trying to save my soul after learning of my identity as same-gender-loving. I didn't make it past three sessions with her.

TIP

As you seek out a therapist or even spiritual director, it's paramount that you have some idea of what their doctrinal beliefs are. Don't be like me and waste your time with someone who has a false sense of purpose and agenda. It's important to get an idea of what they believe because it's possible their beliefs may impact how they show up for you in your search for care.

This section provides greater insight into spiritual direction, based somewhat on what I've learned about the practice over the years. I point out the differences between therapy and spiritual direction and highlight the benefits of spiritual direction in faith deconstruction.

Brief overview of spiritual direction

Just about every person I know who has partaken in spiritual direction has the same thing to say about it: Spiritual direction not only changed their lives but provided clarity. Through spiritual direction, all report, they have a better understanding of themselves, their relationship to God, and their overall life purpose and direction. Each of them has shared with me that spiritual direction brought everything that happened in their past into view more succinctly. Things began to make better sense.

Now, it hasn't all been perfect, and there have been some challenging moments, but they believe themselves better for having made the decision to see spiritual direction. So, then, what *is* spiritual direction?

Wherein therapy is understood as treatment intended to provide healing or relief, spiritual direction is something different. Spiritual direction is viewed as something more relational. It's a practice by which the spiritual director journeys with you, the patient, guiding you through the process of deciphering and discerning where and how God is present in your life. But you're working to discern not only where God is, but where God is leading you. While therapy focuses your mental, emotional, and sometimes psychological health and well-being, spiritual direction is concerned exclusively with your spiritual growth and well-being. The focus is more on your connection and relationship to God.

In spiritual direction, the spiritual director serves as a guide. Their role is to be present, listen, assist, and collaborate. In no way should they be leading or influencing. At no time should they be providing answers or solutions or suggestions that could be seen as impeding your path. They're simply there to be in partnership and in a supportive role to your process. They learned how to do this through formal training. Most certification programs are more than a year long, depending on the program and the course requirements. Before becoming a certified spiritual director, one must have partaken in spiritual direction and are required to undergo supervised practice. Some certificate programs offer in-person or virtual options. Several hybrid programs are also available.

TIP

One more thing to note: Spiritual direction isn't exclusive to Christianity. Hinduism, Buddhism, Judaism, Islam, and some Indigenous practices use it.

Spiritual direction is also popular for those who are spiritual but not religious (SBNR). Those who are SBNR seek clarity on their spiritual path without it having any connection to a specific faith or even God or a god. They're simply seeking guidance and want support in their questions and queries. Spiritual direction becomes an ideal outlet for their efforts in fulfillment and purpose.

Spiritual direction and deconstruction

Spiritual direction has the same potential as therapy in terms of being a useful outlet in faith deconstruction. If faith deconstruction dismantles, spiritual direction provides grounding.

REMEMBER

Keep in mind, faith deconstruction doesn't mean that you completely abandon your belief in God or gods. It doesn't mean that you completely step away from faith. When you deconstruct, you're shedding the baggage of religion, doctrines, rules, and the affiliated structures that have resulted in harmful practices and experiences. In some instances, abandonment may happen. But in other instances, after you deconstruct, you may reconstruct your relation to religion. (Reconstruction is discussed in Chapter 18.) Spiritual direction can play an important role in your reconstruction.

So how is it helpful? One of the main ways is the support that's provided in the journey. Spiritual directors are charged with being partners in your spiritual journey. They're ethically bound to solely be a guide without attempting to lead or direct you through the process. This becomes useful in faith deconstruction because it creates space for you to ask your own questions, seek your own answers, and have your own revelations apart from the influence and perspective of someone else. You're afforded the ability to truly process for yourself with someone skilled in the art of being present with you and listening.

Spiritual direction also allows you to explore intentionally. As discussed in Chapter 12, exploration is an important part of faith deconstruction. Exploring and exposing yourself to other belief systems affords you the opportunity to strengthen and sharpen what you believe and why you believe it. Spiritual direction provides free space to test, explore, and find the necessary language needed for your exploration. And in the process, you may find a greater understanding of whatever you consider to be divine within that exploration and your relationship to it.

WARNING

It's worth noting that you should be careful in your faith deconstruction and spiritual direction journey. While spiritual directors are expected to play the role of supporting actor in your journey, some of them can be biased to the faith tradition they come from. Some spiritual directors see their work as part of their calling. Their relationship to their faith could present problems for you as you question, dissect, and shed your relationship to religious systems and communities. It may be worth considering that possibility when seeking a spiritual director.

I think back to my experience of working with a Christian therapist. The example isn't exact, but it has some overlap. I was looking for someone who would assist me in making sense of things from a spiritual perspective. However, as I quickly realized, she had an agenda. She was incapable of getting beyond her own beliefs as it pertained to my sexuality/sexual identity. There were signs early on, but I was so adamant about making it work that we both set ourselves up for failure. As you're seeking a spiritual director, consider what problems may arise for both of you if you're deconstructing your faith and seeking guidance from someone who may see their role as part of their religious call and affiliation.

TIP

Other things to look for in a spiritual director as you're deconstructing include:

>> Someone who understands religious trauma.

>> Someone familiar with faith deconstruction (maybe even their own).

>> Someone with experience working with people from diverse faith traditions.

Deconstruction Coaching

Maybe therapy or even a spiritual director isn't for you. You've read this chapter and feel like neither of these fit the criteria of what you're seeking and looking for. Maybe you can't get beyond the emotional taboo you still carry regarding therapy. It's just not for you. But on the flip side, spiritual direction also isn't quite for you. You can't imagine sitting with someone talking about where God is in all of this because you're unsure how you feel about God/god or what you believe about a divine entity.

Maybe all of this is true for you. You can't see yourself benefiting from either, but you still feel as though you want and need something or someone to assist you in this journey. In my research for this project, I recently came across faith deconstruction coaching. It could be what you need.

Defining deconstruction coaching

What is *deconstruction coaching?* Being that faith deconstruction is considered a new phenomenon, faith deconstruction coaches aren't formally trained and don't require certification. They're unlike therapists and counselors in that therapists and counselors are trained to focus more on your emotional and mental well-being. And deconstruction coaches are unlike spiritual directors in that spiritual directors are more focused on your spiritual well-being. Faith deconstruction coaches utilize their own lived experience of faith deconstruction to provide support that can be described as more peer-to-peer based. They operate more like a life coach.

Faith deconstruction coaches know what you're experiencing. They've walked the process of deconstructing their faith. They provide a practical understanding to their support. However, since they're not formally trained and unregulated, anyone can call themselves a faith deconstruction coach.

What to look for?

What should you look for in a faith deconstruction coach if you feel as though you want or need one along your journey?

First off, it's a good idea to investigate their background. What work did they do before they became a deconstruction coach? Were they a pastor? A professor? A chaplain? Are they certified as a life coach or even a spiritual director? And what of their own deconstruction journey? Is their story and journey public? What can you glean from their own experience with deconstruction that makes them a viable candidate for coaching?

Other things to keep in mind:

>> Do they have clear boundaries, and are they respectful of where you are in your journey?

>> Do they present themselves as an expert in a way that makes you feel manipulated and controlled?

>> What is their stance on therapy or spiritual direction? Is there a suggestion? Are they supportive of you seeking care and support via these other avenues?

>> What are their policies around pricing and rates, the number of sessions they suggest, and so on?

Again, these are simply suggestions worth considering if you feel faith deconstruction coaching is the route you want to take as part of your deconstruction journey.

REMEMBER

Whatever route you take, whether it's therapy, spiritual direction, or deconstruction coaching, ensure that it's the most viable option for your journey. It may take experimenting with one or all of these as you discern but be sure that whichever one you choose is the best option for you. This journey is yours, and the choice is yours alone.

Chapter **18**

Continuing the Ongoing Quest of Faith

When I was planning this book project, I initially assumed you'd deconstruct your faith as you progressed through these pages. The majority of *For Dummies* books are set up as how-to manuals of sorts, and I'd approached this entire project from that lens. Most of the instruction manual books I've encountered have a clear starting point and endpoint with specific steps to follow.

But faith deconstruction has no step-by-step instructions.

REMEMBER

The suggestion that, by reading this book, you would have accomplished the daunting task of faith deconstruction in its entirety is slightly disingenuous. Deconstruction has no endpoint. Not if you're doing it right. And, to be quite honest, you don't want it to end. The journey of faith should be an ongoing enterprise. It must be.

Just as there are advancements made in just about every industry, there are new discoveries and fresh perspectives on how to live out faith. The task involves being open to new revelations. The journey must exist on a continuum.

This chapter deals with that ongoing process. What does it mean to reconstruct your faith after deconstruction? What is reconstruction, and how does it relate to deconstruction? What should you look forward to, and what are some final takeaways regarding your faith journey?

Life After Deconstruction: The Journey Continues

Dr. Tony Lamair Burks and Rev. Rachel Breyer Mulgrave (you can find out more about each of them in Chapter 11), both had one request in my conversations with them: that this book address not only deconstruction but also reconstruction. They felt it would be irresponsible on my part to omit an important piece of the faith deconstruction experience.

Their insistence led me to really think about reconstruction and its place in faith deconstruction. It also led me to ponder what it looks like because, as I've said about my own deconstruction journey, I had no clue I'd engaged in it (deconstruction or reconstruction for that matter) until I was already in it. Not too long after, a dear friend and covenant brother, Mario Brown-Westbrook, said during an altar call after preaching, "Once you remove something, you have to replace it with something." Brown's statement reminded me of something Mulgrave said during our conversation. "I think about all my friends who deconstructed, and their reconstruction is zodiac signs. They replace certainty for certainty."

Initially, I believed that a piece of reconstruction was replacing one thing — beliefs, practices, understanding, and identity — with another. And to some extent, that's true. But reconstruction involves more than just replacing, rebuilding, or substituting.

The writer Richard Bach is credited with saying, "What a caterpillar calls the end of the world, we call a butterfly." I remembered this quote during my personal and private deliberation about faith reconstruction. I once read somewhere that while the transformation of a caterpillar to a butterfly is considered special and majestic, in reality, the process is far from glamorous. What the caterpillar experiences is close to death. Its caterpillar form is dissolved, and, over time, its cells reorganize themselves to form the beautiful, cherished butterfly. The process, if you remember learning in high school biology, is called *metamorphosis*. While they can't prove it, scientists believe metamorphosis is painful for the caterpillar.

REMEMBER

Deconstruction is a lot like that. There's a dissolution and a transformation. And, for some, it's painful because there's a form of "dying," if you will. It may not be the same "dying to ourselves" found in Matthew 16, Luke 9, or what's suggested in Galatians 2, Romans 12, or John 12 — where one loses themselves for the sake of following Jesus. But there's an end to an existence for the caterpillar to make room for the butterfly. The butterfly form is the opportunity for something new. That's life after deconstruction — a transformation into a new purpose.

This section takes a deeper look at reconstruction, which can also be considered the butterfly stage (not to be confused with the butterfly effect). What is reconstruction? And what happens when you reconstruct your faith?

Reconstruction: What is that?

In Chapter 2, I share a little about a conversation I had with a classmate about faith deconstruction and his thoughts regarding whether deconstruction is the appropriate term for the process. I was introduced to the concept of reconstruction during that conversation. My classmate used the word to suggest that reconstruction is a better fit for faith deconstruction than faith deconstruction. Why? Because reconstruction, as far as he understood it, better aligns with what you experience when you deconstruct your faith than deconstruction does.

To some extent, I think I agree with him. As I've stated, I'm convinced that faith deconstruction isn't truly the breaking up or breaking down of your faith but rather the rethinking of your faith in relation to religion. Deconstruction involves thinking critically about what you believe. What you believe is informed by what you were taught about faith, and that comes from religion.

As you deconstruct, you're in a sense divorcing yourself from those teachings, perspectives, rituals, and practices that you perceive to be harmful, shackling, or no longer in alignment with who you believe yourself to be. You're divorcing or shedding your religion.

TIP

Deconstruction is religion-based, not faith-based. The changes you make in your faith, or what you begin to focus your faith on, are a byproduct of the deconstruction of your religion. (But I'm not here to create a new movement.)

So, what is reconstruction exactly? I've seen it defined or described a few ways, including:

>> A paradigm shift

>> Finding faith after losing it

>> A period of rediscovery

>> The rebuilding of your faith after deconstruction

I've seen faith reconstruction compared to "deep biblical work," (whatever that means), and critics of faith deconstruction have suggested that faith reconstruction is nothing more than a person returning to Jesus. Some deconstructionists who "returned" to Christianity after deconstruction define reconstruction as a recommitment to God, scripture, and their religious community. But again, if we consider the butterfly analogy from before, is a person's return truly a recommitment?

REMEMBER

In other words, how faith reconstruction is defined depends on who you ask.

Reconstruction may look a lot like putting the pieces of your faith identity back together. That may also mean returning to the faith practice you were brought up in. The testimony of Danielle Taylor in Chapter 11 is one example of this. Reconstruction may also look like reconnecting with yourself in such a way that you also connect to the God entity within. Or it may mean realizing that the faith system you once held affiliation with and membership within no longer makes sense for you. That revelation and acceptance signal your reconstruction.

REMEMBER

Reconstruction, like deconstruction, is different for everyone. But at the core of the process is enlightened awareness and choice-making. Reconstruction is the conscious declaration and embrace of your faith identity after you've done the work of evaluation.

Reconstruction: What does it look like?

Reconstruction is a lot like baking. When deconstructing a beloved dish, all the ingredients you know to belong in that dish are there, but they're organized differently. The dish may not look like the same beloved dish, but it still tastes the same if it's done right. In reconstruction, the same faith is there, but it's organized differently. You may or may not believe in the same way you once did, but you didn't lose your faith because its core ingredients — trust, comfort, relationship, and confidence in yourself or whatever you define as the divine — are all still there. Your faith just looks different.

And that's why so many critics of faith deconstruction struggle with it. They don't see its worth or validity because it looks different.

TIP

Faith doesn't require you to think or believe the same way, but religion does.

As I was finishing this chapter, I listened to a podcast I listen to every now and again, *The Jamal Bryant Podcast: Let's Be Clear*. This particular episode featured Delman Coates, senior pastor of Mt. Ennon Baptist Church in Maryland. I've been familiar with Coates, his ministry, and his theology for quite some time, having talked with him several times in my life as a freelance journalist and writer. I have a lot of respect for him and his work, especially the work he's done regarding homosexuality and the Bible. I consider him an ally.

MORE ON DELMAN COATES

Since 2004, Delman Coates has served as the pastor of Mt. Ennon. In his tenure there, he has become one of the foremost voices on theological clarity, biblical literacy, and equity in society at large. A graduate of Morehouse College in Atlanta, Georgia, Harvard Divinity School, and Columbia University, Coates became publicly vocal about his support of marriage equality for the LGBTQ+ community in 2011. As a result, he became a target among many Black clergy in the Maryland area and beyond. In 2025, Coates once again went viral on social media after he began a 10-part sermon series, *Practicing Safe Text*, at Mt. Ennon that addressed three main topics: divorce, sex-outside of marriage, and homosexuality.

In addition to being the pastor of Mt. Ennon Baptist Church, Coates is the founder of Our Money Campaign. Founded in 2019, it's an advocacy group that seeks to empower often neglected and over-looked communities on economic empowerment.

In the episode, Coates pointed out that the inclusion of the four gospels in the Bible is a clear indication of how much diversity of thought, understanding, and perspective is championed histori-cally in Christianity. If that were not the case, four different ver-sions of the life and ministry of Jesus wouldn't have been included.

I couldn't agree with him more. Faith requires trust and confi-dence. Despite your doubts and uncertainty and what some might suggest, you haven't lost your faith. Faith doesn't require blind loyalty to systems or one way of thinking, seeing, or understanding life, society, or even faith for that matter. This is something I've had to learn over the years. These lessons have been part of my reconstruction journey.

Looking Forward

A few years ago, I preached a sermon from Matthew 22:34–38 titled, "Where Do We Go From Here?" The sermon was to a gathering of Black gay men involved in an organization that had experienced a split in its leadership. The split had affected not only the success of that year's gathering, which had been going on for nearly a decade at that point, but their future.

In the sermon, I talked about the fourth and last book written and published by the Rev. Dr. Martin Luther King, Jr. I laid out how King isolated himself from the demands of the civil rights movement to write the book, rented a house in Jamaica with no telephone, and labored over the manuscript before returning to Atlanta to give a keynote address during a meeting of the Southern Christian Leadership Conference. The title of his address shared the name of his final written work, "Where Do We Go From Here?"

I'd never heard of King's book before 2022. In it, King reflected on what the civil rights movement had accomplished up until that point, from the Voting Rights Act of 1965 to their galvanization through nonviolent resistance. He also pointed out how much work was left to be done and the importance of a unified coalition to overcome the ills and evils of society.

In my sermon, I pointed out some of those current ills:

>> The assault of drag queens and trans children

>> The assault on Critical Race Theory, AP African American studies

>> Don't Say Gay

For weeks leading up to that sermon, I struggled. At the time, even though I hadn't published the essay publicly admitting my deconstruction, I was deep in the process. I struggled with how to toe the line of being authentic in my journey while honoring the diverse beliefs, understandings, and religious identities of those in attendance at the gathering. I wanted desperately to honor the differing perspectives, views, and beliefs of as many as possible in the room. I'd never wrestled with an assignment the way I did with this one.

"Where do we go from here?" I asked at one point in the sermon. It wasn't just a question I posed to this group seeking to discern what the future held for them. It was also a question I was asking myself. In thinking about faith deconstruction, faith reconstruction, and looking forward, it's also a question I pose to you. The following sections offer you some things to consider, questions to ask, and final thoughts to look forward to in your faith deconstruction, transformation, and reconstruction.

Continuing to ask questions

Karl Marx once said, "Religion is the opium of the masses." The first time I heard this quote was in seminary. I can't remember if it was part of a reading assignment or if it came up in a conversation because of a reading assignment. But I remember not fully understanding what Marx was trying to say. I understood it to be controversial – that part wasn't lost on me – but I can't say I understood why initially.

Having spent some time in ministry and deconstructing, I can now say that I understand Marx a little more and recognize why his statement riled people not only then, but still today.

The statement is part of a much longer quote from his book, *A Contribution to the Critique of Hegel's Philosophy of Right*. What Marx is getting at in the statement is that religion is commonly used as a tool of distraction and avoidance. Marx believed the working class was less likely to challenge the status quo and fight against injustices if they were more focused on the afterlife. From his perspective, heaven became a mechanism of social control.

What makes opium impactful is the way it numbs you. Used often for pain relief, opium provides the illusion that what was plaguing you — the pain in this example — is no longer there. It's gone. Removed. But the pain *isn't* gone. The pain isn't even removed. And to suggest that it's dulled may not be the most accurate description either.

Opium manipulates. That's what makes it effective and powerful. While you're led to believe you've been freed from that which once caused you discomfort, what happens is you're misled and conditioned to believe you've been relieved. You're tricked. Your body and your brain communicate that pain is altered, albeit temporarily. Your ability to feel and experience the pain is blocked. You're in a state of euphoria.

For Marx, religion does the same. Religion has dulled people and their ability to resist. Going back to Marx's critique of heaven, hell, and the afterlife, I think about how oppressed communities have often adopted the idea that their reward is available to them "on the other side." They're conditioned to believe their plight in the world is to live right, righteously, and holy and that if they do so in this life, God will reward them in the afterlife.

I think about how scripture controlled enslaved Africans when they were brought over on slave ships. Scriptures like Ephesians 6:5 and Colossians 3:22, commonly known as "Slaves obey your masters," conditioned them to believe that what God wanted of them was obedience to those who owned and ruled them. I think about how some of that still exists today and how often those messages are spoken from pulpits on Sunday morning. The message involves being obedient to God's will in exchange for the promise of everlasting life.

The same was and is true when I think about the debate over marriage equality and the argument regarding "biblical marriage." However, throughout the Christian text are examples of men — most of them powerful — taking on several wives. I even think about the story of David and Bethsheba, found in 2 Samuel, where David, as king, saw Bethsheba from the roof of the palace and plotted to have her husband killed so that he could have her. Where's the sanctity of marriage in that passage?

All opioids!

Marx was critical of religion. He believed that instead of what religion was intended to do, religion suppressed. It kept people blind to their realities and conditions. Religion, as Marx saw it, was a tool of oppression. It's been used in countless ways to stifle, control, and overpower the often oppressed, impoverished, and powerless. As you've deconstructed, you've probably made some of these same connections. You've probably seen the contradictions and attempted to reconcile the intent and meaning of these texts with what you believe about yourself, others, faith, and God.

TIP

As you look forward, your work will be to constantly ask questions privately and aloud. As you look forward, your work will be to continue in your quest of seeking understanding and clarity and thinking critically. And as you explore and seek and search, you may have to help others.

REMEMBER

Pay it forward. Also, be gracious and patient and careful with others. They have their own process and pace. They may not be where you are or ready to be where you are. But stay close.

There are still questions I have about my relationship to religion, my relationship to Christianity and other religious systems, and my relationship to God. I'm continuing to work it out. There's an identity component tied to this process for me. The entry point into my faith is through the lens of Christianity. I was born into it. It's been foundational to my development and even my deconstruction. But there continue to be questions I don't yet have answers for.

It's complicated.

As I've journeyed through my faith destruction, I've vacillated between my identity as a Christian and my consideration that Christianity may no longer be where I need to be. This is mostly because of how I relate to the teachings of Jesus as laid out in the New Testament scriptures (most specifically in the gospels) and my exposure to the teachings, beliefs, and practices of other faith systems. I have some affinity and respect for other forms of religious expression, seeing them as related to one another. I pointed out some of these similarities in the 2022 sermon I mentioned earlier. In the closing few minutes of my sermon, I said:

> It also takes knowing who you are and whose you are. If Jesus isn't your point of reference, then take a cue from whomever you choose to worship and/or follow. If it's Buddha, exercise greater loving kindness — acting with compassion towards others. If it's the Prophet Muhammad, practice making good faith — treating others the same way you want to be treated and giving others the same things you want to be given. If it's the Olódùmarè, respect oneself, others, and all sacred items of Ifa and Orisa.

See a pattern here? Let them be your guide, understanding that if we are who we say we are, then let's truly live into it — freely, without conditions. And if you proclaim to exclusively be the master of your fate and captain of your soul, then let the Golden Rule be your guide — doing unto others as you would have them do unto you.

It's possible that what once worked for you, for whatever reason, just doesn't anymore. Your faith should liberate you. It should be the conduit by which you obtain freedom. Check in with yourself from time to time.

REMEMBER

Are you getting everything you believe you need and want to get out of your faith for your own good? Is that faith beneficial to your life and identity? Do you feel that this faith is helping you see the God within, resulting in your feeling closer to the God within you *and* others?

Seeing faith deconstruction as something new to emerge

You have the privilege of having a unique, personal, and individual relationship with your faith. No one should have jurisdiction over what you choose to believe. And no one should be able to dictate what you believe and how you believe it. It's up to you to know that, believe that, and honor that for yourself. Your relationship with God or something divine or whatever you choose to call it is yours alone.

I don't knock anyone who believes in something greater than themselves. I don't have anything against anyone who wants to believe that their survival — whatever that looks like for them — was mitigated by something divine and spiritually led. Do I sometimes question it? Yes, sure. The purpose of this book is not an attack on anyone who chooses to believe in the Divine.

I envy some people's faith. I find it inspiring whenever I come across someone who seems to have unshakeable faith. I consider it admirable that they believe their fate is governed by something or someone they can't see but know to be real. It's awe inspiring.

At the same time, I think about some of the things God or the Divine is given credit for in nuanced ways. I don't believe there's always a spiritual or divine answer for life's coincidences. I also don't know if I believe that my surviving cancer is a blessing from God when others I know, who are just as amazing and gifted and righteous, didn't survive. And I don't know if I believe that they didn't survive because that's what God wanted. Sometimes I don't know if I need to know. Sometimes knowing doesn't matter. Sometimes it just is.

The mysteries of God are just that: mysteries.

There's power in prayer, faith, and hope. Not because of what the outcomes could be or the anticipation of a certain outcome. Not at all. Sometimes that power comes in what it provides when it's most needed. Sometimes that power comes in the reprieve from the challenges that are designed to destroy. In moments of despair and uncertainty, the power of hope may be just what you need to keep going. And that's what's most important about faith and its ability, purpose, and role. In challenging times, it's not answers that you need. It's comfort.

I'm not trying to take that away from you. My intent is to provide you, the reader, some food for thought. Why do you believe what you do? Who taught you to believe what you do? As the spiritual teacher and author Eckhart Tolle once said, "Some changes look negative on the surface, but you will soon realize that space is being created in your life for something new to emerge." That's faith deconstruction.

MORE ON ECKHART TOLLE

Even though Eckhart Tolle considers himself nonreligious, his work pulls from many religious practices, including Zen Buddhism, Hinduism, and what's known as Christian mysticism. Born in Germany, Tolle came to prominence in the late 1990s after the release of his book *The Power of Now: A Guide to Spiritual Awakening*. In all, Tolle has written more than 20 books, with *A New Earth: Awakening to Your Life's Purpose* being one of his most popular and successful titles.

6

The Part of Tens

Find out about ten well-known institutions that were founded on religious principles.

Meet ten famous people whose faith drove their work.

Ponder ten questions worth asking when thinking about your faith.

Chapter **19**

Ten Institutions Founded on Religious Principles

A s stated throughout this book, faith isn't all bad. Or better yet, religious affiliation isn't all bad. As you deconstruct your faith, it is worth being aware of how faith and religion have benefitted society. This chapter points out some of the better-known institutions that were started by faith-based movements, organizations, or denominations.

Note: I've also included one institution that I learned of in the process of doing research for this book. It's only fitting to add it to the list, if for nothing else than educational purposes.

In relation to faith deconstruction, I wrote this chapter to highlight what happens when faith is used in effective and impactful ways to effect change, create equitable spaces, encourage innovation, and create community.

Colleges/Universities

Many of the institutions of higher education began as training grounds for clergy. This is especially true of many ivy league institutions. Their focus was to train minsters responsible for expanding the religious beliefs and commitments of the society at the time.

Many of the most popular ones, like Yale, the College of William & Mary, Princeton, and Columbia, have staked their claim as the oldest or most influential in American history. For this list, I've chosen one because of its history, reputation, and place in the contemporary news cycle at the time of this book's publication.

Harvard University

Founded in 1636 by the Puritans, Harvard was one of the many ivy's initially intended to be a training ground for clergy. Over time, it's believed, the institution shifted its affiliation to Congregationalism and eventually Unitarianism. It doesn't proclaim to have any religious affiliation today. Around the 19th century, the school shifted to being nonsectarian.

Historically Black Colleges/ Universities

Historically Black Colleges and Universities (HBCUs) are known to be the bedrock of Black American education today. Born out of a need to prepare formerly enslaved Africans for the workforce, many of America's HBCUs have been committed to educating some of the world's most successful Black American professionals and leaders. From Thurgood Marshall, Samuel L. Jackson, and Martin Luther King, Jr., to Spike Lee, Alice Walker, Booker T. Washington, and former Vice President Kamala Harris, HBCUs have been the breeding ground for Black excellence.

What you may not know is that many of them were founded in the basements of churches. Morehouse College, Spelman College, and Rust College are three that immediately come to mind. Others have their roots in Christian denominations, including Morris Brown College.

There is a fair amount of debate over which HBCU is the oldest. Two, Wilberforce University and Cheyney University of Pennsylvania, proclaim to be the oldest private and public HBCUs, respectively. Wilberforce also proclaims to be the first Black-owned and operated HBCU. But there is also one other, Lincoln University, that is believed to be the first HBCU to confer degrees.

Cheyney University of Pennsylvania

Cheyney University of Pennsylvania, founded in 1837, is described as the oldest public HBCU in American history. A Quaker philanthropist provided the initial collateral to start the school, seeking to prepare former enslaved Africans and their descendants to be teachers. African Institute was the institution's first name, but eventually it was renamed the Institute for Colored Youth. In 1902 the institute became associated with the name Cheyney after moving to the farm of George Cheyney. Eventually it became the Cheyney Training School for Teachers, Cheyney State College in 1959, and in 1983 Cheyney University of Pennsylvania.

Lincoln University

Receiving its charter from the Commonwealth of Pennsylvania in 1854, Lincoln University was originally established as The Ashmun Institute. In 1866, the name was changed to Lincoln University in honor of the 16th President of the United States, Abraham Lincoln. Its founder, John Miller Dickey, was a minister in the Presbyterian Church, and his wife, Sarah Emlen Cresson, was a Quaker. As a result of Dickey's affiliation, the institution was deeply influenced by the Presbyterian Church, being approved at the time by the Presbytery of New Castle a year before its charter.

Today, the school does not have a specific affiliation with any religious group. Horace Mann Bond became the school's first Black president in 1923.

Wilberforce University

Founded in 1865, Wilberforce University claims to be the oldest private HBCU owned and operated by Black Americans. Named for the abolitionist William Wilberforce, the Methodist Episcopal Church founded the institution alongside the African Methodist Episcopal Church but later sold it to the AME Church under the leadership of bishop Daniel Payne. Payne, who served as its president from 1863 until 1877, was the first Black American to lead a college in the United States.

The University of al-Qarawiyyin

Started as a mosque in 857-859 AD, this institution is considered by the *Guinness Book of World Records* as the oldest university in the world. Located in Fez, Morocco, it's credited today with being one of the leading spiritual and educational centers internationally. In Arabic, the name of the institution means "University of the People."

Hospitals

Hospitals are central to society's well-being and are considered important centers of access and healing. Historically, hospitals were critical tools of faith work. Many were affiliated with Christian movements and developed their missions from what they perceived to be the instructions of Jesus as portrayed in the Bible.

Mt. Sinai Hospital

Until 1866, Mt. Sinai was known as the Jews' Hospital in New York. A group of Jewish charities came together to develop the center in the New York area. Its initial mission was to provide free medical care in New York for indigent Jews.

Mayo Clinic

It's not officially a Catholic institution, but the Mayo Clinic has Catholic roots. The clinic's interesting history began with a natural disaster that impressed upon its founders the importance of caring for the sick. William Worrall Mayo, a self-proclaimed agnostic, joined Mother Alfred Moes, a devout Catholic, to form the Mayo Clinic in Rochester, Minnesota, in 1864.

Charitable, Community, and Membership Orgs

Faith-based institutions aren't limited to churches. They can also be understood as charitable organizations and membership organizations. I wanted to highlight a few whose work and purpose are informed by religious principles.

Habitat for Humanity

In 1976, Habitat for Humanity was founded in Americus, Georgia, to address the needs of the poor, most especially concerns about housing. Self-described as a Christian mission, Habitat believes that every person should have access to decent living. Their work and purpose are informed by what they consider to be three key theological concepts:

>> Putting faith into action

>> The economics of Jesus

>> The theology of the hammer

Divine Nine: Fraternity and Sorority Organizations

Also known as the National Pan-Hellenic Council, Divine Nine (D9) organizations are membership organizations committed to the advancement of society. While their memberships are almost exclusively Black American, they don't exclude other communities from their membership. Their commitment, which was born during a time of racial discrimination and great oppression in American history, is to uplift excellence, racial equity, and justice in society.

Several well-known preachers and pastors have openly criticized the validity of Black fraternities and sororities. Gospel singer and pastor Marvin Winans being the most recent in the summer of 2025. They suggest membership in D9 institutions counters Christian values. But most of the D9 institutions are led by Christian principles of community, service, and charity.

The Divine Nine organizations are:

» Fraternities:

- Alpha Kappa Alpha Fraternity, Inc. (1906)

- Kappa Alpha Psi Fraternity, Inc. (1911)

- Omega Psi Phi Fraternity, Inc. (1911)

- Phi Neta Sigma Fraternity, Inc. (1914)

- Iota Phi Theta Fraternity, Inc. (1963)

» Sororities

- Alpha Kappa Alpha Sorority, Inc. (1908)

- Delta Sigma Theta Sorority, Inc. (1913)

- Zeta Phi Beta Sorority, Inc. (1920)

- Sigma Gamma Rho Sorority, Inc. (1922)

Buddhist Global Relief

Founded in 1008 by Bhikkhu Bodhi, Buddhist Global Relief is committed to combating malnutrition and chronic hunger worldwide. Informed by Buddhist teachings, it seeks to improve poverty worldwide, fight for women's rights, and work to create long-term solutions to hunger and poverty.

Chapter **20**

Ten Influential Figures Whose Faith Motivated Their Work

As I mention in Chapter 6, former President Jimmy Carter referenced his faith in much of his political and community work following his time in the White House. The Rev. Dr. Martin Luther King, Jr., is another example of someone whose faith was hallmark to their work for justice and equity in American and global society. Their motivation, informed by their religious beliefs, can be considered an example of how religion is or can be useful.

But they aren't the only ones in history. The history books, whether digital or analog, are filled with entries of individuals who have seen the world through the lens of their faith and used their religious convictions to enact social change. This chapter highlights ten of them.

As you deconstruct your faith, considering the work of these individuals can help you in evaluating the effectiveness of what you once believed and what role your faith plays in your life and work moving forward.

Bayard Rustin (1912–1987)

In recent years, Bayard Rustin has begun to receive the flowers he so desperately deserved. In 2013, President Barack Obama post-humously awarded Rustin with the Presidential Medal of Freedom for his activism. A decade later, Netflix released the documentary drama *Rustin*, which highlighted his work orchestrating the 1963 March on Washington. Raised by his Quaker grandparents, Rustin is credited with introducing the Rev. Dr. Martin Luther King, Jr. to Mahatma Ghandi and the nonviolence moment. Because he was same-gender-loving, many of King's advisors feared Rustin's reputation would tarnish the work of the Civil Rights Movement and be a hindrance to their work. It was Rustin's faith that informed his work of nonviolence resistance and his beliefs in championing the rights of all people.

Dorothy Day (1897–1980)

Dorothy Day, a journalist and social activist, cofounded the Catholic Worker Movement. In addition to CWM, Day founded the *Catholic Worker* newspaper. She served as its editor from its founding in 1933 until her death in 1980. Her radical faith informed her work. She believed in caring for the poor, that war was morally wrong, and that prayer was more impactful in fighting evil. She also believed that people could and should work together in community, sharing resources with one another and living as simply as possible.

Desmond Tutu (1931–2021)

Desmond Tutu may have been one of the most beloved faith leaders of the past hundred years. A South African bishop in the Anglican church and theologian, his faith and Christian identity deeply informed his work regarding justice, interfaith dialogue, and cooperation. His work regarding apartheid, which he was staunchly against, led to him receiving the Nobel Peace Prize in 1984.

Florence Nightingale (1820–1910)

Florence Nightingale was often referred to as the "Lady with the Lamp." She was believed to be deeply religious, and her faith informed much of her work around patient care and nursing. She contributed greatly to public health and hospital administration, was considered a social reformer, and is considered a major influence in modern nursing.

Marsha P. Johnson (1945–1992)

It's because of Marsha P. Johnson and her work that gay pride celebrations take place across the globe today. A key figure in the 1969 Stonewall uprising in New York and self-described drag queen, Johnson is considered by many a liberation activist. Johnson's faith played a big part in her work regarding justice and liberation. She was reportedly raised in the African Methodist Episcopal Church but also explored Catholicism and other faiths. Historians report that she never stopped believing in Jesus.

Pauli Murray (1910–1985)

Cofounder of the National Organization for Women, Pauli Murray was the first African American to earn a JSD from Yale School of Law. She was a writer, legal scholar, activist, and eventually an Episcopal priest. Her faith informed her work in championing civil rights and dismantling segregation. She believed discrimination to be harmful to humanity at large.

Thich Nhat Hanh (1926–2022)

Often referred to as the father of mindfulness, Thich Nhat Hanh believed that mindfulness helps everyone connect with themselves. "To be mindful is to be yourself," he is quoted as saying. An advocate for peace and nonviolent resistance and one of the foremost influencers of Buddhism in the western world, he was exiled from Vietnam after speaking against the Vietnam War for 39 years. His work and writings moved the Rev. Dr. Martin Luther King to nominate Nhat Hanh for the Nobel Peace Prize.

Malcom X (1925–1965)

Those familiar with the name Malcolm X might believe him to have been radical in his work and teachings. But by the time he died, he was committed to working toward the unity of all people and combating injustice and suffering of every oppressed person. Many historians point out that his conversion from the Nation of Islam to a Sunni Muslim played a role in that shift. Often described as controversial, Malcolm X was instrumental in helping those within the Civil Rights movement understand their work more deeply. One historian pointed out that Malcolm X helped many Black Christians reevaluate their understanding of Black suffering and the role that religion — most specifically Christianity — played in that suffering.

Delores Huerta (b. 1930)

The cofounder of the Farm Workers Association, Delores Huerta has also been a staunch advocate for women rights, immigrants, and people living in poverty for more than 60 years. She's a devout Catholic whose faith informs the work she does in advocating for others. In fact, she sees her faith and commitment to the ministry of Jesus to be a commission to everyone. She believes that to be the kingdom of God, everyone must work and live alongside those often neglected, overlooked, and oppressed by societal systems.

Rev. William Barber II (b. 1963)

Rev. William Barber II is one of the premiere faith leaders and community activists today. He leads Repairers of the Breach and cochairs the Poor People's Campaign. Living with ankylosing spondylitis, Barber has led the charge against poverty, greed, and capitalism for decades. Through initiatives like Moral Mondays, a series of staged protests, Barber and his supporters have shined a light on issues from educational equality, criminal justice reform, and voting rights. His work, informed by his faith, brings together colaborers and collaborators from diverse communities to combat injustice and neglect in society, most specifically in the faith community and political sphere.

Chapter **21**

Ten Questions Worth Asking When Questioning Your Faith

This Part of Tens explores a little more deeply the process of faith deconstruction by considering a few questions worth asking yourself as you evaluate your faith. This isn't an exhaustive list, but these questions are worth pondering.

Is God Real, and Does It Matter?

It's a fair question. And yes, I'm fully aware of its blasphemous nature. Even my suggesting it as a question could cause some to label me a heretic. But it's natural to question whether God exists.

The second half of the question, "Does it matter," is healthy for everyone's faith journey because it allows the opportunity to determine for yourself the value of your faith and the value of your knowing. If you're to define faith as "complete trust and confidence in something," this shouldn't be a terrible question to ask. How else can you measure the strength of your faith?

Who/What Is Jesus to Me?

During a conversation of liberation theologians and deconstructionists, Kristian A. Smith, the technical reviewer for this book, said these words, "For some people, Jesus is a Messiah who saves them. And for some people, Jesus is a model who shows them the way." The statement made me ask myself, "Who or what is Jesus to me?" It's an important question.

How you see Jesus informs how you understand your relationship to him. How you understand your relationship to him informs how you approach your faith and your faith work. If Jesus is a Messiah, your faith becomes more passive. If he is "the way," as Smith puts it, you're potentially more motivated in how you approach and exercise your faith.

What Role Does My Faith Play in How I Show Up for Others?

Faith can be a great motivator. This is not only true for what you believe, but how you live out what you believe. So, what *do* you believe? Do you see yourself as someone who's communal in nature and concerned about the well-being of others? Or could you care less? Are you someone who believes, because of your faith, that someone is unhoused because they were irresponsible, or did your faith teach you to be vocal about the plague of capitalism in society and caring for "the least of these"?

Asking these questions will give you some insight and guidance into how you want to be, if caring about the plight of others is an interest of yours.

Is My Faith Helping or Causing Me Harm?

One of the things I appreciate about concepts like the Greatest Commandment Theology (Chapter 8) is that it equalizes self-love along with love of God and love of others. But for me and many like me, faith has meant carrying around shame and embarrassment. Some struggle with self-care, believing they're to sacrifice themselves for their faith. This is harmful theology.

Where are you on that spectrum? What are your self-care practices? How do you feel about yourself? Do you love yourself, or do see yourself as wretched, sinful, and unworthy of joy, peace, and love?

Who/What Will I Lose?

Many religious communities are great at creating "us versus them" environments. They make their community your complete and entire focus, creating situations where your entire life and being is tied to them. As a result, questioning your faith could result in losing the only community you know.

In questioning what you believe, consider the losses you could experience. What will it mean for you to deconstruct if it also means being excommunicated? Can you handle that? Where is community and support available to you?

What Will I Gain by Challenging What I Believe?

In the same way that you may find yourself considering what you might lose, consider what you might gain. What are the possibilities for deconstructing? Who will you become? What will you learn, and how will it help you grow, mature, and expand your faith? Yes, you may experience loss. But you may also experience great wins and gains. Think about it.

Is My Religious Community a Safe Space for Me?

The healthiest environments are those where people feel safe and secure. In these spaces, people are confident in being who they believe themselves to be and aren't afraid to be their authentic selves. The spaces are breeding grounds for self-awareness and fearlessness. They create not only confident individuals, but courageous leaders.

Does this sound like your religious community? Why or why not? How has your religious space helped you in your growth and self-confidence/self-awareness?

Do People I Love Feel Safe and Welcome in Spaces I Hold Sacred?

Growing up, one of the things I enjoyed most were lock-ins, which were sleepovers held at the church as fundraisers. A few times, I invited a friend from my neighborhood to a lock-in. I wanted to share the joy and fun I'd had with people I considered friends and extended family. Not only did I feel as though they would have a good time, but I believed they would be welcomed by some of the other kids. They did, and they were.

Unfortunately, not everyone has that privilege. I know people who have refused to attend special events, weddings, and even funerals because they didn't feel as though they would be welcome in the space. Why is a space sacred to you if the people you love aren't welcome?

Is My Faith Serving Me Now?

What have you learned about faith, and how have you applied it to your life? What do you need or even require from your faith in this moment? What is the purpose of faith in your life now compared to in your past? It's important to understand what expectations you have of your faith and how to govern those expectations in your present reality.

Has My Faith Ever Truly Served Me?

This question is just as important as the previous one. In Chapter 5, I discuss how some believe that everything is supposed to work out for them because of how they've lived and what they haven't done. This is one of many failures of faith. It makes me wonder, "What has your faith taught you, and how has it served you?" Are you one who believes that your faith will make you immune to the trials and tribulations of life, or are you one who approaches faith with a certain kind of understanding that sustains you when disappointment meets you? Ask yourself which one applies to you and what expectations you have or don't have about your faith.

Index

O

Obatalá, 197
Of Grammatology (Derrida), 27, 29
Ogún, 197
Old Testament, 125
Olodumare, 197
"oral traditions," 199
orientation, 53
origins of faith, 71–72
Orishas
  Eshu, 197
  Obatalá, 197
  Ogún, 197
  Orunmila, 198
  Oshosi, 197
  Oshún, 197
  Oyá, 197
  Shangó, 197
  Yemayá, 197
Orthodox Judaism, 95–96
Orunmila, 198
Oshosi, 197
Oshún, 197
Oyá, 197

P

patriarchy/man-centered society, 41–43
Paulk, D.E., 167–169
Pearson, Carlton D., 169, 219
Pentateuch, 97
Pentecostalism, 103
personal spirituality, 204
philosophical humanism, 213

Pinn, Anthony, 214
polytheistic belief systems
  Hinduism (*see* Hinduism)
  Wicca, 193–194
prayer, 155–156
Praying the Psalms (Brueggemann), 52
Presbyterian Church, 101
proof-texting, 40
proponents, 11
Protestantism, 98
Protestant Reformation, 100
purity culture, 45–46

Q

The Quran, 97, 187

R

Rastafari, 198
Reclamation Collective, 229
reconstruction, 262, 265–266
  definition of, 264
Reconstructionist Judaism, 97
reformation, 35
Reform Judaism, 96
religion, 186, 269
  abuse, 119
  benefits of, 87–90
  definition, 82
  in everyday life, 86–87
  Golden Rule principle, 90–91
  homogeneity, 83
  origins of, 84–87
  problems, 90–91, 117–121

About the Author

Rev. Mashaun D. Simon (he/him/they) is an award-winning journalist, writer, preacher, and thought leader.

A native of metro Atlanta, Mashaun is a Doctor of Ministry candidate at Columbia Theological Seminary. His research engages the relationship between Black church culture, church hurt, and Black LGBTQ+ grief. The former senior pastor of House of Mercy Everlasting (HOME) in College Park, Georgia, he is also a survivor of neuroendocrine carcinoma, a rare form of cancer that makes up about 0.5 percent of all cancer diagnoses.

Mashaun has written for NBC News, the *Atlanta Journal-Constitution*, *Black Enterprise*, *Bloomberg News*, *Ebony Magazine*, *ESSENCE* Magazine, *Queerty*, and the Counter Narrative Project's (CNP's) *The Reckoning*. He has also served as a Local News: US South contributor for GLAAD. Mashaun is the former co-associate editor of *Geez* magazine, a seasonal, nonprofit, ad-free, print magazine about social justice, art, and activism for people at the fringes of faith in both Canada and the US. For three seasons, he cohosted the *B4Nine* podcast, an audio-only, pop culture talk show. In 2025, Mashaun received the NLGJA Excellence in Online Journalism Award.

In addition to his writing, ministry, and community work, which includes serving as the head of the board of the community-based organization HOME Outreach, Inc., Mashaun has successfully created cultural competency and affirmative action programming and training; led several local, regional, and national media relations and marketing campaigns; and provided recruitment messaging support for several institutions of higher education and nonprofit organizations in the metro Atlanta area and beyond.

Mashaun was a 2022 DO GOOD X startup accelerator fellow, a member of the 2022–2023 class of Collegeville Institute's Emerging Writers Fellowship, a member of the inaugural class of Sojourners' Rising Leaders Fellowship (2021–2022), and a CNP narrative justice fellow (2021–2022). He also served on the 2024 CNP leadership council, the AID Atlanta advisory board from 2018–2020, the inaugural PRISM board of Teach for America Metro Atlanta from 2019–2020, and the advisory board for the CNP from 2018–2019. In 2005, Mashaun became the first openly gay student representative on the board of directors for the National Association of Black Journalists. He's also believed to be the first openly gay, Black male president of the Candler Coordinating Council for the Candler School of Theology at Emory University.

Mashaun holds a professional writing degree from Georgia Perimeter College, a bachelor of science in communications from Kennesaw State University, and a master of divinity from Emory University's Candler School of Theology. He lives in Stone Mountain, Georgia, with his husband. To learn more or to contact Mashaun, visit mashaundsimon.com.

Dedication

This book is dedicated to the ones who have hidden their thoughts, struggles, and changes in their theology, as well as their relationship with religion from themselves and loved ones. To everyone who has often felt like they didn't belong, I see you and cherish you.

This book is for you!

Author's Acknowledgments

First and foremost, Jennifer Yee, thank you. You helped make a dream come true. And Chrissy Guthrie, thank you for being my Obi Wan Kenobi. From day one, I knew I needed you. I'm grateful.

Kristian A. Smith, thank you for being part of this journey. I'm glad you said yes!

To my husband, aka roommate, Elvis T. Frison. If no one will cheer me on, you will. And to my sons, Trevon King and Tevin Gadson, the pride felt in my heart is unmatched.

To my mother, I love you. And to my twin, Jaritta Morgan, your encouragement has made me taller and stronger. To the Hickmans and Simons, I hope you know how hard I work to make you proud.

To my covenant brothers Elder Mario Brown, Chris Arrington, Dr. R. Wayne Woodson, and Bishop Elliott Sommerville, thank you for holding and lifting me up all these years.

To my brothers Bishop Troy Sanders and Pastor Pierre D. Cox, you both are painfully missed. If not for you two at the most integral moments of my life, I wouldn't be this person today.

And then to my chosen family, Ristina Gooden, Adrian Daniel, Marques Richards, Dwayne Cox, Mathew Contee, Jr., Lee Jones, Terence Lester, Billy Michael Honor, Terence Mayo, Kylan Pew, Kurtis Sampson, Gloria Thornton, Ed and Myisha Garnes, Randle Eichelberger, and Yvonne Mahoney; my grad quad, Sarah Leer, Joe Evans, Natarsha Sanders; other friends and confidants, Michael Jenkins, Marcus Jackson, Bishop Clarence Laney, and so many others. Each of you were mirrors. You helped me see me through your eyes. I couldn't have done this without you.

Many thanks to everyone from Wiley who touched this project.

Finally, to the nine who shared their stories for this project: Rev. Rachel Breyer Mulgrave, Rev. Dr. Tony Lamair Burks II, Synitta Delano, Jade Foster, Lauren Murphy, Bishop D.E. Paulk, J.S., Danielle Taylor, and Verdell Anthony Wright. Thank you!

I'm a published book author, ya'll! Who would have thought?

Publisher's Acknowledgments

Senior Acquisitions Editor:
Jennifer Yee

Development Editor:
Christina Guthrie

Copy Editor: Karen Davis

Technical Editor: Kristian A. Smith

Production Editor:
Tamilmani Varadharaj

Managing Editor: Sofia Malik

Cover Image: © 1001nights/
Getty Images